Preface

This tutorial series was created to introduce new users to Pro/ENGINEER®. The tutorial has been updated for Release 2000i^2. This release is, once again, a major revision of the software, particularly in regards to the user interface, which is now considerably friendlier and easier to use. The tutorials cover the major concepts and frequently used commands required to advance from a novice to an intermediate user level. Major topics include part and assembly creation, and creation of engineering drawings. The major functions that make Pro/E a parametric solid modeler are illustrated. Although the commands are presented in a click-by-click manner, an effort has been made, in addition to showing/illustrating the command usage, to explain why certain commands are being used and the relation of feature selection and construction to the overall part design philosophy. Moreover, since error recovery is an important skill, considerable time is spent exploring the created models (in fact, intentionally inducing some errors), so that users will become comfortable with the "debugging" phase of model creation. In my experience of teaching numerical methods courses, debugging and error recovery is a skill sadly neglected when students are first taught a programming course, and the same probably applies to CAD.

This series of lessons was originally written for students in the Engineering Graphics and Design course (MecE 265) offered in the Mechanical Engineering program at the University of Alberta **<http://www.mece.ualberta.ca/courses/mec265/>**. This is a required course taken by all students entering the program, and is the only engineering graphics course in their program. We have been using Pro/E since the fall of 1996. Students enter the course with a broad range of backgrounds - some have previous CAD experience, while others have only an introductory programming course. Since students taking the course have a wide range of abilities both in spatial visualization and computer skills, the approach taken in the manual is meant to allow accessability to persons of all levels. These lessons, therefore, were written for new users with no previous experience with CAD, although some familiarity with computers is assumed.

This book is **NOT** a reference for Pro/ENGINEER. There is no index to commands discussed in the lessons. This is for two reasons. First, since Release 18 of Pro/E, all the several thousand pages of reference manuals are available on-line, with good search tools and cross-referencing to allow users to find relevant material quickly. This on-line help is even better in 2000i^2. Secondly, the tutorials are meant to be covered sequentially. Discussion of commands is, by and large, restricted to their use within the context of the lesson (a Just-in-Time delivery!). For this reason, many options to commands are not dealt with in detail all in the same place in the text. Such a discussion would interrupt the flow of the work. So an index might provide a number of locations within the text where a command is used, most of which would not be in the desired context.

Since these tutorials were first written, a number of changes have occurred. The major change in the previous edition was the reorganization of material. The lesson on modeling utilities (the 3 R's) was moved ahead to Lesson #4. This is because students proceeding through the lessons are almost immediately confronted with modeling errors and problems that require knowledge of these commands. Furthermore, the shaft feature (formerly in Lesson #3) was removed in favor of the much more common revolved protrusion. A number of minor errors have been corrected and some additional comments have been inserted at various places in the text to clarify the discussion.

Also new in the previous edition was a multimedia CD-ROM produced by Jack Zecher at IUPU-Indianapolis. In the interests of providing students with multi-modal learning tools and experiences, the CD should help significantly in getting "up the learning curve." The CD follows the text very closely, and although it does not go into all the detail contained in the text, provides an excellent overview of the material in each lesson. We expect that many students will find it advantageous to go through the CD presentation for each lesson (or part thereof) prior to working through the lesson in detail. The CD has been updated for Release $2000i^2$.

Notes for the Latest Edition

In this tutorial for Release $2000i^2$, the same basic sequence of lessons has been retained. Major changes have occurred in the first couple of lessons to deal with the new user interface. Minor effects have been felt throughout the lessons. These changes revolve around usability issues - the same basic functionality of Pro/E is still there. There are new tools for dealing with parent/child relations, a new Sketcher interface, part and drawing templates, new pull-down menus, a new hole creation dialog window, drag-and-drop reordering in the model tree, many new pop-up menus available with a right mouse click, and so on. All in all, the number of command selections and mouse clicks required to use Pro/E has been reduced dramatically with the new interface. Another new addition is the availability of a Web site with VRML models of the Panavise project parts and assembly; see **<http://www.sdcpublications.com/tutorial>**.

Note to Instructors

The Engineering Graphics and Design course at the U of A is a one-term course of 12 weeks, with two lectures and a three hour lab every week. Most lecture time is dedicated to introducing students to the theory and practice of creating engineering drawings (reading drawings, visualization of shape from multiview drawings, layout of multiview drawings, detailing and sectioning practice and standards, and so on). Half the weekly lab activities are devoted to free hand drawing activities such as sketching pictorial views or freehand layout of multiview drawings and solving drawing problems (eg. missing view problems). The other half of the lab each week is spent working with Pro/E, primarily going through these lessons. Students must spend an additional 1 to 2 hours per week with these tutorials.

The tutorials consist of the following:
- 6 lessons on features used in part creation
- 1 lesson on modeling utilities
- 1 lesson on creating engineering drawings
- 2 lessons on creating assemblies and assembly drawings

Each of these will take between 2 to 4 hours to complete (thus usually requiring some time spent out of the regularly scheduled computer lab time). The time required will vary depending on the ability and background of the student. Moreover, additional time would be beneficial for experimentation and exploration of the program. Most of the material can be done by the student on their own time, however there are a few "tricky" bits in some of the lessons. Therefore, it is important to have teaching assistants available (preferably right in the computer lab) who can answer special questions and especially bail out students who get into trouble. Most common causes of confusion are due to not completing the lessons or digesting the material. This is not surprising given the volume of new information or the lack of time in students' schedules. However, I have found that most student questions are answered within the lessons. In addition to the tutorials, some class time (two to three hours) over the duration of the course will be invaluable in demonstration and discussion of some of the broader issues of feature-based modeling. It takes a while for students to realize that just creating the geometry is not sufficient for a design model, and the notion of design intent needs careful treatment and discussion.

It is important for students to keep up the pace with the Pro/E lessons through the course. To that end, laboratory exercises have involved short quizzes (students produce written answers to questions chosen at random from the end of each lesson), creating models of parts sketched on the whiteboard in isometric or multiview, or brought into the lab (usually large models made of styrofoam). Of these, the latter two activities seemed to have been the most successful. It appears that many students, after having gone through the week's lesson (usually only once, and very quickly) do not absorb very much. The second pass through the lesson usually results in considerably more retention. Students really don't feel comfortable or confident until they can make parts from scratch on their own. Each lesson concludes with a number of simple "exercise" parts that can be created using new commands taught in that lesson. In addition to these, a project is also included that consists of a number of parts that are introduced with the early lessons and finally assembled at the end. It would be most beneficial, however, if students could have at their disposal a physical model which they can "reverse engineer".

As a last note, at the U of A the EGD course is a prerequisite to the first "design" course. That course involves a team design-and-build project in which one of the deliverables is a Pro/E model, complete with detailed drawings. Besides being an excellent way to reinforce the learning started in the EGD course, this also gives the students an opportunity to really use Pro/E as it was meant to be - as a design tool. It is important to have this type of follow-up.

Acknowledgments

The inspiration for and initial version of these lessons were based on the Web pages produced by Jessica LoPresti, Cliff Phipps, and Eric Wiebe of the Graphic Communications Program, Department of Mathematics, Science and Technology Education at North Carolina State University. Permission to download and modify their pages is gratefully acknowledged. Since that time (July, 1996) the tutorials have been rewritten/updated five times: initially to accommodate our local conditions and then for Releases 18, 20, 2000i (with another foray into PT/Modeler in between), and now 2000i^2. All of the figures are new and discussion of the commands is considerably amplified.

Some of the objects and parts used in these tutorials are based on illustrations and problem exercises in **Technical Graphics Communication** (Irwin, 1995) by Bertoline, Wiebe, *et al*. This book is an excellent source for examples and additional exercises in part and assembly modeling, and drawing creation.

The Panavise project in this tutorial is based on a product patented by Panavise Products, Inc. and is used with the express written permission of Panavise Products, Inc., Reno, Nevada. The name Panavise is a registered trademark of Panavise Products, Inc., Reno, Nevada, and is used with the express written permission of Panavise Products, Inc. Such permission is gratefully acknowledged.

These tutorials (for Release 16) were first written as Web pages and released in September, 1996. In the 16 months they were available on the Web, they received over 30,000 hits from around the world. This number is indeed gratifying in itself, but in addition, a number of users (students, instructors, industrial users, even a patent lawyer!) have returned comments on the tutorials, which are gratefully acknowledged.

I would like to thank Ian Buttar for his assistance in the computer lab and to the students of the Engineering Graphics and Design course for their comments and suggestions. Notwithstanding their assistance, any errors in the text or command sequences are those of the author!

Acknowledgment is also due to Stephen Schroff for his continued efforts in taking this work to a wider audience.

Jack Zecher at IUPU - Indianapolis has done a great job producing the accompanying CD-ROM.

As always, special thanks are due to my wife, Elaine, for tolerating my late nights and weekends spent on this project. Thanks to Kate for the cookies, and to Jenny for all her special surprises. They deserve a medal for putting up with an absent (and absent-minded) and pre-occupied Dad! Also, thanks are due again to our good friends, Jayne and Rowan Scott, for their continued support and enthusiasm.

To users of this material, I hope you enjoy the lessons.

RWT
Edmonton, Alberta
26 May 2000

Jack Zecher writes:

I would like to express my thanks to Rob Wolter for his continued excellent work on the narration portion of the CD-ROM.

A very special note of appreciation to my wife Karen, for her understanding and tolerance of my schedule during the preparation of this CD-ROM.

Jack Zecher
IUPUI
May, 2000

About the CD-ROM

The CD-ROM was developed to run on PC compatible machines running under the Windows 95, Windows 98 or Windows NT 4.0 (service pack 2 or later) operating system. On most machines the program will self start when you place the CD in the CD-ROM drive. If it does not, you should use "Windows Explorer" or "My Computer" to open the CD-ROM device, and then double click on the executable file *Prolessons.exe*.

The recommended minimum hardware requirements are as follows:
Pentium 133 Mhz
4X CD-ROM drive
32 megabytes of RAM
1024 x 768 video resolution with 16 bit color
Sound card

You may need to make the following adjustments in order to improve the performance of the CD-ROM player under Windows 95 and Windows 98. From the **Start Menu** select the following options:

Settings > Control Panel > System > Performance
File System... > CD-ROM

then set the ***Supplemental cache size:*** to "maximum", and the ***Optimize access pattern for:*** to "No read ahead".

In order to control the volume, you will have to manually adjust the volume control on your speakers, or click on the speaker icon, usually located in the lower right hand corner of the task bar. If you are using headphones, make sure to plug them into the sound card and not the headphone jack located on the CD-ROM drive.

TABLE OF CONTENTS

INTRODUCTION to Pro/ENGINEER

Lesson 1 : Creating Simple Objects

Lesson 2 : HOLES, CUTS, the MODEL TREE, RELATIONS

Lesson 3 : REVOLVED PROTRUSIONS, MIRRORED COPIES, ROUNDS AND CHAMFERS

Lesson 4 : MODELING UTILITIES, PARENT/CHILD RELATIONS, AND THE 3 R'S

Lesson 5 : SKETCHER TOOLS AND DATUM PLANES

Lesson 6 : REVOLVED FEATURES, PATTERNS, and COPIES

Lesson 7 : SWEEPS AND BLENDS

Lesson 8 : CREATING ENGINEERING DRAWINGS

Lesson 9 : ASSEMBLY FUNDAMENTALS

Lesson 10 : ASSEMBLY OPERATIONS

INTRODUCTION to Pro/ENGINEER®

Release 2000i²

A Few Words Before You Dive In...

These tutorials contain information for getting started with Pro/ENGINEER 2000i² (Parametric Technology Corporation, Waltham, MA) and are meant to be used alongside the running Pro/E software. **You will learn the material best by not just executing the command sequences exactly as specified, but also taking time along the way to think about what you are doing and observing how Pro/E operates**. You can also learn a lot by exploring the program on your own and experimenting with the commands and options.

The ten lessons in this book will introduce you to the basic functionality of Pro/E. Please note that this is not a reference manual. Not all the available commands in Pro/E are covered (by a long shot!), nor will a comprehensive discussion of the myriad available options be attempted. The tutorials are meant only to get you started. Nonetheless, upon completion of these lessons (in about 30 or 40 hours!), you should be able to construct relatively complex parts and assemblies, and produce the related engineering drawings. You should also have developed a feel for the design philosophy and methods embedded in Pro/E so that you can explore other commands and understand the on-line reference documentation.

In the early tutorials and as each new function is introduced, commands are presented in considerable detail to explain what is going on and why. As you progress through the lessons, you will be given fewer details about commands that have been covered previously. For example, in Lesson #1 we show you explicitly how to create the default datum planes, mouse click by mouse click. Later on, we will just ask you to "Create the default datum planes" assuming that you know how to do that. Thus, the tutorials build off each other and are meant to be done in the order presented. It is important for you to go through the lessons in sequence and to have a good understanding of the material before you go on to the next lesson. This means that **you may have to go through each lesson (or some portions) more than once**. Each tutorial has some questions and exercises at the end to allow you to check your understanding of the concepts and commands and to give you a starting point for your own exploration of the program. No answers are given here for these questions - you will learn the material best if you have to dig them out for yourself! Each lesson concludes with a project activity that will result in the creation of the assembly shown on the cover page.

The images should correspond with those obtained in the Pro/E windows, and can be used to check your work as you proceed through the tutorials. Figures in this document, however, are only available in black-and-white, whereas in the Pro/E screen color plays an important role in determining the meaning of a line. Where a line interpretation may be ambiguous, the figures are labeled with the appropriate line color or different thickness. Also, some modifications have been made to the default system font in order to make the figures clearer.

These lessons were developed using the Windows NT™ version of the software, however operation under Unix is practically identical.

You are about to learn how to use one of the most sophisticated and powerful solid modeling programs available. It may be the most complex piece of software you have (or will) use. It's power derives from its extremely rich command set, that requires quite a long and steep learning curve to master. Do not be discouraged, as you will find it well worth the effort.

What *IS* Pro/ENGINEER?

Actually, Pro/E is a suite of programs that are used in the design, analysis, and manufacturing of a virtually unlimited range of products. In these tutorials, we will be dealing only with the major front-end module used for part and assembly design and model creation, and production of engineering drawings. There are a wide range of additional modules available to handle tasks ranging from sheet metal operations, piping layout, mold design, wiring harness design, NC machining, and other functions. An add-on package, Pro/MECHANICA (also from Parametric Technology)[1], integrates with Pro/E to perform structural analysis (static stress and deformation, buckling, vibration), thermal analysis, and motion analysis of mechanisms. Pro/MECHANICA can also do sensitivity studies and design optimization, based on the model created in Pro/E.

In a nutshell, Pro/ENGINEER is a *parametric, feature-based solid modeling* system.

"Feature-based" means that you create your parts and assemblies by defining features like extrusions, sweeps, cuts, holes, slots, rounds, and so on, instead of specifying low-level geometry like lines, arcs, and circles. This means that you, the designer, can think of your computer model at a very high level, and leave all the low-level geometric detail for Pro/E to figure out. Features are specified by setting values and attributes of elements such as reference planes or surfaces, direction of creation, pattern parameters, shape, dimensions, and others. The first seven lessons in this book deal with the creation and manipulation of features.

"Parametric" means that the physical shape of the part or assembly is driven by the values assigned to the attributes (primarily dimensions) of its features. You may define or modify a feature's dimensions or other attributes at any time (within limits!). Any changes will automatically propagate through your model. You can also relate the attributes of one feature to another. For example, if your design intent is such that a hole be centered on a block, you can relate the dimensional location of the hole to the block dimensions using a numeric formula; if the block dimensions change, the centered hole position will be re-

---

[1] A companion book, *The Pro/MECHANICA Tutorial* is also available from the publisher, Schroff Development Corp.

computed automatically.

"Solid Modeling" means that the computer model you create is able to contain all the "information" that a real solid object would have. It has volume and therefore, if you provide a value for the density of the material, it has mass and inertia. Unlike a surface model, if you make a hole or cut in a solid model, a new surface is automatically created and the model "knows" which side of this surface is solid material. The most useful thing about solid modeling is that it is impossible to create a computer model that is ambiguous or physically non-realizable, such as the "object" shown in the figure. The figure shows what appears to be a three-pronged tuning fork at the left end, but only has two square prongs coming off the handle at the right end. With solid modeling, you cannot create a "model" such as this that could not physically exist. This is quite easy to do with just 2D, wireframe, or even surface modeling.

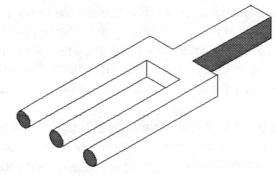

The 3-Pronged Blivot -
A Non-realizable Object

Whether or not the part could actually be manufactured is another story. Here is a cut-away view of a physically possible part, but don't take this to the machine shop and ask them to machine the cavity inside the part! Pro/E will let you make this model, but concerns of manufacturability are up to you.

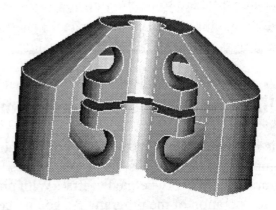

Could your machine shop make this?

An important aspect of feature-based modeling in Pro/E is the concept of **parent/child relationships**. Without going in to a lot of detail at this time, a child feature is one that references a previously created parent feature. For example, the surface of a block might be used as a reference plane to create a slot. A change to the parent feature will potentially affect the child. For example, deleting a parent feature will delete all its children since one or more references required to create the children would no longer exist. Pro/E has special functions available to manage parent/child relationships. This can get pretty complicated with a complex model (a good reason to try to keep your models simple!), so we will leave the details for later (Lesson #4). However, you should keep parent/child relations in mind when you are specifying feature references for a new feature you are creating: If the parent feature is temporary or is likely to change, what effect will this have on the children? Will the references still correctly capture your design intent?

Once your model is created, it is very easy to get Pro/E to produce fully detailed standard format **engineering drawings** almost completely automatically (Lesson #8). In this regard, Pro/E also has **bidirectional associativity** - this means you can change a dimension on the drawing and the shape of the model will automatically change, and vice versa. To a new user of the program, this is almost magic!

Of course, few parts live out their existence in isolation. Thus, a major design function accomplished with Pro/E is the construction of assemblies of parts (Lessons #9 and #10). Assembly is accomplished by specifying physically-based geometric constraints (insert, mate, align, and so on) between part features. Of course, drawings of assemblies can also be created. With assemblies you can see how the different parts will fit together or interfere with each other, or see how they move with respect to each other, for example, in a linkage assembly.

With Release 2000i^2 (which was a major upgrade!), Pro/E has continued the development of the user interface begun in Release 20. The program is more Windows-like than ever. A number of new tools and display "widgets" have been introduced which make the program easier to use. At the same time, for power users, there are a large number of shortcuts which can speed up your work quite a lot. These have made the program easier to use (the interface style will be quite familiar to Windows users) and added a lot of visual excitement to working with the program.

If you do not at some point say (or at least think) "WOW!" while learning how to use Pro/E, then you are very hard to impress indeed.

This sounds like it's pretty complicated!...

It is important to realize that you won't be able to master Pro/E overnight, or even after completing these lessons. Its power derives from its flexibility and rich set of commands. It is natural to feel overwhelmed at first! With practice, you will soon become comfortable with the basic operation of the program. As you proceed through the lessons, you will begin to get a feel for the operation of the program, and the philosophy behind feature based design. Before you know it, you'll feel like a veteran and will gain a tremendous amount of personal satisfaction from being able to competently use Pro/E to assist you in your design tasks. Some work done by students after completing this tutorial is featured in a Project Gallery, available on the Web at the URL <**http://www.mece.ualberta.ca/courses/mec265/vrprojects.htm**>.

To give you a hint of what is to come, you will find that using Pro/E is quite different from previous generation CAD programs. This is a case where not having previous CAD experience might even be an asset since you won't have to unlearn anything! For example, because it is a solid modeling program, all your work is done directly on a 3D model. Spatial visualization is very important and, fortunately, the Pro/E display is very easy to manipulate. Secondly, as with computer programming, with Pro/E you must do a considerable amount of thinking and planning ahead (some fast free-hand sketching ability will come in handy here!) in order to create a clean model of a part or assembly. Don't worry about these issues yet - they will not interfere with your learning the basic operation of the program. As you become more adept with Pro/E, you will naturally want to create more complex models. It is at this time that these high-level issues will assert themselves. In the meantime, have fun and practice, practice, practice.

Overview of the Lessons

A brief synopsis of the ten lessons in this series is given below. Each lesson should take at least 2 to 3 hours to complete - if you go through the lessons too quickly or thoughtlessly, you may not understand or remember the material. For best results, it is suggested that you scan/browse ahead through each lesson completely before going through it in detail. The enclosed CD-ROM has been created for just this task. You will then have a sense of where the lesson is going, and not be tempted to just follow the commands blindly. You need to have a sense of the forest when examining each individual tree!

Lessons 1 through 3, 6 and 7 deal with commands to generate features for individual parts, including extruded and revolved solids, chamfers and rounds, shafts, holes, cuts, sweeps and blends. Copied features and patterns of features are treated in Lesson 6. Lesson 5 deals with special reference features called datum planes and a temporary version of a datum plane called a "make datum". Lesson 4 concerns modeling utilities that are indispensable in dealing with parts composed of many features, in which changes to the fundamental structure of the part model are inevitable during any model development. In order to complete Lesson 4, you will need to download a part file - see the Schroff Development Corp Web page <**http://www.sdcpro.com**> or your instructor for details. Lesson 8 introduces the commands required to create detailed engineering drawings. Finally, Lessons 9 and 10 will introduce you to assembly modeling, in which previously created parts are brought "in session" and assembled using geometric constraints.

Lesson 1 - Getting started / Creating a simple object

How to start Pro/E; representation of Pro/E command syntax; command flow in Pro/E; special mouse functions; Pro/E windows; creating a part; using Sketcher (sketching, alignment, dimension, regeneration); Sketcher constraints; changing the view; saving a part; using part templates.

Lesson 2 - Creating Holes and Cuts

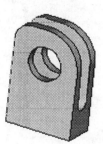

A hole and rounded cut are added to the block created in Lesson #1. More functionality of Sketcher is introduced, including the Intent Manager. Feature database functions are introduced. Changing the part dimensions directly and through relations. Naming features.

Lesson 3 - Creating Revolved Protrusions, Rounds, Chamfers

A new part is modeled using protrusions and a number of different features. Creating mirror copies. Some more drawing tools in Sketcher are introduced.

Lesson 4 - Modeling Utilities, Parent/Child Relations, and the 3 R's

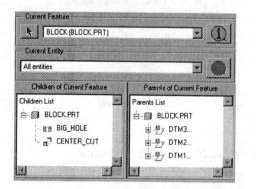

These utilities are used to investigate and edit your model: changing references, change feature shapes, changing the order of feature regeneration, changing feature attributes, and so on. If your model becomes even moderately complex, you will need to know how to do this!

Lesson 5 - Datum Planes

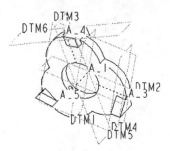

This lesson concentrates on the mysteries of datum planes and "make datums." What are they, how are they created, what can they do for you?

Lesson 6 - Revolved Features, Patterns, and Copies

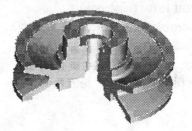

Revolved features are created by revolving a 2D sketch around an axis - very useful for axisymmetric shapes. Patterns are groups of features based on a pattern leader and arranged in a one-dimensional or two-dimensional array; each member of the group can be parametrically modified. A simple copy is a duplicated feature.

Lesson 7 - Sweeps and Blends

These are the most complicated (ie. flexible and powerful) features covered in these lessons. They are both types of solid protrusions, but can also be used to create cuts and slots.

Lesson 8 - Creating an Engineering Drawing

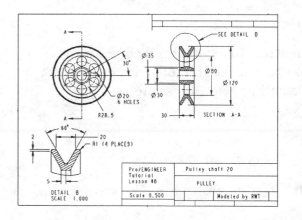

This lesson will introduce you to the process of making dimensioned engineering drawings. Two new parts are created (both parts will also be used in Lesson #9 on assemblies). Much of the work in creating the drawing is done by Pro/E, although a fair amount of manual labor must go into improving the cosmetics of the drawings.

Lesson 9 - Assembly Fundamentals

This lesson will show you how to create an assembly from previously created parts. This involves specifying placement constraints that specify how the parts are to fit together.

Lesson 10 - Assembly Modifications

This lesson will show you how to make modifications to the assembly created in Lesson #9. This includes changing part dimensions, adding assembly features, suppressing and resuming components, creating exploded views, and creating an assembly drawing

Once again, as you go through these lessons, take the time to explore the options available and experiment with the commands. You will learn the material the best when you try to apply it on your own ("flying solo"), perhaps trying to create some of the parts shown in the exercises at the end of each lesson.

On-Line Help

Should you require additional information on any command or function, Pro/E comes with extensive Web-based on-line help. This contains the complete text of *all* reference manuals for the software. There are several ways you can access the on-line help. These are presented towards the end of Lesson #1.

To those of you who have read this far: Congratulations! You are probably anxious to get going with Pro/E. Let's get started...

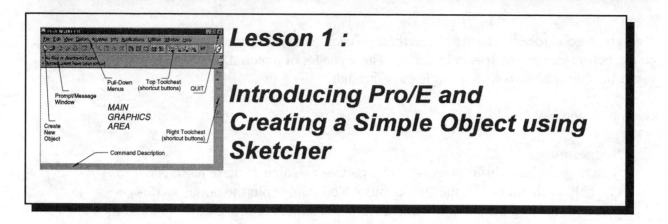

Synopsis

How to start Pro/E; representation of Pro/E command syntax; command flow in Pro/E; special mouse functions; Pro/E windows; creating a part; using Sketcher; Sketcher constraints; changing the view; saving a part; part templates.

Overview of this Lesson

We are going to cover a lot of introductory ground in this lesson. The main objectives are to introduce you to the general procedure for creating features and let you "get into" the Pro/E environment. We will go at quite a slow pace and not really accomplish much in terms of part creation, but the central ideas will be elaborated and emphasized.

1. Starting Pro/ENGINEER
   ‣ Pro/E windows
2. How commands are entered into Pro/ENGINEER
   ‣ menu picks
   ‣ command window
   ‣ special mouse functions
3. How this tutorial will represent the command sequence
4. How to get On-Line Help
5. Creating a Simple Part
   ‣ creating and naming the part
   ‣ creating datum planes
   ‣ creating a solid protrusion using Sketcher
6. Saving the part
7. Sketcher constraints during Regeneration
   ‣ implicit constraints
   ‣ unsuccessful regeneration
   ‣ the "Sadder Mister" sequence
8. View controls: Orientation and Environment
   ‣ naming views
9. Using Part Templates
10. Leaving Pro/ENGINEER

It will be a good idea to browse ahead through each section to get a feel for the direction we are going, before you do the lesson in detail. There is a lot of material here which you probably won't be able to absorb with a single pass-through.

Good luck and have fun!

Suggestion:
You may find it helpful to work with a partner on some of these lessons because you can help each other with the "tricky bits." You might split the duties so that one person is reading the tutorial while the other is doing the Pro/E keyboard and mouse stuff, and then switching duties periodically. It will also be handy to have two people scanning the menus for the desired commands and watching the screen. Pro/E uses a lot of visual queues to alert you to what the program is doing or requires next.

Starting Pro/ENGINEER

To start Pro/ENGINEER, type *proe2000i2* at your system prompt and press the **Enter** key[1]. The program takes a while to load so be patient. The startup is complete when your screen looks like Figure 1. The screen shown in the figure is the bare-bones, default Pro/E screen. If your system has been customized, your interface may look slightly different from this. The main graphics area is, of course, where most of the action will take place. Windows users will be quite at home with the pull-down menus and the use of the short-cut buttons at the top and right side of the screen (called the *toolbars* or *toolchest*). As you move the mouse across the short-cut buttons (several will be grayed out and inactive at this time), a brief description will appear on the bottom of the Pro/E window, and a tool tip window will pop up. The prompt/message window below the top toolchest shows brief system messages (including errors and warnings) during command execution. Pro/E is usually set up to show only the last 2 lines of text in this message area, but you can resize this area by dragging on the lower horizontal border. You can also use the scroll bars at the right to review the message history. The prompt/message area is also where text is typed at command prompts that ask for information such as dimensions and part names.

---

[1] You may have to check this sequence with your local system administrator, as different installations may handle the Pro/E launch differently. Under Windows, there may be an icon on your desktop, or you can look in the Start menu on the Windows Taskbar.

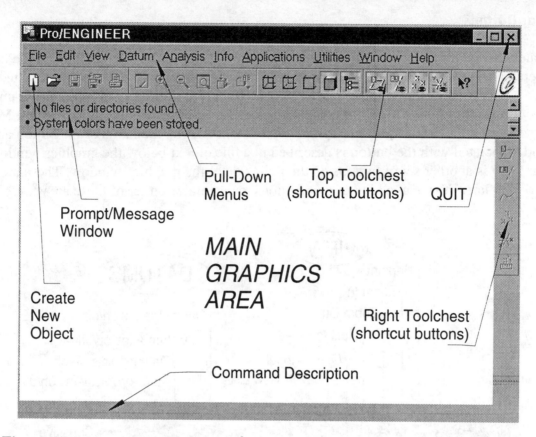

Figure 1 The Pro/ENGINEER 2000i^2 screen (default settings)

We will digress a bit to discuss how this tutorial will deal with command entry.

How commands are entered into Pro/ENGINEER

There are a number of ways that you will be interacting with the program: menu picks, buttons, keyboard entry, and special mouse functions. These are described below.

Pull-Down Menus

The main pull-down menus are presented across the top of the Pro/E window. Click on the *File* menu to open it and scan down the list of available commands. Many of these have direct analogs and similar functions to familiar Windows commands. Move your cursor across to each pull-down menu in turn and have a quick look at the available commands. We will introduce these on as "as-needed" basis as we go through the lessons. Some menu commands will open up a second level menu (these have a ▸ symbol). Commands unavailable in the current context are always grayed out. The available menu choices will also change depending on the current operating mode.

Short-cut Buttons

Immediately below the pull-down menus is a row of short-cut buttons. The buttons in the default screen setup are shown in Figure 2. There are basically four groups of buttons, as indicated on the figure. Other buttons may appear on this row as you enter different parts of the program. Buttons not relevant to the current program status are either not shown or are grayed out. Move your cursor across the buttons, and a pop-up window will tell you the name of the button and the command associated with the button is described in a line of text below the graphics window. Note that there is another set of buttons on the right side of the graphics window. These are discussed a bit later. You can add your own buttons to customize either of these areas[2].

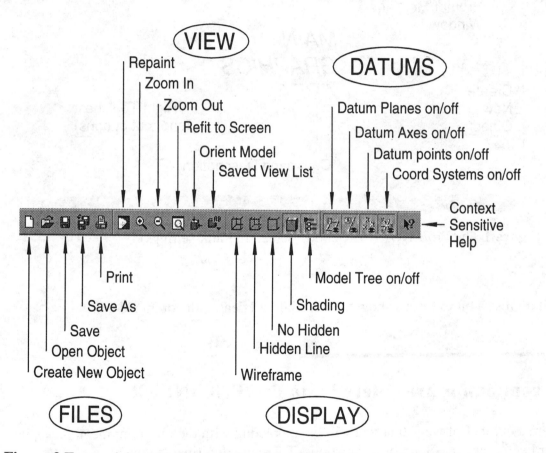

Figure 2 Top toolchest (default) with groups (toolbars) of related buttons

Menu Picks

Many other commands (and command options) are initiated using picks on menus that will appear at the time they are needed. These function menus will show up to the right of the main window, with commands arranged vertically. As you move the mouse pointer up and down within the command menus, a one-line message describing the command under the pointer will

---

[2] Customization of the interface is discussed in Lesson #1 in the *Pro/ENGINEER Advanced Tutorial* available from Schroff Development Corp.

appear at the bottom of the graphics window.

Suggestion:
As you start to learn Pro/E, each time you come to a new menu get in the habit of quickly scanning up and down the listed commands and noting the brief message in the command window. In this way, you will build a familiarity with the location of all the commands.

You execute a command by picking it using the *left* mouse button. Menu choices that are "grayed-out" are either not available on your system or are not valid commands at that particular time. Often, when you pick a command, other menus will pop open below the current one. When these represent options for the current command, the default option will be highlighted. You can select another option by clicking on it. There may be several groups of options on a single menu separated by horizontal lines. Any options not currently valid are grayed out. When all the options in a menu are set the way you want, click on *Done* at the bottom of the option menu window.

Helpful Hint:
Clicking the *middle* mouse button is often synonymous with selecting *Done* or pressing the *Enter* key on the keyboard.

You can often back out of a command menu by pressing an available *Done-return* or *Quit* command, or by pressing a command on a higher menu. At some times, you will be given a chance to *Cancel* a command. This often requires an explicit confirmation, so you don't have to worry about an accidental mouse click canceling some of your work.

Very Important Hint:
Regarding window management, DO NOT maximize the main Pro/E screen, and DO NOT resize or move the main or menu windows. Pro/E is pretty good about placing these so that they don't collide or overlap. If you start messing with the window size and placement, sooner or later you will bury a command menu behind other windows, particularly if your computer has a small screen. This will cause you a lot of confusion. Let Pro/E do its own window management for now.

Pop-Up Menus

One of the big changes in Pro/E 2000i^2 is the number of pop-up menus used. These are available in a number of operating modes by clicking (and holding down) the *right* mouse button. This brings up a pop-up menu at the cursor location which contains currently relevant commands, that is, they are context sensitive. These commands are often listed in the menus to the right, but having them pop-up at the cursor location means you don't have to keep taking your attention off the graphics window.

Command Window

Occasionally, you will enter commands from the keyboard. Generally, we will only use the keyboard to enter alphanumeric data when requested, such as object or file names, numerical values, and so on. Note that when Pro/E is expecting input in the command window, none of the menu picks will be "live."

Helpful Hint:
If your mouse ever seems "dead", that is the menus won't respond to mouse clicks, check the message window; Pro/E is probably waiting for you to type in a response.

You will have to get used to watching three areas on the screen: the menu(s), the graphics window, and the command/message window. At the start, this will get a little hectic at times. Until you become very familiar with the menu picks and command sequence, keep an eye on the one-line message description in the message window. There is often enough information there to help you complete a command sequence.

Special Mouse Functions

Locations within the graphics window and menu commands are generally identified and/or selected using a *left* mouse click. However, all three mouse buttons have been set up to provide shortcuts for operations within the graphics window. The basic ones are shown in Table 1.1. The more comfortable you get with these mouse functions, the quicker you will be able to work. They will become second nature after a while.

Other mouse functions will be introduced a bit later in the lessons. These have to do with the use of a powerful mode of operation of a program (called *Sketcher*) using a new program feature introduced in Pro/E 20 (called the *Intent Manager*). When we get to creating drawings (Lesson #8), we will find some more mouse commands specifically for that mode.

Table 1-1 Pro/ENGINEER Mouse Commands (PART MODE)

Mouse Mode	LEFT	MIDDLE	RIGHT
Regular	Pick	Done Done Select Enter	Query Select or pop-up menu
Dynamic View Control (press and hold CTRL + mouse button...)	(drag) Zoom In/Out	(drag) 3D Spin	(drag) Pan
Zoom Window (press CTRL plus ...)	Click opposite corners of zoom box		
Query Select	Pick	Accept	Next
Mouse Sketch - Draw Entity	Line	Circle	Tangent Arc
Mouse Sketch - Line mode		Abort/End	
Mouse Sketch - Circle mode	Abort/End		
Mouse Sketch - Tangent arc mode		Abort/End	
Sketcher Dimension - Linear	Pick entity	Place Dimension	
Sketcher Dimension - Radius	Pick arc/circle	Place Dimension	
Sketcher Dimension - Diameter	Double pick arc/circle	Place Dimension	

How this tutorial will represent the command sequence

In the early lessons, we will try to discuss each new command as it is entered (usually by selecting from a menu). Eventually, you will be told to enter a long sequence of commands that may span several menus and/or require keyboard input. We will use the following notation in these long sequences:

♦   If you select a command that starts up another menu window, followed by a selection from the new menu, you will see the notation using the ">" sign as follows:

   menu1 > menu2

♦   If a number of picks are to be made from the same menu you will see the notation using the

"|" sign as follows (these are generally selected in a top-to-bottom order in the menu):

option1 | option2 | option3

♦   If you are to enter data through the keyboard, you will see the notation using square
    brackets "*[...]*" as follows:

[block]

In this case, just enter the characters inside the square brackets.

Thus you might see a command sequence in a lesson that looks like this:

Feature > Create > Solid > Protrusion > Extrude | Solid | Done

If a command is launched using a toolbar button, that will be stated in the text.

How to get On-Line Help

Since Release 18 of Pro/E, extensive on-line help has been available. The help pages, consisting
of the entire Pro/E user manual set (many thousands of pages), are viewed using a browser (the
default is Netscape). There are three ways to access the help files:

1. *Right-clicking* on a command in the menus will show a button that you can press to
    bring up the relevant pages in the manual (context sensitive help).

2. Selecting the *Pro/E Help System* command from the *Help* pull-down menu.

3. Click the *What's This* button ⬛ on the right end of the top toolbar. Then click on
    any command or dialog window.

3. Launch your browser and point the URL to the location[3]

file:/el/ptc/proe2000i2/html/usascii/proe/master.htm

where e:/ptc/proe2000i2 is the drive and directory where you have the program
installed. Some installations may have the help files installed on a separate file server.

Once the Help pages are launched (this may take a few seconds), you can page forward or back,
or bring up additional navigation tools by selecting the "Contents" button. These tools include a
contents listing (Figure 3), an index (Figure 4), and a search function (Figure 5). The last two

---

[3]Check this location with your local system administrator.

require some time to load the data.

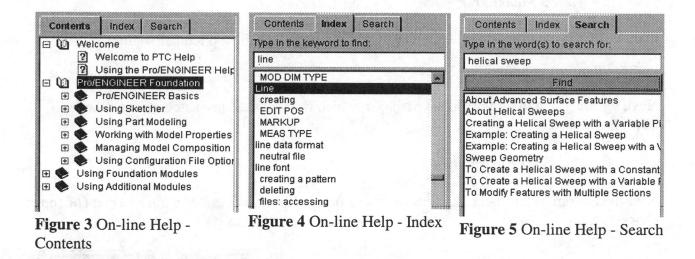

Figure 3 On-line Help -
Contents

Figure 4 On-line Help - Index

Figure 5 On-line Help - Search

Helpful Hint:
When you are finished browsing through the help pages, you should minimize the browser
rather than closing it. This will save you time if you want to start it up again later.

You are strongly urged to explore the on-line help. If you have a few minutes to spare now and
then, browse through the manuals (especially the *Pro/ENGINEER Foundation* sections). In the
beginning, it will be a rare event when you do this and don't pick up something useful. If you
desire and have the local facilities, you can obtain hard copy of these manual pages using your
browser. Your system may have postscript versions of these pages - check with your system
administrator. Be aware of the cost and time involved in printing off large quantities of
documentation.

Creating a Simple Part using Sketcher

In the first two lessons, we will create a simple block with a circular hole and a central slot. By
the end of the second lesson your part should look like Figure 6 below. This doesn't seem like
such a difficult part, but we are going to cover a few very important and fundamental concepts.
Try not to go through this too fast, since the material is crucial to your understanding of how
Pro/E works.

Not only are we going to go slowly here, but we are going to turn off some of the default actions
of Pro/E. This will require us to do several things manually instead of letting the program do
them automatically. This is so that you will have a better understanding of what the many default
actions are and do. Furthermore, eventually you will come across situations where you don't
want the default and you'll need to know what to do.

The first thing to do here is to turn off a special window called the Model Tree. We will be discussing this later on. Close it by selecting

> ### *View > Model Tree*

to turn off the check mark or press the short-cut button in the top toolbar so that it is not pressed in.

Next, we are going to turn off Intent Manager, which is a tool used in Sketcher. From the pull-down menus select

> ### *Utilities > Environment*

Near the bottom of this menu, turn off the check beside *Sketcher Intent Manager*. Then *OK* (not *Close*).

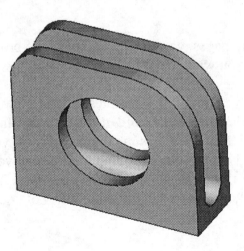

Figure 6 Final block at the end of lesson 2

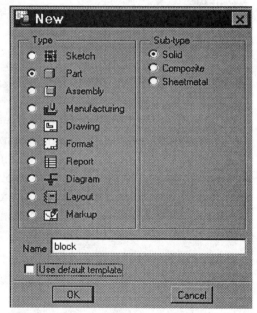

Figure 7 Creating a new part

Creating and Naming the Part

Click the "Create new object" short-cut button (see Figure 2), or select *File > New*. A window will open (Figure 7) showing a list of different types and sub-types of objects to create (parts, assemblies, drawings, and so on). In this lesson we are going to make a single solid object called a *part*. Select

> ### *Part | Solid*

Deselect the *Use Default Template* option at the bottom. Many parts, assemblies, drawings, etc. can be loaded simultaneously (given sufficient computer memory) in the current session. All objects are identified by unique names[4]. A default name for the new part is presented at the bottom of the window, something like **[PRT0001]**. It is almost always better to have a more descriptive name. So, double click (left mouse) on this text to highlight it and then type in

> *[block]*

(without the square brackets) as your part name and press *Enter* or select *OK*.

The *New File Options* dialog window opens, as shown to the right. Since we elected (in the previous window) to not use the default template for this part (NOTE: templates are discussed towards the end of this lesson), Pro/E is presenting a list of alternative templates defined for your system. As mentioned previously, we are going to avoid using defaults this time through. So, for now, select

> *Empty | OK.*

At this time, **BLOCK** should appear in the title area of the graphics window. Also, the **PART** menu should appear to the right of the main window.

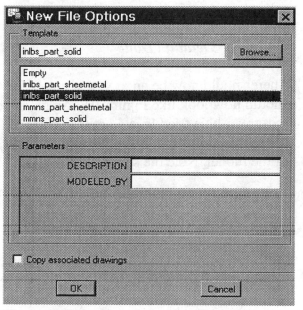

Figure 8 Setting options for new parts

Create Datum Planes and Coordinate System

We will now create the first features of the part: three reference planes to locate it in space. These are called *datum planes*. It is not strictly necessary to have datum planes, but it is a very good practice, particularly if you are going to make a complex part or assembly. The three default datum planes are created using the "Datum Plane" button on the right toolbar, as shown in Figure 9. Do that now.

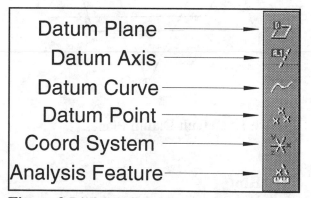

Figure 9 Right toolbar buttons for creation of datums

The datum planes represent three orthogonal planes to be used as references for features to be created later. You can think of these planes as XY, YZ, XZ planes, although you generally aren't concerned with the X,Y,Z form or notation.

---

[4] Pro/E can keep track of objects of different types with the same names. For example a part and a drawing can have the same name since they are different object types.

Your screen should have the datum planes visible, as shown in Figure 10. (If not, see the Hint below.) They will resemble something like a star due to the default 3D viewing direction. Note that each plane has a name: **DTM1**, **DTM2**, and **DTM3**. This view is somewhat hard to visualize, so Figure 11 shows how the datum planes would look if they were solid plates.

Although not strictly necessary for this part, we will establish a datum coordinate system. The command is started using the "Coord System" shortcut button shown in Figure 9. This opens a menu with a number of options for creating the position and orientation of the system. For now, select

Default | Done

There should now be an x, y, z icon labeled CSO in the middle of the datum planes. Your screen should now look like Figure 10. Again, depending on your system settings, you may also have a red-green-blue triad located at the center of the screen. This is called the *Spin Center*. This is not included in the part model but is strictly a display device to help visualize the 3D orientation of the model. Note the sequence red-green-blue (RGB) and the default axis directions (XYZ).

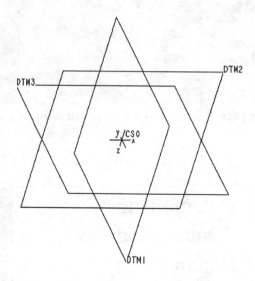

Figure 10 Default Datum Planes

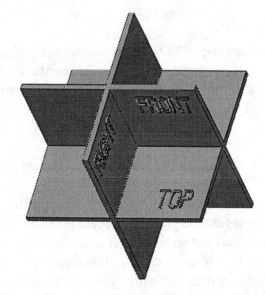

Figure 11 Datum planes represented as solids

Hint:
You can change the visibility of the datum planes in two ways: ① click the "Datum planes" short-cut button in the top toolbar (not the one on the right side - it does something different), or ② select *Utilities > Environment* and change the check box beside Datum Planes. Note that the Environment command lets you change the visibility and display of a number of items. Scan this list quickly before closing the window by clicking *OK*. Many of these environment settings (the most common ones) are duplicated by the short-cut buttons. Turning the datums off does not mean they are deleted, just not displayed. You may turn them back on at any time by re-issuing either of these commands.

Creating a Solid Protrusion using Sketcher

Now its time to start building our part! The *base feature* is the primary shape of a part and is (usually) the first solid feature made in the model. For the block we're working on, it is an extruded polygon. Later, we will add the hole and slot as *child* features. In Pro/E, new geometric features are usually created by specifying some sketching plane, creating a 2D shape or sketch in that plane, and then extending the shape into 3D either by extrusion, sweeping, or revolving. Let's see how that works for the simple block. We will perform the following steps that are common to most solid features:

1. Identify the Feature Type
2. Identify/Specify Feature Elements/Attributes
3. Make a 2D sketch of the basic geometry
4. Generate the feature by manipulating the sketch into 3D by extrusion, revolving, sweeping, blending and so on
5. Preview the feature
6. Accept the new feature

At any time during this process, you can cancel the operation. For the block, the base feature type is a *solid protrusion*. Feature elements include the sketching plane, the sketched shape, extrusion direction and depth. The shape is set up in a program called *Sketcher*.

To start the block, follow this sequence of commands (starting from the **PART** menu):

> *Feature > Create > Solid*
> *Protrusion > Extrude | Solid | Done*

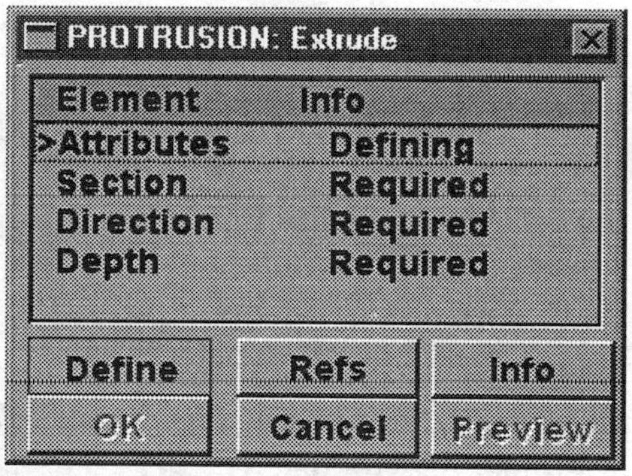

A window will open as shown in Figure 12. This shows the elements that must be defined to specify this feature. The current feature type (extruded protrusion) is shown at the top of the window. The window shows that we are defining the feature attributes. As we go through the process of defining elements, we will use a mix of menu picks and, possibly, some values entered at the keyboard

Figure 12 The Feature Elements Window

(usually numerical). This window will show us a summary of the specified data and record our progress as we create the feature.

As you proceed, you will be asked several questions and be presented with a considerable number of options. We won't go into a lot of detail on all these options now, because you probably want to get on to the good stuff as soon as possible. Just follow the menu picks described below.

First you must specify whether you want the extrusion to happen on one or both sides of the sketch plane (we'll set that up next). For now, choose the following (and remember that a highlighted menu item is pre-selected, and the middle mouse button means *Done*):

One Side | Done

Now (see the message window) you need to choose a sketch plane on which to draw the cross-sectional shape. For the block, the sketch plane will be one of the datum planes. **You can use any planar entity as a sketch plane (including the surface of an object).** The sketch plane is selected by using the left mouse button on either the edge or the nametag of the datum plane (or by clicking on any planar part surface). In this instance, you will use **DTM3** as your sketch plane, so click on the label **DTM3**.

A red arrow will appear somewhere on the edge of **DTM3**. Read the bottom line in the message window. For practice, choose the command *Flip* on the **DIRECTION** menu. This enables you to determine the direction of the extrusion off the sketching plane. For this step, ensure the arrow is pointing down/forward from **DTM3** (in the positive Z direction) using *Flip* if necessary. Then choose *Okay* to commit the direction.

Next, a *sketching reference* plane must be chosen. **This can cause a lot of confusion for new users, so pay attention!** This reference plane is used to orient how we will look at the sketching plane just selected (**DTM3**). Our view is always perpendicular to the sketch plane[5] and one-sided protrusions are always created towards you (coming out of the screen from the sketch). This means, in the present case, that we are going to be looking directly at the yellow side of the datum plane, in the -Z direction. Since we can rotate our view of the sketch arbitrarily around the Z axis, we must tell Pro/E how we want to set the orientation of our view of the sketch. We orient our view by choosing a *reference* plane. This can be any datum plane or planar part surface that is perpendicular to the sketch plane. We specify the direction that plane or surface will face in our view of the sketch (top, right, bottom, or left side of the screen). Unfortunately, Pro/E requires us to specify these in the opposite order - that is, first we select the direction we want the reference to face, then we select the reference plane itself. **Read this paragraph again, since new users are quite liable to end up drawing their sketches upside-down!**

To illustrate this crucial point, consider the images shown in Figure 13. These show two cases where different datums were chosen as the *Top* sketching reference. In both cases, the sketching plane was **DTM3**. On the left, the *Top* reference chosen was **DTM2**. On the right, the *Top* reference chosen was **DTM1**. The identical sketch, shown in the center, was used for both cases. However, notice the difference in the orientation of the part obtained in the final shaded images. Both of these models are displayed in the default orientation (check the datum planes). Clearly, choosing the sketching reference is important, particularly for the base feature.

---

[5]Well, almost always. It is possible to sketch in 3D, in which case you can manipulate your view so that you are not looking perpendicularly at the sketch plane. We will not attempt that here.

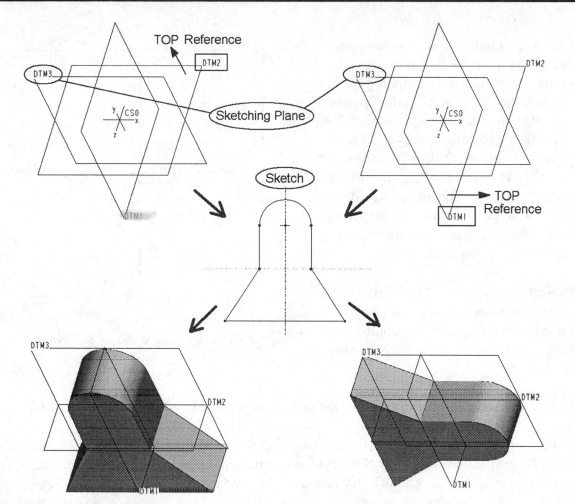

Figure 13 The importance of the sketching reference plane!

Note that there is a default setting available for the sketch reference. Until you get more experience with Pro/E, it is suggested that you avoid this. The default is chosen based on the current view orientation of the part. Therefore, the results can be unpredictable and quite likely not what you want.

Select *Top* from the **SKET VIEW** menu. The plane or surface we select next will face the *Top* of the screen in the sketch we are about to make. Click on **DTM2** (this determines the plane that you want to orient in the direction chosen).

IMPORTANT:
Another window titled "Sketcher Enhancement - Intent Manager" may also open up. We will be discussing this powerful tool a bit later in Lesson 2. For now, *Close* this window.

The graphics window should now appear as shown in Figure 14. The background color may have changed depending on your system settings. Note that the datum plane **DTM3**, that you identified as the sketching plane, is facing towards you (you should see a yellow square). The other datum planes (**DTM1** and **DTM2**) appear in edge view, with a yellow side and a red side. The yellow and red sides of datum planes will be more clear when you view them in 3D in a couple of minutes.

The yellow side (positive) of **DTM2** faces the top of the sketch, exactly as you specified above. Note that we could have obtained the same orientation by selecting *Right > DTM1*.

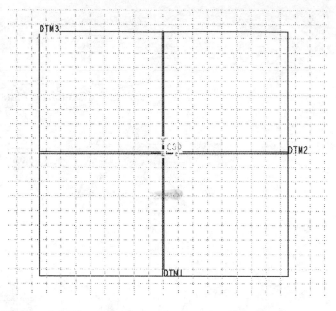

Figure 14 The drawing window in Sketcher

Observe the location and orientation of the coordinate system CSO and the spin center.

The Sketcher menus at the right of the screen are what you will use to create the 2D sketch for the part. Note also that some new short-cut buttons have appeared at the top of the screen. One of these is to turn the dashed grid off - try that now, then use the "Repaint" button to clean up the screen.

Defining the Sketch using Sketcher

The Sketcher menu is now open on the right side of the screen. This is actually the old version of the Sketcher menu used prior to the incorporation of Intent Manager (which occurred in Release 20). As mentioned above, we have turned off Intent Manager for now so that you can understand some of the underlying principles involved in creating a sketch. You need to know this clearly in order to use Intent Manager effectively. Furthermore, there will be rare occasions when you want to turn Intent Manager off and do everything yourself. Some practice with the old Sketcher interface will be useful.

Sketcher is a powerful tool for entering 2D shapes. It is where most of the part geometry creation happens and goes considerably beyond ordinary 2D computer drawing. It is truly a sketching tool since you don't have to be particularly accurate with the geometric shape you give it, as shown in the two figures below.

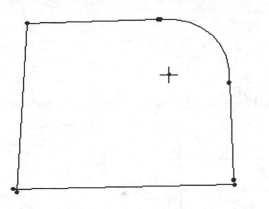

Figure 15 Geometry input by user. Note misaligned vertices, non-parallel edges, non-tangent curves.

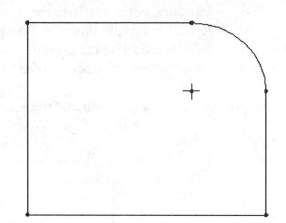

Figure 16 Geometry after processing by Sketcher. Note aligned vertices, parallel edges, tangent curves.

Sketcher is fun (but sometimes also frustrating) to use because it is so smart. Sketcher has a number of built-in rules for interpreting your sketch. For example, lines that "look like" they are at 90 degrees to each other are assumed to be exactly that; lines that "look" horizontal are assumed to be; and so on. The only thing Sketcher requires is that you give it just enough information (not too little or not too much) to be able to construct the shape unambiguously using its internal rule set and the dimensions that you provide.

Familiarity with Sketcher is very important. We won't go into a lot of detail with it at this time, but will gain experience steadily as we progress through the lessons. You would be well-advised to come back later and play around with more of the Sketcher functions as often as you can (perhaps doing some of the exercises at the end of the lesson). In any part creation, you probably spend more time in Sketcher than anywhere else in Pro/E.

Before we proceed, make sure that the **Sketch** and **Mouse Sketch** commands are highlighted. You might also like to review the mouse commands in Table 1-1.

① **Drawing the Sketch**

With the left mouse button, click once at each of the four corners of a rectangle as described below and illustrated in Figure 17. After each click, you will see a straight line rubber-band from the previous position to the cursor position. You do not have to be super accurate with these click positions. You can also sketch beyond the displayed edges of the datum planes - these actually extend off to infinity. The displayed extent of datum planes will (eventually) adjust to the currently displayed object(s). Here are the points to sketch the rectangle:

1.   left-click at the origin (intersection of **DTM1** and **DTM2**)
2.   left-click above the origin on **DTM1**

   3.   left-click horizontally to the right
   4.   left-click straight down on **DTM2**
   5.   left-click back at the origin
   6.   middle-click anywhere on the screen

This will complete the polygon and the screen should look similar to this (minus the balloons):

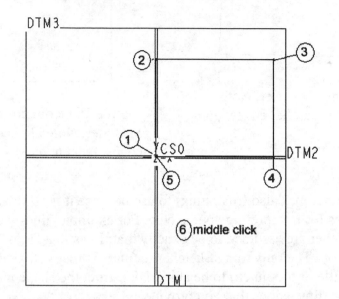

Figure 17 Drawing the Sketch

The sketched entities are shown in light blue (actually, cyan). The visible lines may only be partially seen due to the datum planes. Note that we didn't need to specify any drawing coordinates for the rectangle, nor, for that matter, are any coordinate values displayed anywhere on the screen. This is a significant departure from standard CAD programs. We also didn't need the grid or a snap function (although both of these are available in Pro/E).

To help us see the orientation of the part in 3D wireframe, we'll add a couple of rounded corners on the top corners of the sketch. In the **GEOMETRY** menu, select

      Arc > Fillet

and pick on the top and right lines in the sketch close to but not at the corner. A circular fillet is created to the closest pick point. Then pick on the top and left lines. Your sketch should look like Figure 18. Don't worry if your proportions are slightly different, or the rounded corners are not this size.

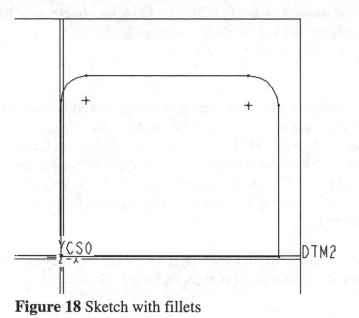

Figure 18 Sketch with fillets

Quick note:
If you make a mistake in drawing your shape, you can choose *Delete* from the
SKETCHER menu and click on whatever you wish to remove. Then replace or add
lines by selecting *Sketch* and *Mouse Sketch* again. We will cover more advanced
Sketcher commands a bit later.

② **Aligning the Sketch**

Next the sketch will be *aligned* with the datum planes. *Aligning is how you specify locational
relations between lines and vertices in your sketch and* **existing** *part features*. By aligning
sketched entities, you are essentially telling Pro/E to "keep this entity in the sketch lined up with
this previously created line, edge, or surface." Here are some important things to note about
alignments:

☞   You can only align new sketched features (in light blue) to previously defined features (in
     white or gray) or datums (planes, axes, curves, or points).
☞   You can't align any part of a sketch to another part of the same sketch.
☞   Alignment does **not** mean "make this line parallel to that one," which is a very common
     misinterpretation with new users.

Explicitly defining alignments is one reason why our sketch doesn't have to be absolutely precise
- Pro/E will make sure that the geometry will be created as you specify using alignments and
dimensions. Select the following

        Alignment > Align > Pick

Read the message in the message window. Click on the **lower horizontal line** of the sketch and then anywhere on the datum **DTM2**. In the message window,

--- ALIGNED ---

appears indicating a successful alignment, and a brown patterned line appears on the sketch at the alignment location. If alignment fails, you will see an error message. Try to align the top horizontal line of the sketch with **DTM2**. **This will fail.** Why? In order for alignment to succeed, the line must be "close" to the object you are aligning to (and remember that alignment does *NOT* mean "make parallel"). In the future, if your sketch is very inaccurate, you might have to zoom out on your sketch to bring the entity and the alignment reference closer together (within a few pixels on the screen).

Align the left vertical line and the plane **DTM1**. You can do this very quickly by double clicking on the sketch line since the datum plane is right underneath it.

③   **Dimensioning the Sketch**

So far, we have told Sketcher *where* our sketch is located using the alignments. Now we have to tell it *how big* the sketch is using dimensions. These (location and size) are two basic requirements for a successful sketch.

Click on **Dimension** in the **SKETCHER** menu. There are many ways to dimension this sketch. What follows is the easiest way (not necessarily the best!). Again, you might like to review the table of special mouse functions (Table 1-1).

Click the **left** mouse button on the lower horizontal edge of the sketch. Position the cursor below the sketch and click the **middle** mouse button. A dimension will appear with letters something like 'sd0'. The **sd** indicates that this is a sketch dimension; the **0** is a dimension identifier/counter generated by Pro/E. Each dimension in a sketch, part, or assembly has a unique identifier - this will be important later when we get to relations. This is the basis of the parametric nature of Pro/E. Dimensions are numbered successively, (eg. sd0, sd1,etc). So, if sd0 has already been used, the next dimension will be labeled sd1.

With *Dimension > Pick* still highlighted, **left** click on the upper and lower horizontal lines. Move the cursor to the right of the sketch and click the **middle** mouse button to place the dimension. Now **left** click on one of the arcs at the top, move away from the arc, and **middle**-click. Dimension the other arc the same way. Your dimensioned sketch should look something like Figure 19. Don't worry if your dimension symbols are different; what matters is the intent of the dimensioning scheme.

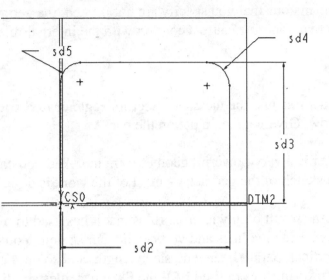

Figure 19 Dimensioned sketch (before regeneration)

④ **Regenerate**

Click on the command ***Regenerate*** on the SKETCHER menu. What does regeneration do? You will recall that Sketcher has a number of built-in rules to interpret your sketch. (We will discuss these rules at length a bit later in this lesson.) Regeneration calls on these rules (if necessary) to "clean up" your freehand drawing, also using the dimensional references and any alignments that you supplied. During regeneration, Sketcher determines correctness of your sketch. The three possible outcomes are

1. geometry underspecified

This is usually caused by missing alignments or incomplete dimensioning. The locations and lines that Sketcher cannot locate are shown in red (this is called "the measles" and everyone gets them sooner or later!). A message appears in the message window telling you to locate the indicated vertices. The ***Dimension*** command is automatically selected, although it may be that you have just forgotten to align some part of the sketch to the existing features.

2. geometry overspecified

There are more dimensional references than are required to specify the geometry. Redundant dimensions are shown in red, and the ***Delete*** command is automatically selected. Click on *any* dimension (ie. not just the red ones) to delete it. Be warned that clicking on any dimension may not necessarily solve your problem, since the problem may be elsewhere in the sketch. Note also that if a sketch is created by aligning all the geometric entities to previously created features, it may not be necessary to supply any dimensions for the new sketch. You may sometimes find that Sketcher needs fewer dimensions than you think it should. This is because it can figure out "missing" dimensions using its internal rule set. This can be good or bad, depending if you want any of those internal rules to be invoked. If any dimensions that you specify are not needed, the geometry is overspecified. If any dimensions that you give cause a conflict with the internal rule set, the regeneration will fail.

3. regeneration successful

Everything went just fine and the message "**Section regenerated successfully**." appears in the message window. Give yourself a pat on the back!

You can see that Sketcher is a very powerful geometry engine. And you can see why you only need to provide a rough sketch of the geometry - most of the work is done by Sketcher.

Sketcher will show you the result of any internal rules that it has used to regenerate your sketch. These appear as symbols beside the lines and vertices in your sketch. You can look for symbols indicating horizontal, vertical, parallel, tangent, same length, and so on. For our simple block, only two or three rules (probably) were fired. All the Sketcher rules are discussed a bit later in this lesson. You might investigate the *Constraints > Explain* command at this time.

⑤   Modifying Dimensional Values

After regeneration, numerical dimension values should appear in place of the 'sd' dimension labels. These values are generated according to the scale of the existing features (or seemingly at random if this is the first solid feature in the model). You need to change these numbers to the desired values.

To do this, select the *Modify* command on the **SKETCHER** menu. Then click on the horizontal dimension - it should turn red. In the message window, a prompt appears asking for the new value. The current value is shown, which will be the value used if you just hit the Enter key (ie. value is unchanged). Usually, you want to enter a new value here. For the horizontal dimension use *20*. After modifying, the dimension value appears in white, but our sketch hasn't changed size or shape. Change the vertical dimension to *30*. The radius of the arc on the right side is *10*, and on the left side is *5*.

⑥   Regenerate the Sketch

This is the step most often missed. After modifying any dimensions or alignments, the sketch must be updated. It is necessary to regenerate the sketch. You can tell when regeneration is needed because some of the dimensions will be showing in white.

Select *Regenerate* from the SKETCHER menu again. You will now see an animation of Sketcher going about its business. This animation will become useful when you create complex sketches, since you will be able to see the reasons why Sketcher might fail or your dimensioning scheme or values are not quite right. In that case, the animation will proceed up to the point where the sketch fails - usually caused by incompatible requirements on the sketch.

At this time your screen should look like Figure 20.

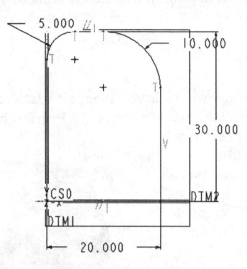

Figure 20 The final regenerated sketch

Assuming that the sketch regenerates successfully, then you are finished with Sketcher for this feature. To complete the process, select *Done* from the bottom of the SKETCHER menu (it may be partially hidden behind one of the smaller menu windows). Be careful that you don't click on *Quit* by mistake, although you can cancel that if you do.

> **Important Note:**
> For the time being, you should **never leave Sketcher with unresolved errors or warnings** that prevent a clean regeneration. Many errors are fatal, but some result only in warnings. Always resolve these problems and get a successful regeneration before leaving, indicated by the message "Section regenerated successfully." You will come to love seeing this message! We will see a few cases later when a warning is generated that we will ignore, but this situation is very rare.

⑦   **Specifying Extrusion Depth**

This is the final element to specify for the base feature (check out the element window). Recall that we set up this feature as a one-sided protrusion off **DTM3** (the sketch plane). To make the block, we will extrude the polygon for a *specified distance* - this is called a **blind** protrusion. From the **SPEC TO** menu, choose

> ***Blind | Done***

You will be prompted in the message window for an extrusion depth. Enter

> *10*

and press return.

A message should indicate that "All elements have been defined." meaning that the extrusion was created successfully.

Ⓐ   **Previewing the Feature**

Before accepting this new feature, we can have a look at it's 3D shape and relation to other features on the part. In the element window, click on the **Preview** button. Make sure the mouse is in the graphics window, then **press and hold down the CTRL key while dragging with the middle mouse button**. This will cause the shaded block to spin around following the mouse. You can do as much spinning as you want. You might note that, when viewed from the left/back/bottom, you will see the red side of the datum planes (these may not be visible while you are spinning). Also, note the new position of the spin center (if it is turned on). You can use the left and right mouse buttons (with CTRL) to zoom and pan in the graphics window.

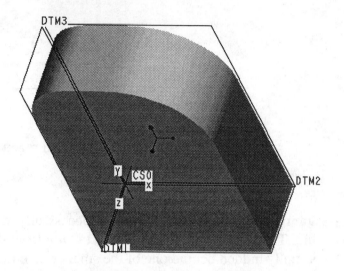

Figure 21 The final SOLID PROTRUSION feature

Ⓑ   **Accepting the Feature**

Once you are satisfied with the feature you have created, click on *OK* in the element window (or middle click). In the present case, you should see the message "Protrusion has been created successfully." in the message window. The final part shown in default view orientation (press CTRL-D or select *View > Default*) should look like Figure 21.

Saving the Part

It is a good idea to periodically save your model, just in case something serious goes wrong. From the top toolchest, select the "Save" button.

In the command window, you will be asked for the name of the object to be saved (remember that you can have more than one loaded into memory at a time). Accept the default **[block.prt]** (this is the *active* part) by pressing the enter key or the middle mouse button. Pro/E will automatically put a .prt extension on the file. In addition, if you save the part a number of times, Pro/E will automatically number each saved version (like block.prt.1, block.prt.2, block.prt.3, and so on). Since these files can get pretty big, you will eventually run out of disk space. So, be aware of how much space you have available. It may be necessary to delete some of the previously saved versions; or you can copy them to a diskette. You can do both of these tasks from within Pro/E - we'll talk about that later.

> **IMPORTANT NOTE:**
> The *Save* command is also available when you are in Sketcher. Executing this command at that time will *not* save the part, but it will save the current sketch with the file extension *sec*. This may be useful if the sketch is complicated and may be used again on a different part. Rather than recreate the sketch, it can be read in from the saved file. In these lessons, none of the sketches are complicated enough to warrant saving them to disk.

Working With Sketcher Constraints during Regeneration

Implicit Constraints

As alluded to above, Sketcher is a powerful geometry engine that is capable of "assuming" things about your input sketch that indicate your design intent. These assumptions are embodied in a number of rules (see Table 1-2) that Sketcher will invoke **if necessary** in order to successfully regenerate your sketch. It will only do this if the specified dimensions and/or alignments are not sufficient to completely define the geometry. You should become familiar with these rules, and learn how to use them to your advantage. Conversely, if you do not want a rule invoked, you must either (a) use explicit dimensions or alignments, or (b) exaggerate the geometry so that if fired, the rule will fail, or (c) tell Pro/E explicitly to disable the constraints. For example, if a line in a sketch must be 2° away from vertical, draw it at 15° and explicitly dimension it, otherwise it will be assumed to be exactly vertical with no dimension required (thus no way to make it 2° off). After the sketch regenerates, you can modify the dimension to the desired 2°. When geometry is driven by an explicitly created dimension, some internal rules will not fire.

Table 1-2 Implicit Rules in Sketcher

Rule	Description
Equal radius and diameter	If you sketch two or more arcs or circles with approximately the same radius, the system may assume that the radii are equal
Symmetry	Entities may be assumed to be symmetric about a centerline
Horizontal and vertical lines	Lines that are approximately horizontal or vertical may be considered to be exactly so.
Parallel and perpendicular lines	Lines that are sketched approximately parallel or perpendicular may be considered to be exactly so.
Tangency	Entities sketched approximately tangent to each other may be assumed to be tangent
Equal segment lengths	Lines of approximately the same length may be assumed to have the same length
Point entities lying on other entities or collinear with other entities	Point entities that lie near lines, arcs, or circles may be considered to be exactly on them. Points that are near the extension of a line may be assumed to lie on it.
Equal coordinates	Endpoints and centers of the arcs may be assumed to have the same X- or the same Y-coordinates
Midpoint of line	If the midpoint of a line is close to a sketch reference, it will be placed on the reference.

When a sketch is regenerated, the rules that have been fired are indicated on the graphics window using one (or more) symbols beside each affected entity. The symbols are shown in Table 1-3 on the next page.

Table 1-3 Graphical Display of Sketcher Constraints

Constraint	Symbol
Horizontal entities	"H"
Vertical entities	"V"
Line segments with equal lengths	"L" with an index in subscript (for example: L_1)
Perpendicular lines	Perpendicularity symbol with or without an index number in subscript
Parallel lines	Parallel symbol with an index in subscript
Equal coordinates	Small thick dashes between the points
Tangent entities	"T"
Midpoint of line	"M"
Symmetry	→ ←
Equal radii	"R" with an index in subscript
Point entity	—O—

An example of a solved sketch with the geometric constraints is shown in Figure 22. Note how few dimensions are required to define this sketch.

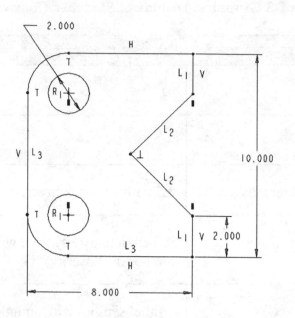

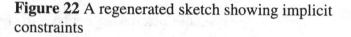

Figure 22 A regenerated sketch showing implicit constraints

Unsuccessful Regeneration of a Sketch

If a sketch cannot be solved using the dimensioning scheme and implicit rules, Pro/ENGINEER issues a message and highlights the error. The basic categories of errors are as follows:

- The sketch does not communicate the intent. For example, a line that you want tangent to an arc is not "close enough" for Sketcher to figure out what to do.
- The sketch is underdimensioned.
- The sketch is overdimensioned.
- The segment is too small. If you have modified dimensions such that a line segment becomes very small, then Sketcher will flag this as an error. If you really do want the short segment, zoom in on the sketch and regenerate again.
- The segment is of zero length. This is similar to the previous error which arises if you have modified dimensions so that in the recomputed position a line segment must have zero length. This is an error that must be fixed in the sketch.
- There are inappropriate sections. For example, a sketch that crosses over itself, or an open sketch for a feature that requires a closed one (eg. for a revolved protrusion).

The "Sadder Mister" Order of Operations

A common "error" that can lead to problems getting a successful regeneration is **NOT** following the sequence below:

> **Sketch**
> > **Align**
> > > **Dimension**
> > > > **Regenerate**
> > > > > **Modify**
> > > > > > **Regenerate**

You can remember this sequence using the acronym "Sadder Mister" taken from the first letter of each step:

S   A   D   R   M   R

Remember that Sketcher will automatically provide values for all new dimensions based on the existing features when it regenerates a sketch. Let it do that! **There is no need to "modify" dimension values prior to the first regeneration, and doing so can often cause you grief! This means, do not Modify a dimension shown in its symbolic (*sdxx*) form!**

Now, all that being said, we will see in the next lesson how the Intent Manager is able to assist you in obtaining a "legal" sketch, usually with considerably fewer commands and mouse clicks and without having to deal with regeneration failures. It is important, however, to understand the basic principles of Sketcher, and the implicit rules, in order to use Intent Manager efficiently. Also, sometimes, you may not want to use Intent Manager.

The exercises at the end of this lesson are to give you practice using Sketcher and to explore commands in the Sketcher menus.

View Controls: Orientation and Environment

In addition to the dynamic viewing capabilities available with the mouse, you can go to predefined orientations. To view the object in the default orientation (called "trimetric"), select the "Saved view list" shortcut button and click on *Default*, the only view currently defined. Alternatively, you can select

> *View > Default*

or press **CTRL-D** (hold the Control key while you press D). Your screen should now look like Figure 21 above.

You can experiment with the *View > Orientation* menu (see Figure 23) to change the display (or use the "Orient model" shortcut button, Figure 2). Read any prompts/messages in the message window. The general procedure for the *Orient by Reference* type is to select a pair of orthogonal surfaces that will face the front, right, top, or left in the desired view. These are called the view references. For example, *Front:DTM3* and *Top:DTM2* will give the same view as our sketch. You can also obtain a new view by an explicit rotation around an axis in the part, or relative to the screen.

Naming Views

Views that you are going to use over and over are usually named so that it is easy to return to them later. When a desired view is obtained (like one of the standard engineering top-front-right orientations), the view can be saved by entering a view name and selecting **Save**. See Figure 23. Once a view has been named, you can easily return to it using the "Saved view list" button. Try this by creating and naming the standard engineering Top, Front, and Right views of the block by selecting the following references:

Standard Engineering View	Reference 1	Reference 2
Top	Front:DTM2	Right:DTM1
Front	Front:DTM3	Top:DTM2
Right	Front:DTM1	Top:DTM2

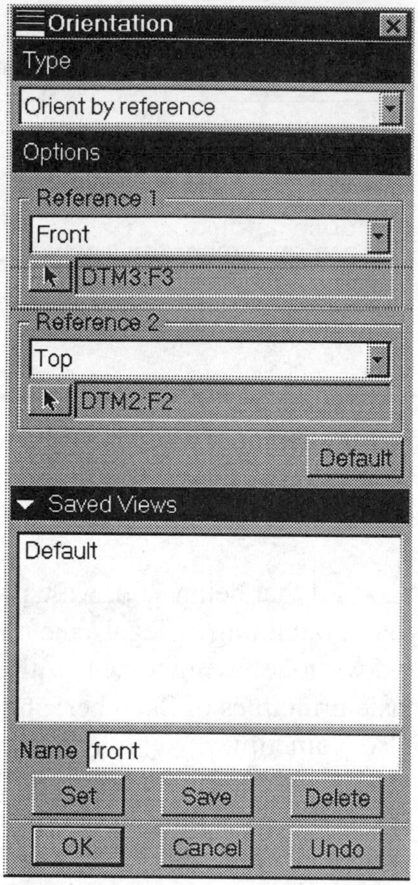

Figure 23 View creation and naming menu

Modifying the View Environment

Try using some of the commands under the **Utilities > Environment** menu. These commands include hidden line, no hidden or turning on/off the datum planes or the coordinate system. The default settings usually show hidden lines and tangent edges as gray lines. Your new settings will take effect when you select **Apply** or leave the **Environment** menu. Note that the most common display styles are easily obtained using the short-cut buttons in the top toolchest. Experiment with these buttons, leaving the view showing wireframe with hidden lines. Note that hidden lines are shown in a slightly darker shade than visible lines. With practice, you will be able to use this visible clue to help you understand the 3D orientation of the part in space.

The view control commands sometimes interact in strange ways. For example, to see a shaded image, select

> **View > Shade**

Note that this view turns off the datum planes. If you dynamically spin this view, the shading will disappear. The "Shading" shortcut button, however, will leave the datum planes visible and you can spin the shaded image.

Using Part Templates

This is one of the exciting enhancements in Pro/E 2000i^2. In the block part created previously, the first thing we did was to create default datum planes. In the last section, we created named views. These are very common features and aspects of part files, and it would be handy if this was done automatically. This is exactly the purpose of part templates.

A template is a previously created "empty" part file that contains the common features and aspects of almost all part files you will ever make. These include, among other things, default datum planes and named views. Pro/E actually has several templates available for parts, drawings, and assemblies. There are variations of the templates for each type of object. One important variation consists of the unit system used for the part (inches or millimeters). Templates also contain some common model parameters and layer definitions[6].

A template is selected when a new model is first created. Let's see how that works. Create a new part (note that you don't have to remove the block - Pro/E can have several parts "in session" at the same time) by selecting

>   *File > New*

or using the "Create New Object" button. The New dialog window opens. Select the options

>   *Part | Solid*

and enter a new name, like *exercise_1*. Remove the check mark beside *Use default template* and then select *OK*.

In the **New File Options** dialog window, the default template is shown at the top. It is likely "inlbs_part_solid". This template is for solid parts with the units set to inch-pound-second. It seems strange to have force and time units in a CAD geometry program. Actually, this is included so that the part units are known by downstream applications like Pro/MECHANICA which perform finite element analysis (FEA) or mechanism dynamics calculations. These programs are very picky about units!

Note that there are templates available for sheet-metal parts and for metric units (millimeter-Newton-second). While we are mentioning units, be aware that if you make a wrong choice of units here, it is still possible to change the units of a part after it has been created.

There are only two model parameters in the default template. *DESCRIPTION* is for an extended title for the part, like "UPPER PUMP HOUSING". This title can (eventually) be called up and placed automatically on a drawing of the part using, you guessed it, a drawing template. Similarly, the *MODELED_BY* parameter is available for you to record your name or initials as the originator of the part. Fill in these parameter fields and select *OK*.

---

[6] Model parameters and layers are discussed in the *Advanced Tutorial*.

The new part is created which automatically displays the default datums. They are even named for you (we will see how to name features in lesson 2): instead of DTM1, we have **RIGHT**. **TOP** replaces DTM2, and **FRONT** replaces DTM3. The part also contains a coordinate system, named views (look in the Saved Views List), and other data that we'll discover as we go through the lessons. The named views correspond to the standard engineering views. Thus, it is important to note that if you are planning on using a drawing template (discussed in Lesson #8), your model orientation relative to the default datums is critical. The top-front-right views of the part are the ones that will be automatically placed on the drawing later. If your model is upside down or backwards in these named views, then so will be your drawing. This is embarrassing!

Now, having created this new part, you are all set up to do some of the exercises at the end of the lesson!

Leaving Pro/ENGINEER

When you want to quit Pro/E entirely, after you have saved your part(s), you can leave by using the *Exit* command in the **File** menu or the X at the top-right corner. Depending on how your system has been set up, Pro/E may prompt you to save your part and any sketches you made. In these lessons, you do not need to save the sketches. If you are sure you have saved the most recent version of the part, you don't need to do that again.

This completes Lesson #1. You are strongly encouraged to experiment with any of the commands that have been presented in this lesson. Create new parts for your experiments since we will need the block part in its present form for the next lesson. The only way to become proficient with Pro/E is to use it a lot!

In the next lesson we will add some more features to the block, discover the magic of relations, and spend some time learning about the Intent Manager in Sketcher.

Questions for Review

Here are some questions you should be able to answer at this time:

1. What is meant by a blind protrusion?
2. What is the purpose of the sketching reference plane?
3. What aspect of feature creation results in the parametric nature of the model?
4. What mouse action can be used to spin the object?
5. What is meant by alignment?
6. What three outcomes are possible when you regenerate a sketch? What do these mean?
7. What is the correct order of the following activities for using Sketcher:
    ◆ sketch drawing
    ◆ modify dimensions
    ◆ regenerate
    ◆ alignments
    ◆ place dimensions
    ◆ regenerate
8. Why do datum planes have a red and yellow side?
9. What is the purpose of the datum planes?
10. When you look at a sketch, in which direction will a one-sided solid protrusion occur?
11. How do you specify the name of a part?
12. What are three ways to get on-line help?
13. When you are in Mouse Sketch mode, what do the three mouse buttons do?
14. How can you get a shaded image of the part?
15. What mouse action can be used to zoom in on the part?
16. How do you turn the datum plane visibility on and off?
17. Give as many of the Sketcher implicit rules as you can.
18. How do you save a part?
19. What is the difference in operation between *View > Shade* and the "Shading" shortcut button?
20. What is a template?
21. What is your system's default template?
22. Where does your system store your part files when they are saved?
23. What is meant by the *active* part?
24. How does Sketcher determine the radius of a fillet created on two lines?
25. Try to create sketches/procedures that cause the errors noted in the section "Unsuccessful Regeneration of a Sketch" on page 1-28.

Exercises

Here are some simple shapes that you can make with a single solid protrusion. They should give you some practice using the Sketcher drawing tools and internal rules. Create these with Intent Manager turned off. Choose your own dimensions and pay attention to alignments and internal constraints. The objects should appear in roughly the same orientation in default view.

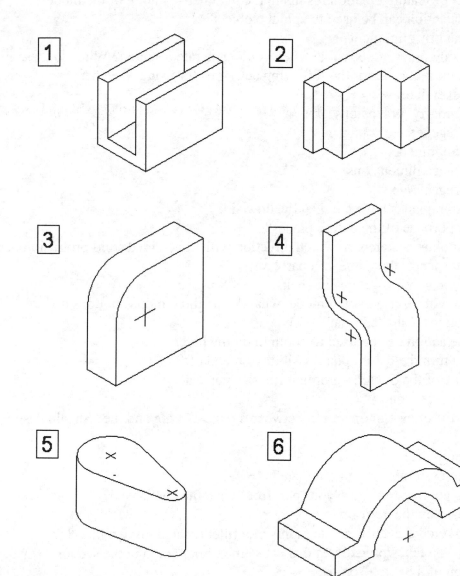

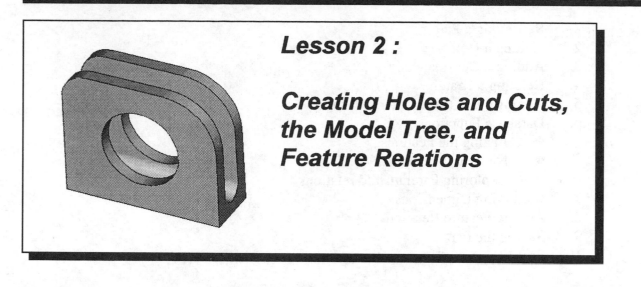

Lesson 2 :

Creating Holes and Cuts, the Model Tree, and Feature Relations

Synopsis

A hole and rectangular slot are added to the block created in Lesson #1. Introduction to the Intent Manager in Sketcher. Feature database functions are introduced: listing and naming features. Modifying dimensions of the part features; adding relations to control part geometry. Implementing *design intent*.

Overview of this Lesson

We will continue with the creation of the block part you started in Lesson 1. We are going to add two features to the block: a circular hole and a central slot. The circular hole feature does not require Sketcher, but the slot will. Then, to introduce and demonstrate some of the capability of Pro/E, we will modify some part dimensions, and then add a couple of relations to adjust the geometry automatically. We will also look at some Pro/E commands that let us keep track of the feature database we are creating.

When we are finished this lesson, the block part should look like Figure 1. Although not obvious from the figure, there are a number of different ways we can create the geometry. This goes to the subject of *design intent*, which will be discussed towards the end of the lesson. Coupled with this is an introduction to the functionality in Sketcher called the Intent Manager.

Here are the major steps we will follow. You can jump ahead to any of these for information purposes, but the steps should be completed in order:

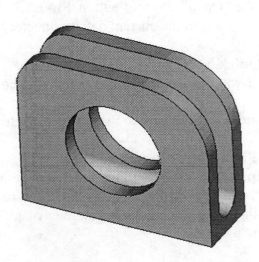

Figure 1 Final Part

1. Retrieving a Part
2. Adding a Hole
3. Adding a Cut (manually)
4. Deleting a Feature
5. Adding a Cut (using Intent Manager)
6. Database Functions
    ♦   Listing the Features
    ♦   Naming the Features
    ♦   Exploring Parent/Child relations
7. Modifying Dimensions
8. Adding Feature Relations
9. Saving the Part
10. Pro/E Files saved automatically

As usual, we will not discuss all command options in each menu in detail although some important modeling and Pro/E concepts will be elaborated. As you come across each new menu, you should quickly scan up and down the command list to familiarize yourself with the location of the available commands/options.

Retrieving a Part

If you haven't already, login to the computer and bring up Pro/Engineer. If you are already in Pro/E, make sure there are no parts in the current session (select *File > Erase > Current*; then select *File > Erase > Not Displayed* to remove any other parts in the session).

Retrieve the block part using the command sequence:

>   *File > Open*

or use the "Open" shortcut button. Pro/E will bring up a list of all the objects (parts, assemblies, drawings, etc.) in the current default directory.

>   **Quick Note:**
>   If you need to change the default directory, use the commands:
>   *File > Working Directory*
>   and select the path to the desired directory for your *block.prt* file from the last lesson.

In the **File Open** dialog window, files in the current directory are listed. Left click on the file **block.prt**, then select the *Preview* button at the bottom. This preview function, new in Pro/E 2000i^2, will be useful when your directory starts to fill up with part files by making it easier to select the file you want. Note that the dynamic view controls (spin, zoom, pan) work in the preview window.

With **block.prt** highlighted select the *Open* button (or middle click). Pro/E will bring the part into the session and display it in the default orientation as shown in Figure 2. Close the Model Tree window if it comes up and make sure Intent Manager is turned off. Both of these can be set using *Utilities > Environment*.

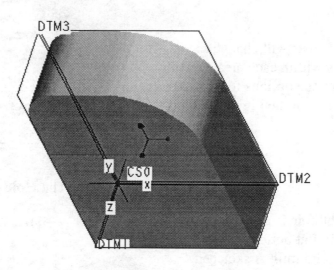

Figure 2 The *base feature* of the block

Adding a Hole

The next feature we'll add to the block is the central hole. There are almost as many versions of holes as there are of protrusions - that is, a lot! Beginning at the **PART** menu, the command sequence is:

> *Feature > Create > Solid > Hole*

You might wonder what a "solid hole" is! This is just Pro/E's way of organizing geometric elements - a solid is basically a 3D primitive that involves "mass", as opposed to a surface, datum, etc. which doesn't. It happens to be a hole because when it is combined with the existing features it results in material removal from the part.

The Hole dialog window is now open and should appear as in Figure 3.

There are four areas in this dialog:

- Hole Type
- Hole Dimension
- Hole Placement
- Hole Note Preview

The contents of these areas will change as you select various options within each area. Starting at the top of the window, the options for the various hole types are illustrated in the Figures below.

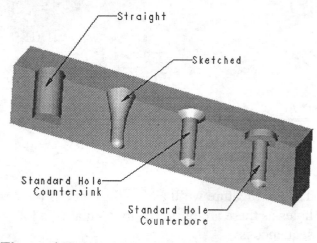

Figure 3 The **Hole** dialog window

Hole Type: A straight hole is a simple cylindrical hole with a flat bottom, essentially what you get with an end mill. A sketched hole involves the use of Sketcher to define the hole cross sectional shape. This shape is revolved through 360° to create the hole. This obviously gives considerable freedom in the hole geometry. This is handy for holes with several steps or unusual curved profiles. The standard holes (including threads) can be countersunk, counterbore, neither, or both! Notice the shape at the bottom of the holes. Standard hole sizes are built-in for common bolts and thread specifications. If you pick a common thread specification, this will automatically create a note (that can be included in a drawing, for example).

Figure 4 Hole types

Hole Dimension and Depth: The primary dimension for a hole is its diameter. A number of options are available to determine the depth of the hole. These are shown in Figure 5. If the hole is created "both sides" from the placement plane, then the hole depth can be defined separately in each direction.

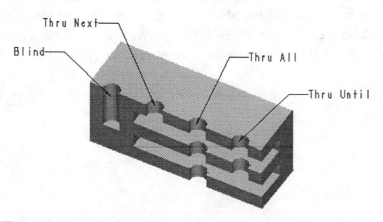

Figure 5 Hole depth options

Hole Placement: Finally, there are two basic methods of determining the hole placement, as shown in Figure 6. These use a linear dimensioning scheme (on the left) and a radial/angular dimensioning scheme (on the right). Linear placement will positioned the hole using linear dimensions from selected references to its center point. The references are typically surfaces of the part or datum planes. Radial placement requires an axis, a radial distance from the axis, and an angular distance from a planar reference.

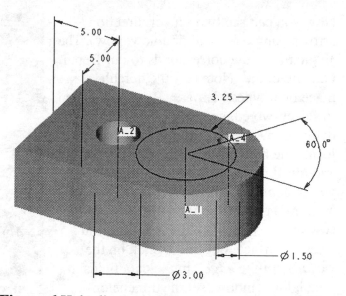

Figure 6 Hole dimensioning schemes: linear (left) and radial (right)

Basically, you fill in the dialog window from top to bottom. We will come back later to explore this window some more. For now, all we want is a straight, 'thru all' hole using linear placement on the front surface of the block. This is the easiest hole imaginable to create.

In the **Hole Type** area, select **Straight Hole**. In the **Dimension** area, enter a diameter of **10**. In the **Depth One** pull-down list, select **Thru All**. The appearance of the window will change, and in the **Placement** area, the Primary Reference button is pre-selected. Pro/E is asking for the surface where you want to place the hole (also called the placement plane).

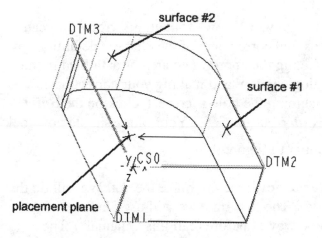

Click on the front face of the block at the approximate location of the hole center (mid-way between the left and right faces, 2/3 of the way up from the bottom). You do not have to be very accurate with this since we will be setting exact dimensions next.

Figure 7 Surfaces and dimensions required for linear placement of a hole

Now you can see two sets of direction arrows (single red and double yellow). The single red arrow corresponds to our Depth One direction[1]. Note that the default placement type is **Linear**. Pro/E wants you to select two edges, axes, planar surfaces or datum planes for linear dimensions to locate the hole center. We will use the right and top surfaces of the block (make sure you pick on the flat surface at the top). You might like to spin the block so that the two surfaces are visible. Each time you select a surface, be sure to click on the *surface* not the *edge*. In the data fields in the dialog window, set the dimensions to place the hole **10 units from the right face, 10 units from the top face**.

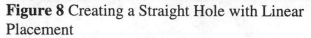

Figure 8 Creating a Straight Hole with Linear Placement

This completes the definition of the hole. The completed dialog window for this hole is shown in Figure 8. Before you leave this window, select the ***Preview*** button 🔳 to see the hole. An outline of the hole will appear. Use Ctrl-middle mouse button to spin the part. Note that an axis line has been added automatically.

If the preview shows something wrong, you can go back and correct any of the element definitions by selecting the appropriate area or data field in the dialog window and making your corrections. Assuming the hole is correct, click on the ***Build Feature*** button ✅. Your block should now look similar to Figure 9.

We are now ready to make the cut. We will do this twice. The first time we will use Sketcher in the same way as before (call this "manual"). The second time, we will introduce a very powerful tool called the Intent Manager.

Before we proceed, change the display to **Hidden Line**.

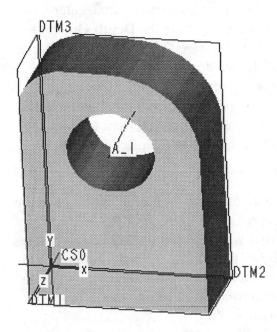

Figure 9 Hole feature added

---

[1]You might ask yourself how Pro/E knows this!

Adding a Cut (manual)

To complete the block, we will cut away the central portion by creating a feature that subtracts material from the part. We have two feature choices here: a slot[2] or a cut. These are quite similar, and the difference between them is subtle. Both features involve the creation of a 2D sketch that represents a cross section view of one or more cutting surfaces. The sketch of the cutting surface(s) can contain straight or curved lines or a combination of these as long as the cutting surface doesn't intersect itself. It is possible to have several disjoint closed cutting surfaces in the same sketch (although this is not advisable). The sketch is then extruded, revolved, or swept through the part. The difference between a slot and a cut is as follows:

slot

The 2D sketch is a closed section. Material is removed from inside the section as it is extruded or revolved. Slots are usually created normal to a part surface to create pockets.

cut

The 2D sketch can be an open or closed section. You will get to specify which side of the cut surface the material is removed from. Cuts are the major "sculpturing" tool used to create the exterior/interior shape of a part.

We will use a cut feature in this lesson. You might like to come back and create the same geometry using a slot. Execute the following command sequence, starting in the **PART** menu:

Feature > Create > Solid > Cut > Extrude | Solid | Done

Once again, it seems strange that the cut feature is obtained by selecting a solid feature! Think of what you are creating as a negative solid. In any case, the term "cut" is self-explanatory. Extrude means that the feature will be created normal to our sketch, rather than revolved around an axis.

The element window will now open up (note the title on this window) and we will proceed through the definition of the various elements. First, we have to specify how the cut will be extruded from our sketch. Select

One Side | Done

Now we choose the sketch plane. We will sketch the outline of the slot on the right end of the block (see Figure 10), and let it extrude through to the left end. The following selections should be highlighted (if not, just select them)

Setup New > Plane > Pick

------

[2]The availability of the slot feature depends on your system configuration settings. See your system administrator if the slot feature is not available.

Click on the *right* face of the block (assuming you are in the default orientation). A red arrow should appear showing the direction of feature creation. The arrow should be horizontal on the screen and pointing into the block (to the left). You can change the direction of the arrow using *Flip*. For now, make sure it is pointing into the block and click on *Okay*.

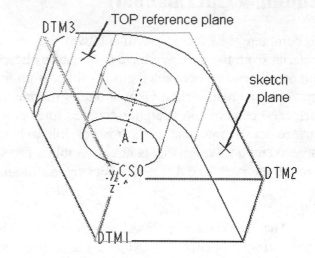

You now need to pick a reference plane to orient your view of the sketch. Remember that **cuts are always created away from you as you look at the sketching plane**. Choose *Top* in the **SKET VIEW** menu and click on the *top* surface of the block (ie. the selected surface of the block will face the top of the screen).

Figure 10 Sketching and reference planes for the cut

Think about this: would we get the same view using *Left* and **DTM3**?

You should now be in Sketcher, looking directly at the right face of the block. If you have hidden lines turned on, you should see gray lines representing the contour of the hole. You can turn off the grid lines using one of the shortcut buttons.

Important Note:

To repeat: When Pro/E sets up the sketching orientation, the direction of view is such that cuts or slots will extend into the screen (away from you) while protrusions will extend out of the screen (towards you). When you first open a sketch window, be sure to understand the orientation of the sketch. Sometimes you will end up looking at the part the "wrong way around", that is from the reverse direction from what you were expecting. This is where some good 3D visualization skill comes in very handy! When you are in Sketcher you can use the *Ctrl-middle* mouse button to spin the part and sketch to check your orientation. To return to the normal view, select *Sketch View* in the Sketcher menu.

If they aren't already, select

Sketch > Mouse Sketch

Use mouse clicks at the positions indicated in
Figure 11 as follows:

Point   Mouse clicks
①   left - start of line
②   left - end of line
          middle - abort line creation
②   right - start tangent arc
③   right - end tangent arc
③   left - start of line
④   left - end of line
          middle - abort line creation

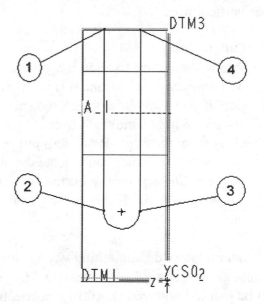

You might like to review the mouse function
commands in Table 1-1 if you don't understand
this sequence. Note that the cut is open at the
top (between 1 and 4). As usual when using
Sketcher, accuracy is not as important as
indicating the intent of your design. You should

Figure 11 End view of block showing sketch
creation sequence

make sure, however, that the end points of the vertical lines are reasonably close to the top edge
of the block. If you have created extraneous lines, or make a mistake, select *Delete* and click on
the line. Then select *Sketch* to resume line creation.

Once you have the sketch drawn, you will then constrain or align it to the existing geometry.
Here, we want to align the end points of the vertical lines with the top *surface* of the block. Why
not just with the top edge shown on the sketch? Suppose that we just pick the top edge. There are
actually three entities there: the edge view of the top surface and the two tangents of the corner
fillets. It is not clear which entity will be picked for the alignment. Then, suppose the alignment
is made to one of the tangent edges of a rounded corner. What would happen if we come back
later and delete that rounded corner? We will have lost our tangent edge, and the cut feature
would not be able to make the alignment and its regeneration would fail.

   IMPORTANT HINT:
   It is always preferable to select surfaces as references rather than edges. Surfaces are less
   likely to "disappear" during model modifications and changes.

To make sure we align to the top surface, spin the part a little bit so that this surface is visible.
Select

         Alignment > Align

Click the left mouse button on the **end point** of one of the vertical lines (a small red + sign
appears), and then on the top surface of the block. The message

-- ALIGNED--

should appear in the message window. ***Repaint*** the screen and repeat this procedure with the other vertical line.

> **Quick Note:**
> When attempting to align the vertical lines, ensure you pick the END POINT. You will know you have done it right when small red cross appears on the end point of the line. If you accidentally pick the entire line (all in red), just select the ***Alignment*** command again and try it over. If you don't spin the part and the end point is too far away from the edge, Pro/E will tell you that "Entities cannot be aligned." This just means that Sketcher can't locate the alignment that you want. You might try to zoom out (use ***Ctrl-left*** mouse button) to bring the end point visually closer to the edge. Try ***Alignment*** again. If this doesn't work, you may have to delete the line and draw a new one.

Let's intentionally do something wrong here to see what happens. Select the ***Regenerate*** command. You should get a message "*Underdimensioned Section*" and the vertices of the lines will be marked with red crosses (a case of the "measles") and the arc will turn red. This is telling you that Sketcher doesn't have enough information to place or solve the section.

Add dimensions for the height and width of the sketch. If you spun the part to help with the alignment, get back to the 2D sketch with ***Sketch View***. Then, select

Dimension

from the Sketcher menu. You should avoid placing the dimensions on top of the part or where it can obscure your sketch. Remember that there are two types of dimensions needed: size and location. Sketcher must be able to figure out **how big** something is and **where** it is. Remember to pick the entity with the left button and place the dimension on the sketch using the middle button. Dimension the sketch as shown in the figure at the right. To dimension the center of the arc, click on the arc itself and the line you want to dimension it to. Sketcher will ask if you want a Center or Tangent dimension. Select ***Center***. To dimension the arc

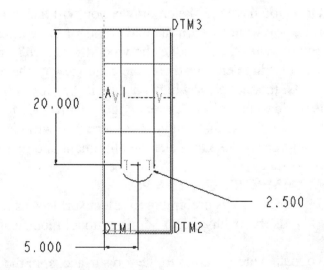

Figure 12 Dimensions of the cut

radius, just click on the arc and middle click to place the radius dimension.

> **Quick Note:**
> Remember SADRMR - do not modify the dimension values until after regeneration!

Again, let's do something intentionally wrong to see how Pro/E handles it. Dimension the distance between the two vertical lines of the sketch. When you regenerate the sketch, you should receive a message about overdimensioning, or unrequired dimensions. The redundant dimension(s) will be highlighted in red, and the ***Delete*** command will be automatically picked. You can click on either the highlighted one or the arc radius to remove the redundancy. For now, click on the red dimension between the vertical edges.

Now click on ***Regenerate*** again. You should get the much-desired message "*Section Regenerated Successfully*" however the actual size of the section is probably not exactly what you want. Notice the constraint labels placed on the sketch beside the various lines. Select

> ***Modify***

to set the dimensions. Click on the numerical dimension (it should turn red) then type in the desired values (the new dimension should appear in white) as follows:

The height is **20**, the radius is **2.5**, the center of the arc is **5** from the left edge of the block.

Then click on ***Regenerate*** again and watch the animation of your sketch as it changes shape. Regeneration should be successful and your screen should now look something like Figure 12.

You have now completed the definition of the sketch of the cut, so select ***Done*** at the bottom of the Sketcher menu.

The red direction arrow should once again appear on the screen. Read the message window! Technically, what we have created is an *open section*, and Pro/E must be told on which side of the edge the material should be removed. Zoom way in if this is not clear. Orient the arrow so that it is pointing into the slot. Click on ***Okay***.

Now Pro/E has to be told how far to extrude the sketch. Spin the model using ***Ctrl-middle*** mouse button, read the message window, and look at the direction arrow. When prompted for the depth in the message window, select

> ***Thru All | Done.***

The message window should tell you that *"All elements have been defined"*. Select ***Preview*** to have a look at the new feature. It is almost always a good idea to preview a feature and spin it around to make sure it is what you want. You can come back to fix any errors later, but it is easier to do it now. If everything is as you want it, select ***OK***.

The block is now completed. Let's get back to the default view direction:

> ***View > Default***

or use the "Saved view list" and select ***Default***. Your screen should look like Figure 13.

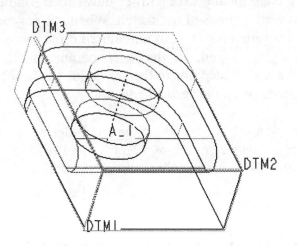

Figure 13 Final part shown in wireframe

Getting a Shaded Image of the Part

There are two ways to get a shaded image. The easiest is to select the "Shading" shortcut button. The second is to select the following:

View > Shade

Note that the datums are automatically turned off with this command. Also, the display shortcut buttons (datum planes, axes, points, etc.) are no longer operational. If you spin the part, the shading disappears and the shortcut buttons are operational again.

A bit later in the lessons, we will discuss how to get hard copy and/or export this image, for example, to use in a design report. We will also find out how to change the color of the part - this will be useful when we make an assembly. Before continuing, select the commands

View > Repaint

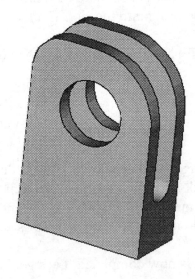

Figure 14 Part shown in shaded view

to get back to a wire frame, or use the "Repaint" shortcut button.

Save the part using *File > Save* or select the "Save" shortcut button.

Deleting a Feature

In preparation for what we want to do next, we are going to delete the cut. There are two ways to delete a feature. We will go part way through the first and then quit, so that we can see the second way. Select

> *Feature > Delete*

and click on one of the surfaces formed by the cut (not edges, since you run the risk of selecting the entire block instead of just the cut). The cut highlights. If you click *Done* (don't do that now), the cut will be deleted from the model database. Instead, let's look at another way. To back out of the current delete command, in the **DELETE/SUPP** menu (SUPP is short for *Suppress*, which we'll discuss in Lesson #4), select *Quit Del/Sup*. Repaint the screen.

Bring up the model tree (*View > Model Tree*) or select the "Model Tree" shortcut button. The model tree window opens showing you a schematic representation of the model database. See Figure 15. The tree shows all the features in the model, including datums. Equally important, it shows you the order that features were created (the regeneration sequence). Thus, the cut, which was made last, is at the bottom of the tree. We will be discussing the model tree and some of its other functions a bit later in the lesson.

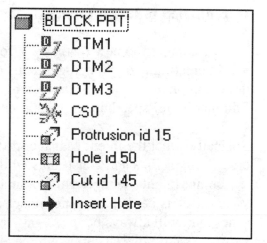

Figure 15 The Model Tree

Left click on the *cut* feature in the model tree. The feature on the model highlights. Hold down the *right* mouse button with the cursor in the model tree to see a pop-up menu. Select *Delete*. You will be asked to confirm the deletion. Select *OK*. The cut is removed. You can use the pop-up menu in the model tree to perform other tasks such as modifying dimensions or obtaining parent/child information about features. For now, close the model tree window with the short-cut button.

Sketching Using Intent Manager

We will create the cut again using commands and functions in Sketcher associated with a very powerful tool called Intent Manager. To turn Intent Manager on, select

>   *Utilities > Environment*

and turn on the check mark beside *Sketcher Intent Manager*. Apply this change and close the environment window. Then select

>   *Feature > Create > Solid > Cut > Extrude | Solid | Done*
>   *One Side | Done*

Select the right surface of the block as the sketching plane, and the top surface as the *Top* reference plane. You should now be in Sketcher but with a different menu than before, appearing as a right toolchest. There is also a new window, called **References**, and a couple of brown/orange patterned lines. What is all this about? We'll digress a bit to talk about Intent Manager and how it works.

Introduction to Intent Manager

Intent Manager is a new (actually introduced in Pro/E Release 20), high-level tool that will assist you in creating and managing dimensions and constraints in a sketch. At first glance, it appears quite complicated and will take a while to get used to but after a little use and practice you should find that it will speed up the creation of sketches considerably.

Basically, what the Intent Manager does is automatically create dimensions and constraints while you are sketching. Intent Manager will automatically ensure that your sketch is neither over- nor under-constrained at all times, and will always be in a legal "regenerated" state. How does it do this? There are three aspects to Intent Manager that you should understand. These are concerned with Sketching references, constraints, and dimensioning.

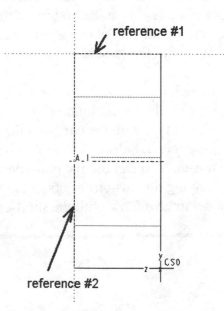

Sketching References

When you enter Sketcher with Intent Manager turned on, two sketching references are automatically created/selected for you. These are the orange/brown lines. Intent Manager determines these based on your Sketch reference and previously created features. The references will be used by Intent Manager to locate (using alignments) and dimension your sketch. The references are how Intent Manager "knows" about your existing part geometry.

Figure 16 Specifying Sketcher references

You can override these default references very easily, if desired, and you can have many references selected at once. The minimum number is normally two. You can add references to the sketch at any time.

The current references are listed in the **References** window as surfaces of the base protrusion. Click on each of these in the window to see the reference highlight on the part. It is easy to remove these and/or add new references if desired. For example, pick the reference that highlights the vertical reference on the right side of the sketch (on the datum plane), then select the *Delete* button. Notice that the *Reference Status* changes to *Partially Placed*. By removing this reference, Intent Manager has no way of locating the sketch left to right. Now pick on the left edge of the part in the graphics window (actually the front surface, remember we are looking at the block from the right side!). Now an orange reference line is shown there and the *Reference Status* is *Fully Placed*. See Figure 16. We can now proceed with our sketch. *Close* the **References** window.

Constraint Management

While you move the cursor around the screen, you will find that it will snap to positions where the possible constraints (the implicit Sketcher rules) will be automatically fired. Try sketching some arcs and lines. As you sketch, these constraints (indicated on the screen with red symbols: "V", "H", and so on) appear and disappear automatically as the cursor moves past the references or other sketched entities. You have the option of turning off any of the constraints on-the-fly (using the right mouse button), or locking them in, as you sketch (Pro/E uses the term "dynamically" to describe this). These include things like alignments, tangency points, equal line segment lengths, perpendicularity, and so on.

Automatic Dimensioning

Once an entity is created, it will be automatically dimensioned based on "known" geometry. These dimensions can be to the chosen references or to other parts of the sketch. The dimensions created automatically by Intent Manager are called "weak" since they can be over-ridden by dimensions that you create explicitly. A weak dimension appears in gray on the screen. A dimension that you create is called "strong" and appears in yellow. There is no possibility of over-dimensioning since a strong dimension will take precedence, and any weak dimensions that are not required will be automatically deleted from the sketch (without asking for confirmation). You can promote a weak dimension to be a strong dimension, but not vice versa. This "strengthening" can be done by an explicit command, or by modifying the dimension value.

The result of these three behaviors is that your sketch is always in a regenerated state. No more battling with a sketch that won't regenerate for some mysterious reason!

Why do you need to worry about sketching references and weak and strong dimensions, since the sketch is always "correct" anyway, that is, it is always regenerated? The answer is that Intent Manager's automatic system cannot determine what your *design intent* is. There are usually many ways to define a sketch. As we will see in the exercise below, each of these schemes will have a different purpose or intent. The reference and dimensioning scheme that Intent Manager produces may not be the one you want. The Intent Manager choices can be overridden very easily. For example, by explicitly creating your own (strong) dimensions, you will over-ride the Intent

Manager (weak) dimensioning scheme.

Before we start sketching, turn off the grid and
datum planes. Let's examine the new toolchest on
the right side of the graphics window. Move the
mouse over the various buttons to see the tool tip
pop-ups. The Sketcher menu is shown in Figure
17. Notice that several of the buttons have
flyouts, indicated with the ➤ symbol. Selecting
the flyout gives access to related commands.

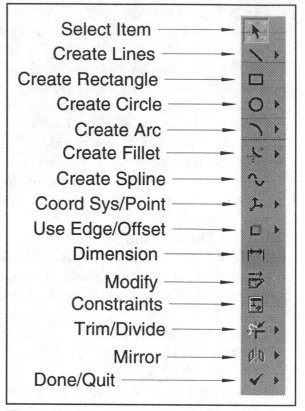

Figure 17 The Sketcher toolchest

Using Sketcher with Intent Manager

Now we can go ahead and sketch our cut. Select
the "Create Lines" button. Move the cursor
around on the screen. As you get close to the
reference lines, the cursor will snap to the lines,
and small red constraint symbols will appear.

We will create the same sketch we did previously
(see Figure 11). Start at the top of the sketch by
clicking at point ①. As we move the cursor away
from this point, the line will snap to the
horizontal or vertical references, showing a
constraint symbol. Left click at point ②, noting
the "V" constraint on the line. Middle click to
end line creation. The weak dimensions will immediately appear in gray. We now want to create
a tangent arc. Right click (and hold the mouse button down) anywhere in the graphics window
and select *3 Point/Tangent Arc* from the pop-up menu. Left click at the lower end of the
sketched line (point ②) and move the cursor around.
Again, as you move the cursor around you will see
potential alignments and constraints that might be fired.
Bring the end of the tangent arc to point ③ and left click.
The weak radius dimension shows immediately. Right
click again on the screen and select *Line*. Left click at
point ③ and create the line back up to the top of the block
(point ④), using the automatic alignment on the top
reference. To get out of line creation mode, middle click.

The sketch is now complete and regenerated, however the
values of the dimensions are probably not correct or
placed where you want them. So we have some clean-up
to do. First, let's reposition the dimensions. Move the
cursor over each dimension; it highlights in magenta. Left
click on one of the dimensions and drag it (it will appear
in red during motion) to the position shown in Figure 18.

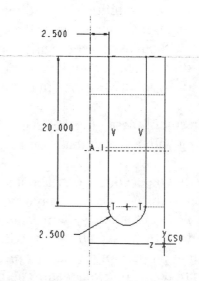

Figure 18 Sketch of cut (design
intent alternative #1)

Repeat for the other dimensions. Now, double-click on each dimension and enter the values shown in Figure 18. Repaint the screen. Note that the weak (gray) dimensions are now strong (yellow) - a weak dimension is strengthened by modifying it.

Before we accept this sketch for the cut feature, we are going to look at a couple of different ways of dimensioning the cut. These are related to the subject of Design Intent that was introduced earlier

Capturing Design Intent in the Sketch

The notion of *"Design Intent"* is one of the more abstract ideas associated with using Pro/E. It is difficult to explain, but easy to demonstrate! Basically, it refers to the fact that there are always alternate ways of creating the model and of creating the sketch for a feature. For our simple cut, there are a number of possible dimensioning schemes that would all describe the same geometry. We must choose from these alternatives based on how we want the feature to relate to the rest of the part (or to itself). This is called *design intent*. Design intent is implemented in a number of ways: feature selection, feature order, feature references, dimensioning schemes, and relations (we'll see those in a few minutes). In this exercise, we will see how different design intents might be implemented in the dimensioning scheme for our cut.

In the sketch created above, we have implemented the following intent:
1.   The width of the cut is controlled by an explicit dimension (the radius of the arc at the bottom).
2.   The depth of the cut is controlled by the vertical distance from the top of the part to the center of the radius.
3.   The front of the cut is a controlled distance from the front of the part.

We will modify the sketch to implement a couple of alternative design intents. First, change the radius of the arc to *2.0* (remember all you need to do is double-click on it).

Design Intent Alternative #2

Suppose that we want the radius to be determined automatically based on the thickness of the remaining material at the front and back of the block after the cut is created. We have an explicit dimension for the front thickness already. We want to add a corresponding explicit dimension for the thickness at the back. Select the "Dimension" button in the toolchest (or hold down the right mouse button and select *Dimension*). Click on the right vertical edge of the sketch, then on the right edge of the block (the back surface). Place the dimension using a

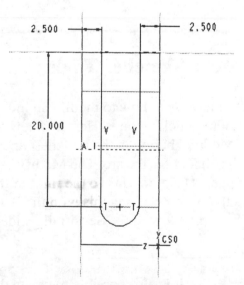

Figure 19 Sketch of cut (design intent alternative #2)

middle click.

We have now over-dimensioned the sketch and Pro/E will highlight all the entities (dimensions and constraints) involved in the conflict. The Resolve Sketch window opens which lists the dimensions and constraints involved in the redundancy. Highlight the dimension for the arc radius (should be 2.0), then select *Delete*. We are now properly constrained and dimensioned. Change the value of the dimension to the rear surface to *2.5*, as shown in Figure 19.

Our sketch now expresses a different design intent that results in the same geometry. We will see shortly how we can set up an explicit requirement for the two thickness dimensions to be equal[3].

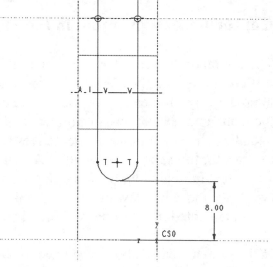

Design Intent Alternative #3

Let's change the intent for the vertical dimension. Select

> *Dimension*

again from the right-mouse pop-up menu. Left click on the arc and on the edge at the bottom of the block. Middle click to place the dimension and in the small window that opens at the right select

Figure 20 Sketch of cut (design intent alternative #3)

Tangent > Close. We are again informed of conflicting dimensions and constraints. Why are the top thickness dimensions in conflict? Click on the 20 dimension to delete it. We have yet another expression of design intent for exactly the same geometry as shown in Figure 20.

More Sketcher Tools

We have seen how to modify an individual dimension by double-clicking on it. Here is a new tool. Select the "Modify" button in the toolchest and click on the tangency dimension for the arc. The Modify Dimensions window appears (Figure 21). To the right of the dimension value is a thumbwheel. Drag this with the left mouse button. Experiment with the Sensitivity slider. Return the

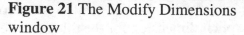

Figure 21 The Modify Dimensions window

---

[3] It is also possible to create the sketch so that both thicknesses are driven by a single dimension on the sketch. Can you figure out how to do that? It involves adding a couple of lines to the sketch and having Intent Manager invoke the *equal length* rules.

dimension to its original value (**8.0**) by typing it into the data field and hitting ***Enter***.

Now left click on the two horizontal dimensions at the top of the cut. As these are selected they will appear in the Modify window. Check the box beside *Lock Scale*. Now drag the thumbwheel beside the 8.0 dimension. All dimensions are changed simultaneously, in approximately the same proportion. Remove the check beside both *Lock Scale* and *Regenerate*. The latter option will delay the simultaneous and/or immediate regeneration whenever a single dimension is changed. This is sometimes necessary when you want to change a lot of dimension values at the same time, but don't want to regenerate until all new values are entered. This would avoid trying to regenerate to a geometry with some old and some new dimensions, which may be incompatible. When you are finished experimenting, return the dimensions to the original values (or select the X symbol in the Modify window).

Another useful command in Sketcher is ***Undo***. There are several ways to access this: using the button at the top of the screen, holding down the right mouse button and select ***Undo***, or just clicking the right mouse button in the graphics window. Each time you select this command, you move backwards through any changes you have made in the sketch, one at a time. You can move forward again using ***Redo***.

Return the dimensions to the values shown in Figure 20, and select the *Done* button in the Sketcher toolchest.

To complete the feature creation, we have to specify the material removal side and the depth (***Thru All***). Do that now, following the screen prompts. When all elements have been defined, select ***Preview***, spin the part to make sure the cut is created correctly, and then select ***OK***.

To learn more about Intent Manager, the next time you start Pro/E and enter Sketcher for the first time, select the ***Overview*** button in the Sketcher Enhancement splash window. Assuming your system has been set up properly, a Web page discussing various aspects of the Intent Manager should come up. Take a few minutes to study this, since Intent Manager is a tool that can save you a lot of time if you know how to use it effectively.

Database Functions

Listing the Part Features

The part we have created is quite simple - only seven features. You can get a list of the features in a part by the command sequence (starting in the pull-down menus):

> ***Info > Feature List*** (and ***> Screen*** depending on your system setup)

A window will open showing you a list of the features in the order that you created them. Each feature has associated with it a feature number (showing the order of feature creation), an internal feature ID (assigned automatically by Pro/E), a name, type, and current status. You should see seven features listed. The name field is currently blank for the last three features (protrusion, hole, cut). *Close* this window.

You can also get this information in a more usable and flexible form by selecting (from the pull-down menu)

> *View > Model Tree*

or selecting the "Model Tree" button in the top toolchest. We have seen this window before - in its simplest form it just shows you the features in the model. To display more information, select

> *View > Model Tree Setup > Column Display*

In the list of Display items, double-click on on **Feat #**, **Feat Type**, and **Status**. These will be moved to the Displayed list on the right. Now adjust the width of the columns by highlighting each entry in the Displayed list and using the Width data field at the bottom (try Feat # = 4, Feat Type = 10, Status = 10). Then select *OK*. The model tree window should look like this

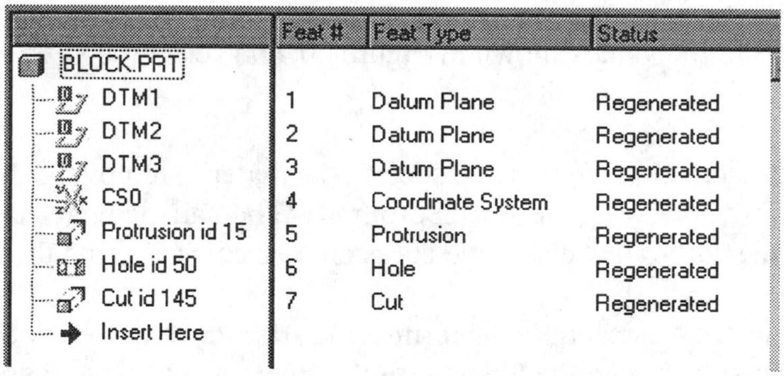

	Feat #	Feat Type	Status
BLOCK.PRT			
DTM1	1	Datum Plane	Regenerated
DTM2	2	Datum Plane	Regenerated
DTM3	3	Datum Plane	Regenerated
CS0	4	Coordinate System	Regenerated
Protrusion id 15	5	Protrusion	Regenerated
Hole id 50	6	Hole	Regenerated
Cut id 145	7	Cut	Regenerated
Insert Here			

Figure 22 The model tree with added columns

In the left half of the model tree window, click on the line containing feature #6 (the hole). On the model in the graphics window, the hole will highlight in red. Try clicking on the next feature (the cut). This is a handy way to locate and identify features in a complicated model. Save this model tree layout for future use using

> *Utilities > Model Tree Settings > Save > [tree.cfg] | Save*

Note the configuration file name. Next time you open the model tree (for this session or any other) you can immediately recover these settings using

> *Utilities > Model Tree Settings > Load > [tree.cfg] | Open*

The model tree has other uses that we will get into a bit later in the tutorials. For now, just close the model tree window (either select *View > Model Tree*, or click the "Model Tree" shortcut button on the top toolbar).

Note that the command *Info > Model Tree* will create a file containing the current model tree information. This can be printed out, and is sometimes useful when working on very large, complicated models.

Naming the Part Features

Naming features will be a very useful practice when you start to deal with parts with even a moderate number of features (say more than 10). From the **PART** menu, (if you are still in the **FEATURE** menu just select **Done** to get back) select

> *Set Up > Name > Feature*

Spin the part so that you can see the cylindrical surface of the hole, and then click on it with the left mouse button. The edges of the hole should highlight in red. In the command window, enter a name for the hole feature:

> *[big_hole]*

Click on the cut surface of the slot, and name it *center_cut*. Finally, click on one of the side surfaces of the block, and name the feature *block*. When you are finished naming the features, select *Done* to return to the **PART SETUP** menu.

Now call up the feature list again (*Info > Feature List*). You will see each of the features in the table identified by their name. *Close* this information window.

Call up the model tree (*View > Model Tree*) to see each feature in the left window identified by name. Close the model tree and repaint the screen.

IMPORTANT:
> Just a reminder to periodically save your model. Now is a good time. Trying using the keyboard command CTRL-S (hold down the Ctrl key and press S).

Parent/Child Relations

When a new feature is created, any previously created feature that the new one uses for reference is called a *PARENT* feature. The new feature is called a *CHILD*. It is crucial to keep track of these parent/child relations. Any modification to a parent feature can potentially change (ie. damage if the change is undesired!) one or more of its children. In the extreme case, deleting a parent will normally result in deletion of all child features that reference it (and their children...). In these cases, Pro/E will ask you to confirm the deletion. If you don't want to delete the child, you will have to change its references using techniques discussed in Lesson #4. Sometimes, if you make extreme modifications to a parent (like deleting the arc on the corner of the block), the child will be unable to regenerate (because it may lose an alignment, for example). This is a symptom of a poor feature selection and/or referencing scheme. So it is important to be aware of what parent/child relations are present when new features are added. Be aware of the intent of your part geometry and build the model accordingly.

It is useful to know, therefore, what parent/child relations exist in a part. Pro/E has a number of functions to help. To start with, from the pull-down menu select

Info > Parent/Child

Click on the side of the block. The Reference Information Window opens (Figure 23). This window lists all the parents and children of the currently selected feature (shown at the top). You can click on any listed feature and it will highlight on the model. If you click on the part name in either list, you will see all the parents or all the children.

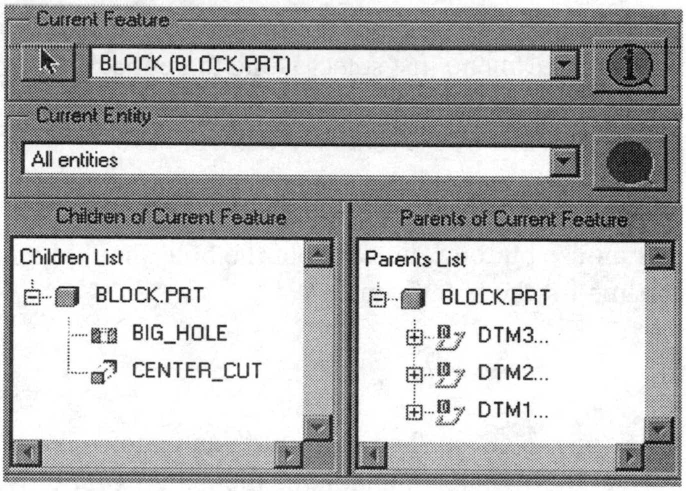

Observe that the hole is a child of the feature named *block*. This relation exists because the sides of the block were used as dimensioning or sketching references when the hole was created. We could have

Figure 23 Getting parent/child information

referenced the hole entirely to the datum planes, for example. This might offer some advantages, but also some disadvantages. An advantage would be that we would not be restricted in how we could change the shape of the block (make it a semi-cylinder for example) without affecting the definitions of the hole. On the other hand, if we did that and then moved the block away from its current position relative to the datum planes, the hole wouldn't go with it. These are design intent considerations.

Select the feature *big_hole* and use the right mouse pop-up menu to select *Set Current*. This switches focus to the hole, and the window now shows parents and children of the hole. This shows that the *block* feature is a parent of the hole. Does the block have any parents? The answer is yes - the three datum planes. Check this out using *Set Current*. Note that the datum planes were not included in the list of parents of the hole - **the parent/child relations do not explicitly extend to grandparents or grandchildren!**

Close the Reference Information Window.

As you might expect, parent/child relations can become quite complicated when the model starts to accumulate features (A good reason to keep your models as simple as possible, and to think about your modeling strategy *before* you start creating anything!). A parent can have many children, and a child can have several parents. Choosing (dare one say *designing?*) the best parent/child scheme for a part is a major difference of Pro/E from previous CAD programs. It is important (but very difficult) to plan ahead for *all* possible design changes that might occur that would be affected by the existing parent/child relations. Poor planning of the model organization and setup will almost guarantee big problems later on if the model must be changed in any way. Fortunately, Pro/Engineer provides a number of utility functions to help you manage the parent/child relations in a model. These include changing the dimensioning scheme and/or replacing current relations with new ones (called rerouting). In the worst case, reference elements of a feature can be redefined. We will be discussing these functions at length in lesson #4. For now, you might keep as a general rule that, as in many things, simpler is better.

Modifying Dimensions

Now we will see one of the powerful capabilities of Pro/Engineer. Once a feature has been created, it is very easy to modify its shape via its dimensions. From the **PART** menu, select

> *Modify > Value*

and click on the side of the block. You should see the length, width, height, and radius dimensions. Click on the number that shows the length dimension (currently 20) to change it. A clicked dimension turns red. Enter a new value for the dimension, say *30*. The dimension turns white. The shape of the part will not change until you regenerate the part by selecting

> *Regenerate*

from the **PART** menu. You notice that the hole has stayed in the same position relative to the right end of the part. That's how the hole was defined (*Linear* placement). Also, the central slot continues all the way through the now-lengthened part (*Thru All* depth).

Try modifying some of the other dimensions, either of the block or the hole or slot. Here is a nifty way to do that: open the model tree and put the mouse cursor on the name of a feature and click (and hold) the right mouse button. From the pop-up menu, select *Modify*. All the chosen feature's dimensions will appear. Click on any dimension and enter a new value. Notice that you are now in the Modify menu - you can click on any feature listed in the model tree and its dimensions will appear. You can still dynamically alter your view at any time if some dimensions become obscured or hard to read. The dimensions will stay on the screen until you select *Regenerate* or *Repaint*.

You might try some "silly" dimensions (for example, make the diameter of the hole bigger than the height of the block), to see what Pro/E will do - in particular, what messages does it give you? Try changing the location of the hole so that it is completely off the left end of the block. If you get into serious trouble here, just erase the part from the current session (*File > Erase > Current*), and retrieve the previously-saved part (You did save it, right?) from disk (*File > Open > block.prt*). Before you proceed, return the dimensions to their original values.

Note that when the dimensions are changed, Pro/E will still maintain all the geometric constraints that you set up during feature creation. A simple example of this is alignments - the edges of the cut forming the slot were aligned with the top face of the block. If the block height is increased, the slot still stays in the same relation to the new top face. If a feature is *completely* defined by this type of constraint (ie. all geometry is defined with alignments with previously created features), then you will not be able to modify it directly by its dimensions since it has none! You will only be able to affect it via its parent(s) dimensions.

The type of constraints discussed in the last paragraph might be called implicit constraints since they are built into the model. There is another way that we can define relations between dimensions of features that is even more powerful - these are feature relations.

Feature Relations

A *Relation* is an explicit algebraic formula that allows a dimension to be automatically computed from other dimensions in the part (or in other parts, for example, in an assembly). This is another way of implementing design intent. We will set up two simple relations to ensure that the hole in the block is always centered along its length, and mid-way between the top and bottom faces.

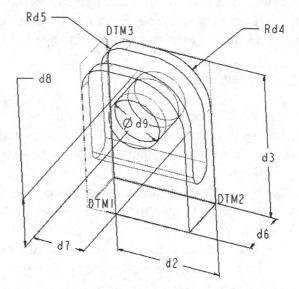

From the **PART** menu, select *Relations*. Click on the block and the hole surface. Your screen should look like Figure 24 with dimensions d2, d3, d4, and so on.

IMPORTANT: Your dimension labels might be numbered differently from these. Note *your* labels!

Figure 24 Symbolic dimension labels used for relations

Pro/E maintains symbolic names that can be used to set up relations between the dimensions. In Figure 24, the length of the block is d2, and the position of the hole from the right face is d7. **Check to see if these are the symbols used in your model.** We can force the hole to be placed at the midpoint of the block by setting up a relation as follows: Select

> *Add*

and then type in the following two lines (press the enter key at the end of each line and **use your own dimension labels!**):

> /* hole centered mid-length
> d7 = d2 / 2

When these lines have been entered, just press the enter key to quit the entry mode. The first line of the relation, starting with **/***, is a comment line that describes the nature of the relation. This comment is not mandatory, but is a very good idea for clarity. You can put any text here that you like. The second line defines the relation itself - the distance from the end face to the center of the hole is half the length of the block.

Let's add another dimension to make sure the hole is half-way up from the bottom of the block. The relevant dimensions are d8 and d3 in Figure 24. Select

> *Add*

and type in the following (again make sure that these are the correct symbolic names used in your model):

> */* hole centered mid-height*
> *d8 = d3 / 2*

To make sure these have been entered correctly, select **Show Rel**. This will also show you the value that has resulted from the relation.

It is always a good idea to check out the dimension relations as soon as you have created them. In the **RELATIONS** menu, select **Switch Dim** to display the dimensions in numerical form, then in the **MODEL REL** menu select **Done**. In the **PART** menu, select **Modify** or use the right mouse button in the model tree. Click on the block and change the length and height dimensions to **30** and **25**, respectively. **Regenerate** the part. If all goes well, the hole should be exactly centered on the block. While we're here, change the diameter of the hole to **15**. Don't forget to **Regenerate**.

Try to use **Modify** to change either of the dimensions that locate the hole that are explicitly controlled by relations - Pro/E won't let you! And it even tells you what relation is driving that dimension.

You might like to try to set up some relations that will keep the sides of the slot exactly 2 units in from the front and back surfaces of the block no matter its depth. This will involve the two horizontal dimensions in the sketch of the cut.

More about relations:

Relations can take the following forms:

/* explicitly define a dimension
d4 = 4
/* explicitly define a parameter
length_of_block = 30
/* use a parameter
d6 = length_of_block

d12 = length_of_block / 2
/* set up a limiting value for a dimension
d4 > 2

Explicitly defined dimensions are just that - they create constant values for dimensions that cannot be overridden. The right hand side of a relation can contain almost any form of arithmetic expression (including functions like sin, cos, tan, ...). The final inequality form can be used to monitor the geometry during regeneration of the part. If the inequality is violated, then Pro/E will catch the violation and show you a warning message.

All the relations for a part go into a special database that is consulted when the part is regenerated. These relations are evaluated in a top-down manner, so that the order of relations is important (just like the order of feature creation). You can't have two relations that define the same dimension, and a relation is evaluated based on the current values on its right hand side. If one of the right-hand side values is changed by a subsequent relation, then the dimension will be incorrect. Pro/E has a utility function that will let you reorder the relations to avoid this. When re-ordering, Pro/E assumes that each relation is preceded by a single comment line that will be moved with the relation when the database is reordered.

Saving the Part

We are at the end of this lesson. Before you leave, make sure that you save the current part, that should look something like the figure at the right.

>   *File > Save*

or use Ctrl-S. You can now exit from Pro/E.

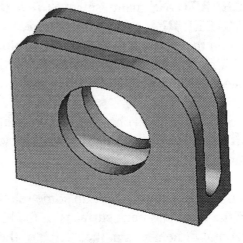

Figure 25 Final part shape

Pro/E Files saved automatically

Have a look at the files in your default disk space or Pro/E working directory. You should see files listed that include the following forms:

block.prt.1   block.prt.2   block.prt.3 . . . .

Each time you save a part, a new file is created with an automatically increasing counter. Thus, you always have a back-up available if something goes very wrong. On the other hand, this can eat up your disk space very quickly since the part files can get pretty large. If you are sure you do not need the previous files, you can remove them. Since it is always a good idea to keep back-ups, you might consider copying final part files to another storage location anyway (see your system documentation for this).

Pro/Engineer will also write a number of other files to your disk space. These might include the following:

trail.txt.1
> This is a record of all keystrokes, commands, and mouse clicks you made during a session. For an advanced user, this may be useful to recover from catastrophic failures!

feature.lst
> The same list of features obtained using *Info > Feature List*

rels.inf
> Dimension relations

reviewref.inf
> Information on parent/child relations

and other *.inf files.

Unless you have a good reason to keep these, remove them from your disk space as soon as you leave Pro/E (and not before!).

In the next lesson we will look at a number of new features, including revolved protrusions, rounds, chamfers, and slots that will considerably extend our "vocabulary" of part-creation features. In the meantime, here are some questions for you. Some review material we have covered and others will require you to do some exploring on your own.

Questions for Review

1. What elements are required to define a simple hole?
2. What is meant by linear placement of a hole?
3. When aligning a vertex in a sketch, how do you know you have selected just the end point and not the entire line?
4. When aligning, you can align to a vertex, edge, or plane. In what circumstances would each of these be useful?
5. What is the difference between a slot and a cut?
6. Why is a cut (that removes material) treated as a solid feature?
7. What is the difference between the terms "protrusion" and "extrude"?
8. What is a useful method for visualizing a new sketch relative to the part?

9. What are two methods of obtaining a feature list?

10. What command is used to name features?

11. Suppose you are creating a new feature. All elements have been defined, but upon Previewing the feature, you find an error - for example, the depth is not correctly defined. How can you fix this?

12. Suppose you have a very complex part with many features and you want to identify/locate (ie. show graphically) a specific feature in the model. How would you do it?

13. When might you want to turn off *Regenerate* in the **Modify Dimensions** dialog window?

14. Once a feature has been created, how can you change its dimensions?

15. What do we call an explicit equation that computes a dimensional value?

16. What are the "junk" files that Pro/E creates in your disk space? How do you get rid of them?

17. What commands (ie. what do they do) are available by selecting the Geom Tools command in the old Sketcher (non-Intent Manager version)?

18. Why is it not a good idea to modify dimensions in the old Sketcher before regenerating the sketch for the first time?

19. How can you go back and edit a previously defined relation?

20. How can you find out the internal symbolic names for feature dimensions?

21. What is the difference between the Feature Number and the Internal ID?

22. What is the first thing you have to do when you have entered Sketcher with the Intent Manager turned on?

23. What is the meaning of the gray dimensions in Sketcher? What about the yellow, red, and white ones?

24. How can you strengthen a dimension?

25. Where did we see the *Lock Scale* option?

26. How do you over-ride the default dimensions placed by Intent Manager?

27. How do you change the location of the dimensions (on the screen) after they have been placed by Intent Manager?

28. What does the right mouse button do when you are in the Intent Manager?

29. Find out how to turn off the constraints presented by Intent Manager.

30. What is the minimum number of Sketcher References needed by Intent Manager? The maximum number? What do these do?

31. What is meant by "design intent?" Describe the ways design intent was implemented for the part created in this lesson.

32. Examine some simple everyday objects and describe how you might implement design intent in a computer model of the object.

33. Can you turn on the Intent Manager part way through the creation of a sketch?

Exercises

Here are some simple shapes you should be able to make using the features covered in the first two lessons. Before starting in on any new part, take a few minutes to plan your modeling strategy. For example, where should the datum planes be located? This will pay dividends in the ease with which you can model the part, and particularly with how you will be able to modify it afterwards.

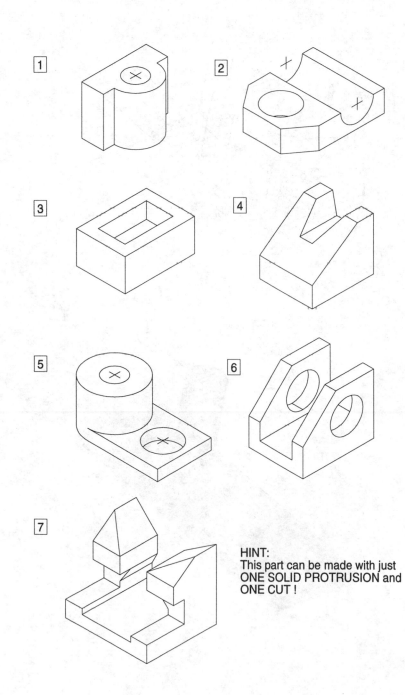

HINT:
This part can be made with just
ONE SOLID PROTRUSION and
ONE CUT !

Project

Here is the first part in our assembly project. It uses only the features covered in the first two lessons. All units are in millimeters. As usual, take a few minutes to plan your modeling strategy. For example, where should the datum planes be located? How should you orient the part in the Front-Top-Right system of datums (assuming you are using a template). Which is the base feature?

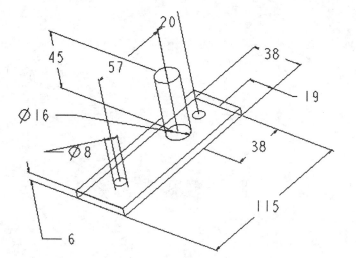

Lesson 3 :

Revolved Protrusions, Mirrored Copies, Rounds and Chamfers

Synopsis

A new part is modeled using a number of different feature creation commands and options: both sides protrusions, an axisymmetric (revolved) protrusion, a cut, rounds, and chamfer. Mirrored features. We will intentionally make some modeling errors to see how Pro/E responds.

Overview of this Lesson

This lesson will introduce you to a number of new features, and give you some practice using ones introduced in the first two lessons. We will discover some new commands in Sketcher. The steps should be completed in order. Remember to scan through each section before starting to enter the commands - it is important to know what the goal is when you are going through the feature creation steps. If you can't finish the part in one session, remember to save it so that you can retrieve it later and carry on. The finished part should look like Figure 1.

1. Creating the Base Feature
2. Adding a Revolved Protrusion
3. Adding a Pocket with a Cut
4. Adding Holes
5. Adding Rounds and Fillets
6. Adding a Chamfer
7. Save the Part!
8. What Can Go Wrong?

Figure 1 Finished Part

IMPORTANT:

Be sure to complete the last section - you will learn a lot about how Pro/E works, beyond finding which button to click. This is important for your proficient use of the program.

As usual there are some Questions for Review at the end, some exercises, and another part for the project.

The instructions are going to be a bit more terse this lesson, especially for commands we have covered previously. You should be getting in the habit of scanning both the command menus and the message line in the command/message window. Remember, if the mouse seems to be dead, then Pro/E is probably waiting for you to respond to a prompt via keyboard entry. By now, you should also be fairly comfortable with the dynamic view controls obtained with the mouse. As a reminder, here there are again:

Ctrl-left (drag)	**Zoom in/out**
Ctrl-middle (drag)	**3D spin**
Ctrl-right (drag)	**Pan**
Ctrl-left (pick) then left (pick)	**Window zoom**

So, get started by launching Pro/E as usual. If you are already in Pro/E with another part active, then choose *File > Erase > Current*.

Study the object in Figure 1 carefully before proceeding. Also, from now on it is assumed that you will be using Intent Manager in Sketcher.

Creating the Base Feature

Create a solid part named *guide_pin* using the "Create new object" button or select:

>   *File > New > Part | Solid | [guide_pin]*

Use the default part template. When the part comes up, you can close the Model Tree.

The rectangular block at the base of the part will be our first (base) solid feature. We will be creating the base feature so that the **FRONT** and **RIGHT** datum planes can be used for mirroring of features we will create later. Whenever you have symmetry in a part, it is a good idea to use the datum planes on the plane(s) of symmetry. Thus, we will create the first feature as a blind symmetric extrusion coming off both sides of the sketching plane.

>   *Feature > Create > Solid > Protrusion > Extrude | Solid | Done*
>   *Both Sides > Done*

Now you need to select a sketch plane and reference plane. Choose **FRONT** as the sketch plane. The red extrusion direction arrow appears. Read the message window -- for a *both sides* protrusion, the direction arrow indicates our *direction of view* of the sketch plane, not the direction of extrusion. The same applies to a *both sides* cut (which is also symmetric about the sketching plane). Make sure the direction arrow is pointing up/back unto the screen and select *Okay*. For the sketching reference plane, make sure *Right* is selected in **SKET VIEW** menu, then pick on the label or edge of **RIGHT**. Note that in Sketcher you are now looking at the positive (yellow) side of **FRONT**, with the positive (yellow) side of **RIGHT** facing to the right. Could we have also used *Top* and **TOP**?

It is assumed that you are using Intent Manager[1]. If so, the sketching references will have been selected automatically for you. If you entered Sketcher with Intent Manager turned off, turn it on now using

> *Sketch > Intent Manager*

and select RIGHT and TOP as your references. Remember that you can always turn Intent Manager on as long as you have a currently regenerated sketch (or, as in this case, no sketch at all!).

The base feature will be created symmetrically about **RIGHT**. This placement means that the axis of the vertical revolved protrusion we'll create later can be aligned with the vertical datum planes that cross in the center of the base. This is an example of the planning ahead you must do. This one was easy - only "one move ahead." Like good chess players, good modelers are always looking many "moves" ahead.

Before we start the sketch, recall the sequence we want to follow when using Intent Manager:

- make sure the desired references are selected
- sketch the geometry using the chosen references for alignments, constraints, etc.
- modify the constraints if required to implement your design intent
- modify the dimension scheme so that it implements your design intent
- modify the dimension values

This is essentially the same SADRMR order discussed previously. With Intent Manager the first four steps (SADR) occur more-or-less simultaneously and automatically.

The sketch we are going to create is shown in Figure 3. Turn off the datum planes, as they will not be needed for a while. You can create the entire sketch using a single polyline (left click, left click, ...), finishing with a single middle click when you are back at the starting point. Middle click again to leave *Line* mode. Intent Manager will put all the weak dimensions on the sketch. Move the dimensions off the part and observe the constraints implemented by Intent Manager. We can implement a left-to-right symmetry about RIGHT as follows:

Use the flyout on the "Line" button to select the "Centerline" button, OR right click on the graphics window to get the pop-up menu and select *Centerline*. Sketch a vertical centerline on the vertical reference. When the centerline appears, if your sketch is already close to being symmetric about this line, Sketcher may automatically apply the symmetry constraint.

---

[1]It would actually be a good idea to use both versions of Sketcher for a while. When you have created the sketch one way, then delete it and use the other.

If not, select the "Constraints" button in the Sketcher toolbar. This opens the window shown in Figure 2 with the nine possible constraints. Select the symmetry constraint (lower left) and read the message window. Click on the vertical centerline and then the two lower vertices. Note that with symmetry constraining the sketch, the dimensioning scheme has changed. Check out the symbols that indicate the symmetry. Repeat this process for the two vertices on the top edge of the sketch. The sketch should now look similar to Figure 3.

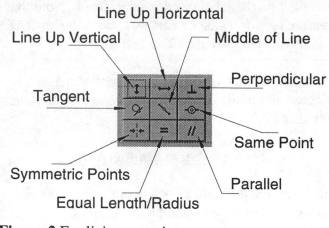

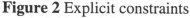

Figure 2 Explicit constraints

So far, we have the geometry and constraints set the way we want, but probably not the desired dimension scheme or values. We want the dimensioning scheme shown in Figure 3. If any of these dimensions are missing, create them explicitly. Recall that these are strong dimensions and Intent Manager will remove redundant weak dimensions automatically. To dimension the angle, click on the two intersecting lines and middle click to place the dimension. Sketcher assumes that if two lines intersect you must want the angle between them.

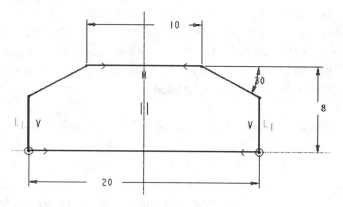

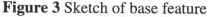

Figure 3 Sketch of base feature

Once you have the dimensioning scheme you want, you can modify the dimension values. Here is a very useful procedure to do this on the base feature. Shift-click with the left mouse button to select all the linear dimensions (not the angle!). Select the "Modify" button. The three dimensions will appear in the Modify Dimensions window.

IMPORTANT: check the **Lock Scale** option, since we want to change all dimensions simultaneously.

Now, select the dimension for the block width and enter 20 into the data field. The other dimensions will change at the same time. Now uncheck the **Lock Scale** option. Enter new values for the other dimensions according to Figure 3. Finally, close this window and change the angle dimension (hint: double-click on the dimension).

This should complete the sketch. So, select the "Done" button at the bottom of the Sketcher toolbar.

We now specify the depth of the extrusion. For a *both-sides blind* protrusion, this is the *total* width of the block, which will be symmetric about the sketching plane. If you want to go different distances on each side of the sketch plane you would use *2-Sided Blind*. Select:

> *Blind | Done*

and enter a depth of *10*. You can now *Preview* the protrusion.

Assuming everything is satisfactory, select *OK* and you should have a shape resembling that shown in Figure 4. To get the same orientation as the figure select:

> *View > Default*

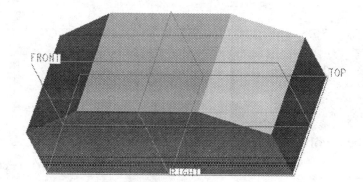

Figure 4 Base protrusion completed

Adding a Revolved Protrusion

We'll now add the vertical axisymmetric shape onto the top of the base feature. In 3D solid modeling terms, this is a "revolved solid", created by taking a 2D sketch and rotating it around a specified axis. In Pro/E, we can use revolved features to create protrusions or cuts. The angle of the rotation is adjustable. For this part we will do a 360° revolve. Depending on the model, the sketch can be either an open or closed curve. **The sketch must also include the axis of rotation**.

Starting at the **PART** menu:

> *Feature > Create > Solid > Protrusion > Revolve | Solid | Done*
> *One Side > Done*

Select **FRONT** as the sketching plane, and the upper surface of the base feature as the horizontal (*Top*) sketching reference plane. Why not select the **TOP** datum for this? The answer is in the sketch!

Quick Note:
   For the revolved section, only a half cross-sectional shape is required since it will be revolved through a full 360°. See Figure 5.

Create the sketch shown in Figure 6. To place the centerline (the axis of rotation) along the vertical reference hold down the right mouse button in the sketch window and select *Centerline*. Click once on the vertical reference; the centerline will automatically snap to vertical when you click to create the second point on the reference.

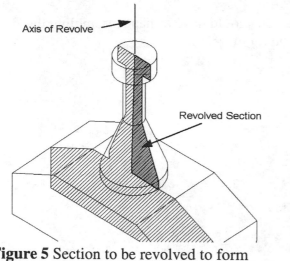

Figure 5 Section to be revolved to form protrusion

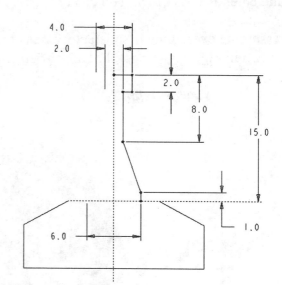

Figure 6 Sketch for revolved protrusion

Here is a trick for dimensioning the diameter of a revolved feature (the horizontal dimensions in the sketch): left click on the outer edge, then on the center line, again on the outer edge, then middle click to place the dimension.

After finishing the sketch, select "Done" button. The common error made here is forgetting to create the centerline used as the axis of rotation. Sketcher will catch this mistake and prompt you if you try to leave Sketcher without the centerline. You should get in the habit of always creating the revolve centerline first. If you have several centerlines in the sketch (they can also be used as construction lines), hold down the right mouse button to find the *Axis of Revolution* command.

Follow the prompts in the message window. Since this is an open curve, you will have to tell Pro/E which side of the curve is to be made solid.

Finally, in the **REV TO** menu, specify a *360 °* rotation.

All elements should now be defined. *Preview* the part (it should look like Figure 7) and select *OK*. Note that an axis **A_1** has been defined. This axis is now available as a reference for new features.

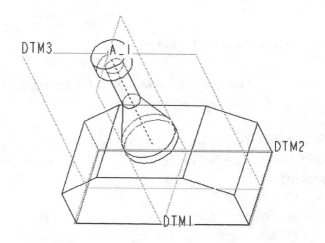

Figure 7 Revolved protrusion completed

Adding a Pocket

We'll now use a cut feature to cut a pocket on one side of the base. For the following, turn off the display of the datum planes. Our design intent here will be to leave a 1 unit[2] thick edge around the pocket - Sketcher has a useful tool for doing this. Select

> *Feature > Create > Solid > Cut*
> *Extrude | Solid | Done*
> *One Side | Done*

Pick the front surface of the base for the sketching plane. The feature creation direction should automatically be into the block - check this and select *OK*. Select **Top** and pick the top surface of the block as the sketching reference plane. We will now create our sketch using only a single dimension - the thickness of the edge around the pocket!

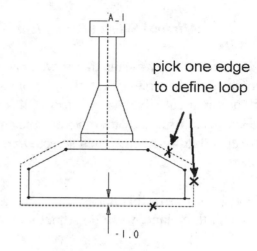

Figure 8 Picking edge to define loop

On the flyout from the "Use Edge/Offset" button in Sketcher (see Figure 17 in Lesson #2), select the "Offset" button. In the **TYPE** window, select the *Loop* option. Pick on one of the right or bottom edges as shown in Figure 8. A small red arrow will appear on one of the edges showing an offset direction. Read the message window. If the arrow is pointing outwards, enter an offset value of *-1*, otherwise enter *1*. The sketch for our pocket is now complete. Select the "Done" button.

The material removal direction arrow should point to the interior of our sketch.

Spin the object to see the feature creation direction arrow. For the depth of the cut, select *Blind | Done* and enter a depth of *4*. *Preview* the feature and select *OK*. The resulting pocket should look like Figure 9.

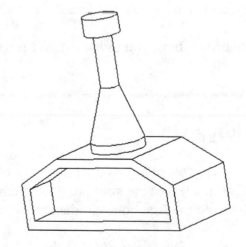

Figure 9 Pocket added using cut feature

---

[2] Incidentally, what are your units? These are the units of the default template. We'll introduce part units and how to change them in Lesson #8.

Creating a Mirror Copy

Since the part is symmetrical, we can easily create
the pocket on the back of the base by mirroring the
first one. Make sure the datum planes are turned
off. Select (in the **FEAT** menu)

> *Copy*
> *Mirror | Select | Dependent | Done*

A *Dependent* copy means that if we change the
geometry of the first pocket, the mirrored pocket
will automatically be changed too. Click on one of
the surfaces formed by the pocket - the entire
pocket should turn red. Then select *Done Sel >
Done*.

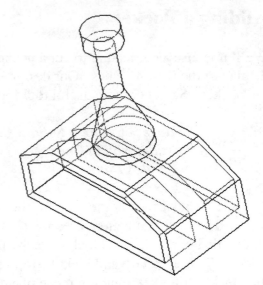

Figure 10 Part with mirrored pocket

We want to mirror this pocket through the **FRONT** datum plane, which is currently turned off.
To select this plane, we'll do something a little different:

> *Plane > Sel By Menu > Datum > Name > FRONT*

The *Sel By Menu* command is handy if, as in this case, the feature is not displayed or if the model
becomes very complicated with many datum planes and/or features. In this case, it is helpful if
the features are all named (see Lesson #2). The result is shown in Figure 10.

By the way, have you saved the part recently?

Adding Holes

We already came across the hole feature in Lesson #2. We are going to add four holes as shown
in Figure 13. We are going to do something a little different with the depth specification. We
will create the first hole and then mirror it across the datums.

> *Create > Solid > Hole*

In the dialog window, select a *Straight* hole and enter a diameter of *2.0*. From the Depth One
pull-down list, select *Thru Next*.

We will use a linear placement for the hole. This means two linear dimensions from orthogonal references. For the primary reference (the placement plane), click on the sloping surface of the base at approximately the position where we want the hole center to be. This is shown in Figure 11. For linear dimensioning references, we want to use **FRONT** and the upper edge of the end surface of the base. This is one time where we must use an edge as a dimensioning reference, which we normally want to avoid. (Why?) The distance from each reference will be *3*. Here is a quick and easy way to pick the references that you should know...

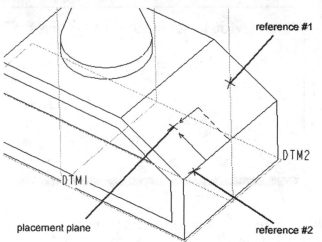

Figure 11 Placement plane and linear references

Using *Query Select*

If you have trouble selecting an entity on a crowded screen, for example, just the top edge of the right surface, here is a handy tool. When required to select or pick an entity in the graphics window (even a hidden one), instead of clicking with the *left* button to select it, first click the *right* mouse button. This is called a *Query Select* as you can see by the highlighted entry in the **GET SELECT** menu at the right. Now *left click* on or close to the desired entity. For example, on our part click at approximately the edge where the two surfaces meet (reference #2 in Figure 11). Depending on exactly where you pick, you might see either one of the surfaces highlight or the desired edge. There are, in fact, quite a number of possible entities that might be selected at the pick point. Now, unless your system administrator has turned this off, all the entities at or close to (within a few pixels) the pick point are listed in the **Query Bin** window that appears on the right, as in Figure 12. We can now select from this list of features. The first feature on the list is highlighted in the window and on the model.

Click the *right* mouse button to move to the next feature on the list. It will highlight. You can cycle through all the features at that pick location (including hidden surfaces) using the right mouse button until the one you want is highlighted. At the bottom of the list, you'll have to use the up arrow to move back to the top. You can also select directly by left clicking on a listed feature in the **Query Bin** window. When the feature you want is highlighted, both in the Query Bin and on the model, then *middle* click to accept it. These mouse functions are summarized in Table 1-1 back in Lesson #1. The following diagram might help you remember this sequence better:

```
Edge:F5(PROTRUSION)
Surf:F5(PROTRUSION)
Surf:F7(CUT)
Edge:F7(CUT)
Surf:F7(CUT)
Surf:F5(PROTRUSION)



↓  ↑              Accept
```

Figure 12 The Query Bin

Mouse sequence for *QUERY SELECT* function:

	Right	enter *Query Select* mode
Left		pick location on screen
	Right	*Next* feature
	Right	*Next* feature, ...
	Middle	*Accept* feature

Query Select is a very powerful and necessary function, so be sure you understand this sequence of mouse clicks.

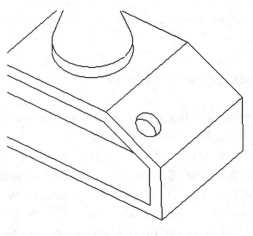

Now, we'll get back to creating our hole. Once the dimension references and values are entered you can *Preview* the hole. The finished hole is shown in Figure 13. *Thru Next*, as might be expected, creates the hole until it passes through the next surface it comes to[3]. Thus, it doesn't go all the way through the part. A blind hole may have achieved the same geometry, but would not be in keeping with our design intent. Why? If all is well, accept the hole using the *Build Feature* button (with the check mark on it).

Figure 13 First hole

We can use the mirror command to make copies of the hole. When executing the following, try using *Query Select* and *Sel By Menu*. The command sequence is

> *Copy*
> *Mirror | Select | Dependent | Done*
> ...pick the hole using *Query Select*...
> *Done Sel > Done* (middle click twice)
> ...pick **RIGHT** using *Sel By Menu*

The new mirrored hole should appear. Repeat this process to mirror both holes to the back at the same time:

---

[3] The only restriction on *Thru Next* is that the sketch or hole must be entirely within the terminating surface. That is, if only part of the sketch or hole intersects the surface, the feature will just keep going through! We will see some examples of the problems this might cause when we get to the last section of this lesson.

Copy
Mirror | Select | Dependent | Done
...pick on the both holes...
Done Sel > Done (middle click twice)
...pick on FRONT

The part should now look like Figure 14. The
figure does not show the axes created with each
hole.

Having Problems Mirroring?

If you have trouble creating mirrored features, it is
likely that your underlying geometry is not
perfectly symmetrical about the mirror plane. We
should not have that problem here, because we
used the symmetry constraints on our base sketch,
and a both-sides blind protrusion, which is also
automatically symmetric. If you ever do have

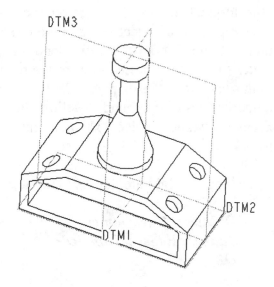

Figure 14 Holes added to base

problems, you may have to *Modify* the geometry to ensure that its dimensions are exactly correct.
We will investigate this problem later on in this lesson. Geometric conditions at the location of
the mirrored featured must be "legal" for the creation of the feature. For example, if the left side
of the block did not have the same slope as the right side at the location of the hole, we should
expect problems trying to do the mirror operation from right to left.

Adding Rounds and Fillets

We are going to add a couple of *rounds* to the top of the guide pin, and the edge where the shaft
meets the base. Technically, these are called a round and a fillet, respectively. (A round removes
material from an edge, while a fillet adds material.) Both are obtained using more-or-less the
same command sequence:

> *Create > Solid > Round > Simple | Done*
> *Constant | Edge Chain | Done > One by One*

You can see that there are a lot of options for this command! You might like to come back some
time and experiment to explore some of these options. We chose this sequence to produce a
simple constant radius round of a single edge.

Select the visible edge where the base of the shaft meets the block. Note that only half the circular edge is highlighted in blue. Spin the object to pick and highlight the other half of the circular edge. Select *Done* in the **CHAIN** menu. In the **RADIUS TYPE** menu select *Enter* to enter a specific radius of the round - in this case, *0.5*. The display will show the tangent edges of the round in yellow. In the Elements window, select **OK** to accept the round.

If the tangent edges are not visible, select

Utilities > Environment
Tangent Edges > Dimmed
OK

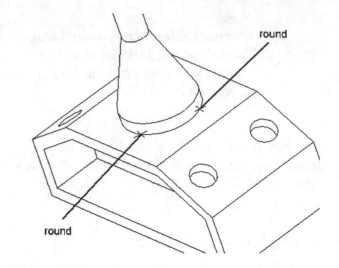

Figure 15 Creating a fillet at the base

You might like to shade the image to see the round a bit better.

Repeat the same sequence to create rounds on the two circular edges at the top of the guide pin. These are also simple, constant radius rounds and both will be created at the same time. This time use *Tangnt Chain* instead of *One by One*. Pick both circular edges as shown in Figure 16. The entire top circular edge will be selected with a single pick, since all edges are tangent. Then select *Done* and enter a radius of *0.25* for both rounds. Select **OK** in the Elements window and shade the part.

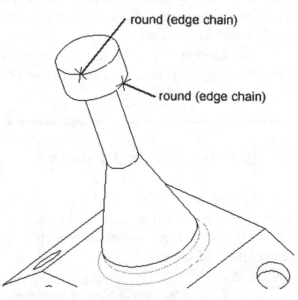

Figure 16 Use *Tangnt Chain* on top edges

Adding a Chamfer

The last feature that we will add to this part is a 45° chamfer all around the edge of the pocket.

Create > Solid > Chamfer > Edge > 45 x d

Use *0.25* for the chamfer dimension and click on all the edges shown in the figure at the right. If you accidentally select a wrong edge, pick *Unsel Last* or *Unsel Item* from the **GET SELECT** menu.

Click on *Done Sel > Done Refs*

Preview the part, and select *OK* if you are satisfied. Now shade the image using

> *View > Shade*

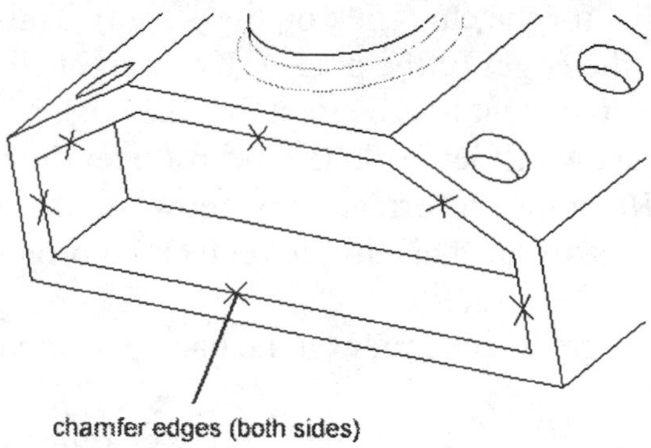

You should see the part in its final form similar to Figure 18. Return to a wireframe with *View > Repaint*.

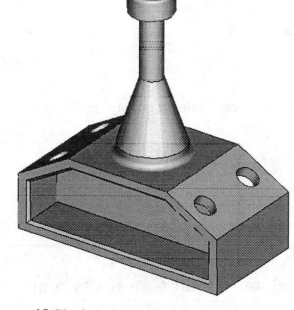

Figure 17 Edges for chamfering

Figure 18 Shaded view of completed part

Now, in preparation for what we are going to do later, we will try to mirror the chamfer to the pocket on the back face of the base using mirror plane **FRONT**. This seems like a reasonable kind of thing to do. Use the *Copy > Mirror | Select | Dependent* command. When you select the chamfer by picking on any of the chamfered surfaces, they will all highlight, since they all belong to the same feature. When it comes to selecting the mirror plane, select **FRONT**. Now the problems start! Pro/E is unable to create the mirrored feature. A Failure Diagnostic Window opens up with a couple of statements about the chamfer being aborted and an edge being unsuitable or missing. What's going on here? Click on the *<Resolve Hints>* field. This tells us how we can get some more information about this. *Close* the diagnostics window. To find out which reference is invalid, select *Investigate > Show Ref*. This brings up the Reference Information window that we have seen before. In the list of parents on the right side, expand the list for the cut (click on the + sign). This brings up a list of all the references of the failed feature - the edges of the pocket. If you right click on any listed edge and select *Entity Info*, you will see a statement to the effect that the edge is "not in the geometry." Hmmm...it appears that Pro/E just won't let us do this mirror operation. We need to back out of this command. Close the Reference Information window. In the **RESOLVE FEAT** menu, select *Quick Fix > Delete > Continue*. This doesn't delete the original chamfer, just our attempted copy.

To get the chamfer on the back pocket we have two options:

1.   Delete the existing chamfer and create a new one containing both edge sets
2.   Redefine the existing chamfer by adding new edges to the feature (this involves commands discussed in Lesson #4).

For now, you might as well try the first of these two. This will complete the part.

Saving the Part

Don't forget to save your part:

> *File > Save*

(or use CTRL-S) and if you have been saving regularly, get rid of previous copies of the part file by using

> *File > Delete > Old Versions > [guide_pin]*

and press the enter key (or middle click).

Exploring the Model, or "What Can Go Wrong?"

Now comes the fun stuff! Here are some things you can try with this part. This is probably the most important part of this lesson, so DO NOT SKIP THIS SECTION!! We will review what we covered in Lessons #1 and #2. More importantly, some of things we'll try will show you how Pro/E responds to some types of modeling errors such as the failure to mirror the chamfer. Being comfortable with these methods to respond when an error is generated/indicated is an important aspect of your modeling proficiency.

1.   In Lesson #2, we found out how to name the features of a part. Do that now for the *guide_pin*, using whatever names you like. Obtain a feature list using
> *Info > Feature List*
> or
> *Window > Model Tree*
2.   Use the *Modify* command to make the following changes to various features of the model.

Regenerate the part after making each dimensional change. Observe what Pro/E does and see if you can explain why. You can usually recover from any errors that occur by selecting *Undo Changes*, or *Quick Fix > Delete*. If things really go wrong, you should be able to use *File > Erase > Current*, and retrieve your copy of the part file.

▸ change the radius of the round on the base of the revolved protrusion to the following values: (*0.75, 1.5, 3.0*). For each value, see if you can predict what Pro/E will do before you actually execute the regenerate command. Reset to the initial value after these modifications. In all previous releases of Pro/E, the R1.5 and R3.0 rounds would have failed. Can you figure out why? In 2000i^2, the round feature is much more robust.

▸ change the diameter of the first hole to the following values: (*1.0, 4.0*). Again, try to predict how Pro/E will handle these changes. Reset to the initial value after these modifications. Try changing the diameter of one of the mirrored holes on the back of the part. When you click on this hole, where do the placement dimensions show up on the screen?

▸ change the location of the first hole from 3 to **1.5** away from the datum plane **FRONT**. Where does the hole now terminate? Why? Now change the same dimension to **5**. What happens and why? Reset to the initial value after these modifications.

▸ change the location of one of the holes from 3 to **1.0** away from the edge reference on the end of the block. Where does the hole now terminate? Why? Now change the same dimension to (*7.0, 8.0*). What happens and why? Reset to the initial value after these modifications.

▸ change the height of the base block from 8.0 to **6.0**. Then change it to **4.0**. Explain what happens and reset to the initial value after these modifications.

▸ change the depth of the base block to (*9.0, 8.2, 8.0*). What happens each time? Reset to the initial value after these modifications.

▸ change the length of the base block to (*16.0, 12.0*). Shade the view. What happens each time? Reset to the initial value after these modifications.

▸ change the radius of the base of the revolved protrusion to the following values: (*8.0, 9.0, 9.5*). What happens?

▸ change the radius of the rounds on the top of the revolved protrusion to the following: (*0.75, 1.5*). What happens?

▸ change the edge offset dimension for the pocket to the following: (*2.0, 3.5*).

▸ change the depth dimension for the slot to the following: (*4.5, 5.5*).

3. Set up a relation so that the distance of the holes from the datum *FRONT* is such that the hole is always centered on the depth of the pocket. Add another relation that will give a warning if the web between the two pockets down the center of the part becomes less than 1.50 thick. Finally, add relations so that all rounds, fillets, and chamfers have the same dimension.

4. Examine the parent/child relations in the model. What are the parents of the pocket? of the rounds? What are the children of the revolved protrusion? Do the relations added in question 3 change the parent/child relations?

5. Delete the front pocket and all its children. Now, try to create it again. What happens to the holes? Since this new feature will be added after the holes, you might anticipate some changes in the model. This points out again the importance of feature creation order.

6. Explain why centering the base feature (the block) on the datums was a good idea.

7.   Try to delete the revolved protrusion. What happens?

8.   Try to delete one of the corner holes. What happens?

Well that's a lot of exercises and is enough to think about for this lesson. Select *File > Exit*.
When you quit Pro/E, you might also have to check out your disk space usage and delete any
files that you don't want to keep (for example: trail.txt).

In the next lesson we will discuss Pro/E utilities for dealing with features, including examining
parent/child relations in detail, suppressing and resuming features, and the 3 R's (Redefine,
Reroute, and Reorder). These are often necessary when creating a complex model, and to
recover from modeling errors or poor model planning.

Questions for Review

1.   What are the dynamic view controls available with the three mouse buttons? (there are 4
     functions)

2.   When sketching with Intent Manager, why should you deal with and set up your constraints
     before setting up the dimensioning scheme? Why do you set the dimension values last?

3.   What is *Query Select* and what is the sequence of mouse buttons to do this?

4.   What surfaces can be legally chosen as sketching planes?

5.   In Sketcher, how do you easily create an arc tangent to a line at an endpoint?

6.   What does the *Thru Next* depth specification do? What is a requirement for this?

7.   In Sketcher, where are the *Trim* and *Intersect* commands? What do they do?

8.   What elements are required to create a **revolved protrusion**?

9.   What is meant by a **linear** hole? What are the alternatives?

10. What is meant by a **sketched** hole? What are the alternatives?

11. What is meant by a **dependent** copy?

12. What is the difference between *One by One* and *Tangent Chain* when selecting edges?

13. What is the difference between a round and a fillet?

14. What types of chamfer are available?

15. When you are creating a mirrored copy can you:
     ▸   select more than one feature to mirror at once?
     ▸   select more than one mirror plane at the
         same time?

16. What happens when a chamfer meets a round
     at the corner of a part?

17. What happens when two rounds of different
     radii meet at a corner of a part?

18. The figure at the right shows a sketch of two
     four-sided polygons. What is the difference
     between these polygons?

19. Where do the placement dimensions of a
     mirrored feature appear under *Modify*?

20. What are the options for setting the depth of a
     blind, both-sides protrusion?

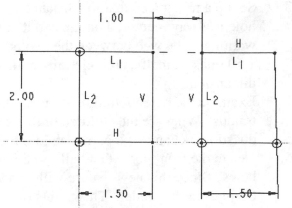

Figure for Question 18

21. Could the rounds we made on the top be created as part of the **revolved protrusion**? What advantages/disadvantages would there be?

22. Describe some of the ways that Pro/E indicates an error in a sketch regeneration.

23. Describe some of the ways that Pro/E indicates an error in part regeneration.

Exercises

Here are some simple parts to make that use the features introduced in this lesson.

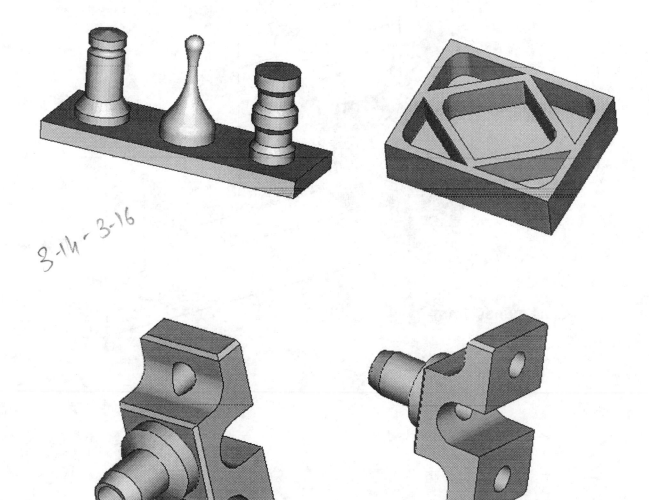

3-14 ~ 3-16

Project

Here is another part for the vise project, using features introduced in this lesson (a revolved protrusion, some mirrored cuts, and some rounds). All units are in millimeters.

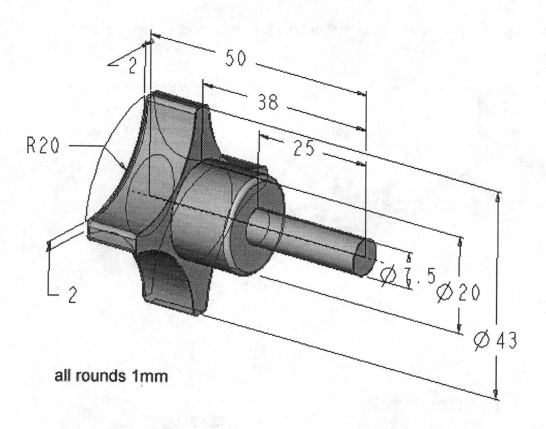

all rounds 1mm

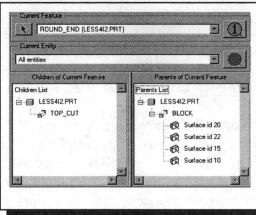

Lesson 4 :

*Modeling Utilities,
Parent/Child Relations,
and the 3 R's*

Synopsis

This lesson deals with important utilities that are used to explore and edit your model: finding relationships between features, changing references, changing feature shapes, changing the order of feature regeneration, changing feature attributes, and so on. If your model becomes even moderately complex, you will need to know how to do this!

Overview of this Lesson

When you are modeling with Pro/ENGINEER, it is almost inevitable that you will have to change the geometry and/or structure of your model at some point. This could be because you discover a better or more convenient way to lay out the features, or the design of the part changes so that your model no longer captures the design intent as accurately or cleanly as you would like. Sometimes, you just plain run into difficulty trying to modify the model, usually caused by the logical structure of the features, or have made errors in creating the model. In this lesson we will discuss Pro/E utilities for dealing with features, including obtaining information about parent/child relations, suppressing and resuming features, the 3 R's (*Redefine*, *Reroute*, and *Reorder* commands), and using Insert Mode.

This lesson is in three sections:

1. Obtaining Information about the Model
    ▸ Regeneration Sequence
    ▸ Obtaining a Feature List and Using the Model Tree
    ▸ Getting Information about a Specific Feature
    ▸ Parent/Child Relations
2. Suppressing and Resuming Features
    ▸ Suppressing/Resuming a Single Feature
    ▸ Suppressing/Resuming a Feature with Children
3. Modifying Feature Definitions - the 3 R's
    ▸ Reroute

- ‣ Redefine
- ‣ Reorder
- ‣ Insert Mode

As usual, there are Questions for Review, Exercises, and a Project part at the end of the lesson.

These utilities are most useful when dealing with complex parts with many features. In this lesson, to illustrate these commands we will only look at the application to a very simple part that will be provided for you. This part has a number of modeling "errors" that we will try to fix. For the operations we will perform in this lesson, for this simple part it may actually be easier to just create a new part and start over again. However, when your parts get more complex, and contain many features, starting over will not be an option and these utilities will be indispensable.
In order to do this lesson, you will have to obtain a copy of the file *less4i2.prt.1* that is available from your instructor or from the Schroff Development Corporation home page on the Web (go to **http://www.schroff.com/sdcpublications/PET_download.htm** Note that this is case sensitive). Use your Web browser to download this file and copy it to your Pro/E working directory - full instructions to do this are on the Web page.

Once you have the part file in hand, launch Pro/E, retrieve the part and continue on with the lesson. The part should look like this (select *View > Default*)

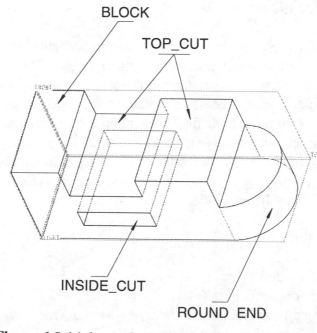

Figure 1 Initial part for Lesson #4

This model contains the default datum planes and four features. The base feature is a rectangular block. The other features are another solid protrusion and two cuts. The features are named as shown in Figure 1.

Obtaining Information about the Model

Once your model gets reasonably complex, or if you "inherit" a model from another source such as we are doing here, one of the important things to do is to have a clear idea of the structure of the model. Which features were created first? Which features depend on other features? How do the features reference each other? Answers to all these questions are available!

The Regeneration Sequence

The order of feature creation during part regeneration is called the *regeneration sequence.* Features are regenerated in the order in which they were first created. (We will talk about changing the order of the regeneration sequence in a later section of this lesson.) To observe the regeneration sequence select the following commands, starting in the pull-down menu:

> *Info > Regen Info > Beginning*

Selecting the ***Continue*** command will step you through the creation of the model one feature at a time. The message window will tell you which feature is currently being created. As you progress through the sequence, the menu gives you a chance to get more information about the feature currently being created, including its dimensions.

For example, for feature #6, you can get the information shown in Figure 2 by selecting ***Info Feat*** when the cut is highlighted or immediately after it has been created. This shows you the *feature number* (#6), the *internal feature ID* (52), the ID's and feature numbers of the parents and children of this feature, the *feature type* (an extruded cut), dimensions, and other parameters. Note that the depth of this feature is indicated as *Blind, Depth=10*. This will be important later on. Also, note the difference between the feature number (the placement within the regeneration sequence) and the feature ID

```
PART NAME = LESS4I2

FEATURE NUMBER        6
INTERNAL FEATURE ID   52
PARENTS = 7(#4) 28(#5)
CHILDREN = 149(#7)

CUT: Extrude

NO. ELEMENT NAME     INFO                                              STATUS
--- ------------ -----------                                          ------
 1  Attributes   One Side                                            Defined
 2  Section      Sk. plane - Surface of feat #4 (PROTRUSION)         Defined
 3  MaterialSide                                                     Defined
 4  Direction                                                        Defined
 5  Depth        Blind, depth = 10                                   Defined

NAME = TOP_CUT
SECTION NAME = S2D0003
OPEN SECTION


FEATURE'S DIMENSIONS:
d12 = 5.00
d13 = 7.50
d14 = 3.50
```

Figure 2 Information obtained with ***Info Feat***

(Pro/E's internal bookkeeping). It will be possible to change the feature number, but, once created, you can never change a feature's ID.

Exit this window by pressing ***Close***, then continue through the regeneration sequence until you are back to the normal screen with the message "Regeneration completed successfully.".

The Feature List and other Feature Information

You can call up a table summary of all the features in the model by selecting:

Info > Feature List

This brings up the table shown at the right. This shows the feature number and ID in the first two columns, a name for the feature (if defined), the type of feature, and current regeneration status. If you have many features, it is a good idea to name them - there is nothing worse than seeing a whole bunch of features all identified with just "Hole" or "Cut" in this table.

```
MODEL NAME       : LE88412
FEATURE LINK LIST:
*******************

Num  ID      Name        Type          Sup Order   Regen Status

0001 000001  RIGHT       DATUM PLANE               Regenerated
0002 000003  TOP         DATUM PLANE               Regenerated
0003 000005  FRONT       DATUM PLANE               Regenerated
0004 000007  BLOCK       PROTRUSION                Regenerated
0005 000028  ROUND_END   PROTRUSION                Regenerated
0006 000052  TOP_CUT     CUT                       Regenerated
0007 000149  INSIDE_CUT  CUT                       Regenerated
```

Figure 3 List of all features in the part

By the way, whenever you see a text/data window like this in Pro/E, the text is automatically saved to a file in your disk space. Observe the file name in parentheses at the top of the window. You can use *File > Save As* in this window to save to a different file. You will undoubtedly want to delete these files later (see Lesson #2) - look for files with the extension *lst* or *inf*. *Close* this window.

If you issue the command sequence:

Info > Model

you will get a long output of information about all the features in the model (essentially a listing like Figure 3 for the entire part). For example, part way through this listing you will see the table shown in Figure 4 which tells you some of the details about feature #5 (the rounded protrusion), including its parent (#4 - the block), and children (#6 - the top cut, #7 - the inside cut). *Close* this window.

```
*******************
FEATURE NUMBER        5
INTERNAL FEATURE ID  28
PARENTS = 7(#4)
CHILDREN = 52(#6) 149(#7)

PROTRUSION: Extrude

NO. ELEMENT NAME    INFO                                          STATUS
--- ------------ -----------                                      ------
 1  Attributes   One Side                                        Defined
 2  Section      Sk. plane - Surface of feat #4 (PROTRUSION)      Defined
 3  MaterialSide                                                  Defined
 4  Direction                                                     Defined
 5  Depth        Blind, depth = 5                                 Defined

NAME = ROUND_END
SECTION NAME = S2D0002
OPEN SECTION

FEATURE'S DIMENSIONS:
d9 = 5.00
*******************
```

Figure 4 Listing for feature #5

If you want model information for a single feature, say the rounded protrusion, select:

Info > Feature

and click on the rounded end of the part. This is the same window as above. *Close* the window, and select *Quit Sel* in the **GET SELECT** menu.

The Model Tree

The model tree was introduced in Lesson #2. Call it up using the commands

> *View > Model Tree*

or select the "Model Tree" shortcut button. Use

> *View > Model Tree Settings > Column Display*

to add and format columns. The usual columns you will use are *Feat #*, *Feat Type*, and *Status*. Also, while we're here, select

> *View > Model Tree Settings > Item Display*

This brings up a dialog window with a number of checkboxes for selecting items to be displayed in the model tree. For example, remove the check mark beside **Datum Plane**, then select *Apply*. This might be useful if the part contains many datum planes which are cluttering up the view of the model tree feature structure. Turn the datum plane display back on and exit the window with *OK*. (What happens if you *Close* this window instead?)

The model tree should now look like Figure 5.

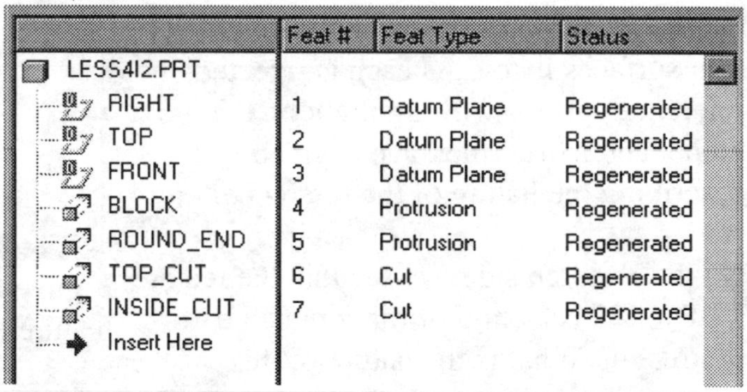

Left click on any of the feature names shown in the left column of the model tree to see it highlighted in the model. (If the feature doesn't highlight, make sure that **Highlight** is checked in the *View > Model Tree Setup* menu.) This is an easy way to explore the structure of the database and the features in the model. But the model tree can do much more!

	Feat #	Feat Type	Status
LESS4I2.PRT			
RIGHT	1	Datum Plane	Regenerated
TOP	2	Datum Plane	Regenerated
FRONT	3	Datum Plane	Regenerated
BLOCK	4	Protrusion	Regenerated
ROUND_END	5	Protrusion	Regenerated
TOP_CUT	6	Cut	Regenerated
INSIDE_CUT	7	Cut	Regenerated
Insert Here			

Figure 5 The Model Tree with added columns

Make sure you are in **Part** mode, and hold down the right mouse button on one of the features listed in the model tree. This brings up a menu containing the following commands:

- ▸ Delete
- ▸ Suppress
- ▸ Modify
- ▸ Redefine
- ▸ Reroute
- ▸ Pattern
- ▸ Note Create
- ▸ Info which brings up the menu
  - • Feat Info
  - • Model Inf

- Parent/Child Info

We have seen the *Modify* and *Delete* commands before, as well as the *Feat Info* and *Model Info* commands. These are available in the **FEATURE** and **INFO** menus, respectively. The other commands **Redefine**, **Reroute**, and **Suppress** are among the main topics in this lesson, and are discussed at length below. These commands are also available in the **FEATURE** menu. *Close* the model tree window.

Parent/Child Relations

Using the commands given above, you can find out the regeneration sequence and internal ID numbers of parent and child features. There are several commands for exploring the parent/child relations in the model in considerably more detail. To get at them, issue the commands:

Info > Parent/Child

Click on the round protrusion. The Reference Information Window (Figure 6) opens. Expand the lists in the Children and Parents areas.

On the parents side, click on each of the four surfaces listed. As each is selected, the reference surface will highlight on the model and a brief message is given describing the nature of the reference.

On the children side, we see that the feature TOP_CUT is a child of the rounded end protrusion. What is the nature of this reference? Highlight this feature, then hold down the right mouse button and in the pop-up menu select *Set Current*.

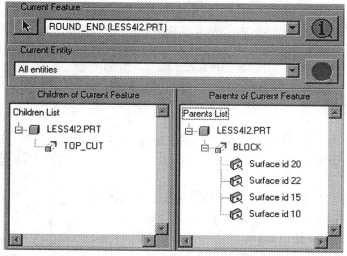

Figure 6 The Reference Information Window for feature ROUND_END

The Reference Information Window now shows TOP_CUT as the current feature, and lists its parents and children. Expand these lists (Figure 7). Notice the surface listed under ROUND_END in the parents area. Select this surface and it is highlighted on the model. The message tells us that this was used as the horizontal sketcher reference for the cut feature #6 (TOP_CUT). This will be important to us later. The other four parent surfaces of TOP_CUT correspond to the following:

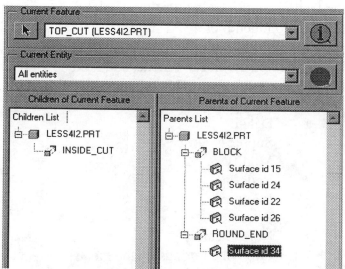

Figure 7 The Reference Information Window for feature TOP_CUT

1. the front of the block - sketching plane
2. top of block - dimensioning ref used for aligning/dimensioning the cut
3. right end of block - dimensioning ref used for aligning/dimensioning the cut
4. left surface of block - dimensioning ref used for dimensioning reference

If you repeat this process for the inside cut, you should see the following references:

1. the front of the block - sketching plane
2. the right horizontal surface of the top cut - horizontal reference plane
3. the base of the block - dimension reference
4. left vertical surface of the top cut - alignment/dimension reference
5. right vertical surface of the top cut - alignment/dimension reference

Now that we have explored the model a bit, you should have a good idea of how it was set up. Before we go on to ways that we can modify the model, let's have a look at a useful utility for dealing with features. Select *Close* in the **Reference Information Window** menu.

Suppressing and Resuming Features

When you are working with a very complex model, or when you don't want to accidentally pick on an existing feature as a reference for a new one, you can temporarily remove one or more features from the regeneration sequence. This is called *suppressing* the feature(s). It is important to note that this does not mean deleting the feature(s), it just means that they are skipped over when Pro/E regenerates the model. This will speed up the regeneration process thus saving you time. It also speeds up the screen refresh rate when doing 3D spins and shading.

When a feature is suppressed, it generally means that all its children will be suppressed as well. To bring it back, you can *resume* it. Let's see how suppress and resume work.

Issue the following commands:

Feature > Suppress > Normal | Select | Pick

and pick on a surface formed by the inside cut. Select *Done* in the **SELECT FEAT** menu. The part will regenerate without the cut as shown in Figure 8.

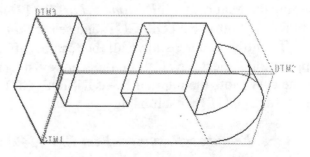

Figure 8 Part regenerated with cut suppressed

Check out the new feature list:

> *Info > Feature List*

or call up the model tree (make sure that *View > Model Tree Setup > Item Display > Suppressed Objects* is checked). If you use the model tree, leave its window open for the following. In the model tree, notice the small black square beside the suppressed feature.

You will note that the suppressed feature no longer has a feature number (but it still has an ID), and the last column shows its status as suppressed. To get the slot back into the geometry, issue the commands

> *Feature > Resume > Last Set | Done*

Now, try to suppress the TOP_CUT. Select

> *Feature > Suppress*

and click on a surface of the cut. You will be informed that the cut has a child (shown in blue), and you will have to decide what to do with it. The **CHILD** menu opens to give you some options. For now, select *Suppress > Done* to suppress both cuts together. You should see the part as shown below:

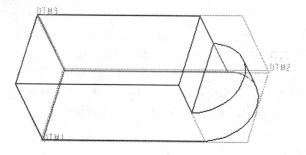

Figure 9 Part with both cuts suppressed

Resume the features with *Resume > Last Set | Done*. In the model tree, try holding down the right mouse button on TOP_CUT, and select *Suppress* from the pop-up window. This operates a bit differently - you are shown all the features affected and merely asked to confirm the suppression. Select *OK*. Call up the feature list again (*Info > Feature List*) and observe the data for the cuts. Note the internal ID of INSIDE_CUT is 149. Close that window, and try to resume the INSIDE_CUT by itself using

> *Feature > Resume > Feat ID > [149] > Done*

You should find that both the selected feature and its parent (the other cut) are resumed - you can't resume a child without also resuming it's parent(s).

Using suppress and resume can make your life easier by eliminating unnecessary detail in a model when you don't need it. For example, if your part is a valve, you don't need all the bolt holes in the flange if you are working on some other unrelated features of the valve. If you are setting up a model for Finite Element Modeling (FEM) for stress analysis, for example, you would usually suppress all fine detail in the model (chamfers, rounds, etc.) in order to simplify it. Suppressing features also prevents you from inadvertently creating references to features that you don't want (like two axes that may coincide, but may be separated later). Finally, suppressing unneeded features will also speed up the regeneration of the part.

Features that are suppressed are still included in the part data base, and will be saved (with their suppress/resume status) along with the part when you save your model to a disk file. When we get to drawings and assemblies in the last lessons, remember that suppressed features are carried over into these objects as well. That is, a suppressed feature will stay suppressed when you add its part to an assembly, or display the part in a drawing.

Modifying Feature Definitions - the 3 R's

No self-respecting CAD program would prevent you from going back and changing portions of the model. In previous lessons, we have used the *Modify* command to change dimension values only. We need some tools to let us edit the basic structure of the model. So, now we will look at ways to modify the parent/child relations in the part, and to modify the geometric shape of some features.

Suppose we want to take the original *less4i2.prt* and modify it to form the part shown in Figure 10. This involves the following changes (some of these are not visible in the figure):

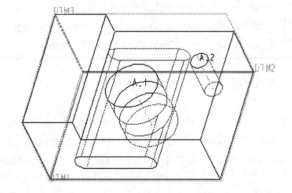

Figure 10 Final modified part

1.   deleting the rounded end
2.   changing the shape of the inner cut
3.   changing the dimensioning scheme of the inner cut
4.   changing the references of the inner cut
5.   changing the shape of the cut on the top surface
6.   changing the feature references of the top cut
7.   increase the width of the part
8.   change the depth attribute of the top cut
9.   add a couple of vertical holes

Some of these changes will require modifications to the parent/child relations that were used when the part was created. This will also result in a cleaner model.

If you haven't gone through Section 1 of this lesson on obtaining model information, now is a good time to do so, since a good understanding of the existing parent/child relations is essential for what follows.

To see what we are up against, try to delete the rounded end of the part (the first thing on our "to do" list) using

> *Feature > Delete*

and clicking on the feature. You will be notified that the feature has a child (the top cut, shown in blue) and asked what you want to do with it. (Furthermore, the inside cut is a child of the top cut, as we discovered earlier.) We do not want to delete either cut. If you select

> *Show Ref > Next*

you will see that the top face of the rounded end is a reference surface for the cut. This was used as the *Top* reference for the cut's sketch. We could change that reference now (using *Reroute*), but we'll deal with that possibility later. We could also delete the child along with the parent. We would then have to decide what to do with the children of the children (that is, the inside cut) and so on! For now, do neither and select

> *Done/Return > Quit > Quit Del/Sup*

We'll deal with our desired changes one at a time, and not necessarily in the order given above. For example, before we can delete the rounded end, we have to do something about its child references. Some careful thought and planning is necessary here. When you get proficient with Pro/E, you will be able to manage these changes more efficiently. Our main tools to use here are the 3 R's: *Redefine*, *Reroute*, and *Reorder*.

① Changing a Sketch using *REDEFINE*

The first thing we'll do is change the shape of the inner cut from its current rectangular shape to one with rounded ends. This requires a change in the sketch geometry of the feature. We'll take the opportunity to change the dimensioning scheme as well.

The redefine command allows you to change almost everything about a feature except its type (you can't change a extruded solid into a revolved cut, or even an extruded cut into a revolved cut!). From the **FEATURE** menu select

> *Redefine*

and click on the inside cut. (Or select the command from the model tree using a right mouse click.) The feature element window will open (Figure 11).

This is the same window we saw when a new feature is being created. Click on the line that says *Section*, then select the *Define* button. In the **SECTION** menu, select *Sketch*. Now we can use Sketcher to modify the sketched shape of the slot. Make sure that Intent Manager is turned on. The final shape is shown in Figure 12.

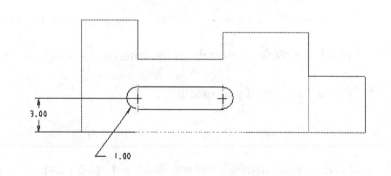

Figure 11 Feature element window for the inner cut

First, shift-click (hold down the shift key while picking with the left mouse button) on the vertical sketched lines at each end. Then, hold down the right mouse button and from the pop-up menu select

> *Delete*

Now add two circular arcs. Again, hold down the right mouse button and from the pop-up menu select

> *3 Point / Tangent End*

and sketch the arcs at each end. Now change (if necessary) the dimensioning scheme to the one shown in Figure 12. Note that the ends of the straight part of the slot are still aligned with the vertical faces of the cut. We will deal with those later. When the sketch is complete, select the "Done" button. In the attribute window, select *Preview* if desired, then the *OK* button. If all went well, you should get the message

Figure 12 New sketch for the inner cut

> "Feature redefined successfully."

② Changing a Feature Reference using *REROUTE*

Recall that the horizontal sketching reference for the inner cut was on the top cut, and we are planning on changing the shape of the top cut to remove that surface. We will have to change the reference for the inner cut to something else. This is done using the *Reroute* command.

In the **FEAT** menu, select

Reroute

and click on the inner cut (or, of course, use the pop-up menu in the model tree). You will be asked if you want to "*roll back*" the model. Rolling back means temporarily returning to the part status when the inner cut was created. This is like suppressing all features created after the cut. This is a good idea, since then it will not be possible to (accidentally) select a new reference that is "younger" than the cut (ie. created after it). It is a good idea to **ALWAYS ROLL BACK THE PART!** It is curious that this is not the Pro/E default (although if you have a seriously complex model, this situation might change!) - you will have to enter a *y* (or click the *Yes* button) to cause the roll back to occur. This doesn't do anything for this simple model at this time because the cut was the last feature created.

The general procedure in a reroute operation is to step through all the references for the feature being changed. In the **REROUTE** menu that appears, as you step through the sequence of current references, you have the options of selecting an alternate reference, keeping the same reference, or obtaining feature/reference information. As you step through the references, they will be highlighted on the part. Read the message in the message window - it will tell you what the currently highlighted reference is used for. For the inner cut, we want to:

1.   keep the same sketching plane (*Same Ref*)
2.   select a different horizontal reference for Sketcher (*Alternate*). A good one is the top surface of the block; an even better one is the horizontal datum plane (yellow side). Click on either of these now.
3.   keep all the same alignment and dimensioning references (*Same Ref*, *Same Ref*, ...)

When you have cycled through all the references, you should get the message

"Feature rerouted successfully"

If you have rolled back the part, any features suppressed during the roll back will be resumed.

Go and check with *Info > Parent/Child* and click on the inside cut to confirm that the horizontal surface of the top cut is no longer referenced. There should still be a couple of references to the top cut, though. These are alignment constraints in the sketch of the inside cut. We'll have to change these if we are going to modify the top cut as planned.

③ Changing the Sketcher Constraints using *REDEFINE*

As we saw earlier, the ends of the straight part of the inner cut are aligned with the vertical faces of the top cut. See Figure 13. To change these alignments, we need to redefine the sketch. So, select

Redefine

and click on the inside cut (or, as usual, select this in the model tree). Select

Section > Define > Sketch

Turn off the datum plane display and make sure that the Intent Manager is on. We want to do something with the sketch references so in the pull-down menu select

> *Sketch > References*

Click on the left edge of the part. This should add an entry in the References window. Now, select the other listed references (these will both be to feature #6, the top cut) and select the Delete button. The other two vertical (orange) references should disappear.

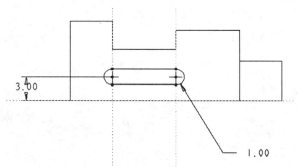

Figure 13 Old alignment references in the inside cut sketch

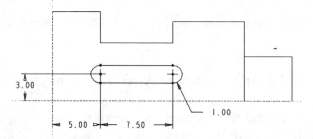

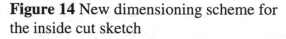

Figure 14 New dimensioning scheme for the inside cut sketch

Set up the new dimensioning scheme as shown in Figure 14. Intent Manager will do some of this for you automatically. To dimension to the center of the arcs, pick on the arc itself (not its center point!). A small window will open asking if you want to dimension to the center or tangent to the arc. Close out Sketcher and accept the redefined feature.

Return to the **FEATURE** menu. To make sure that there is now no relation between the top cut and the inside cut, select

> *Info > Parent/Child*

and click on the top cut - the inner cut is no longer a child!

④ **Changing a Feature Reference using *REROUTE***

Recall that the rounded end is a parent of the top cut via supplying the horizontal sketching reference. We need to break this connection before we can delete the rounded end (which is on our "to do" list). The command to do this is

> *Feature > Reroute*

Pick on the top cut, and roll back the part. Notice that the inside cut disappears (temporarily). Keep the same sketching plane (*Same Ref*), but select a new horizontal reference (*Alternate*) like the top of the block or the horizontal datum. This is all we have to reroute, so select *Done*. You should get the message

"Feature rerouted successfully"

Check out the rounded end with

> *Info > Parent/Child*

and click on the rounded end to see that it now has no children. Go ahead and delete it with

> *Feature > Delete*

pick on the rounded end, then *Done* in the **SELECT FEAT** menu.

⑤ **Changing Feature Attributes using** *REDEFINE*

We want to change the shape of the cut to get rid
of the step. We will also change its depth attribute.
To see why this is necessary, select *Modify* in the
PART menu and change the depth of the block
from 10 to *15* and regenerate. As you recall, the
top cut had a blind depth of 10, so it doesn't go all
the way through the new block as show at the
right.

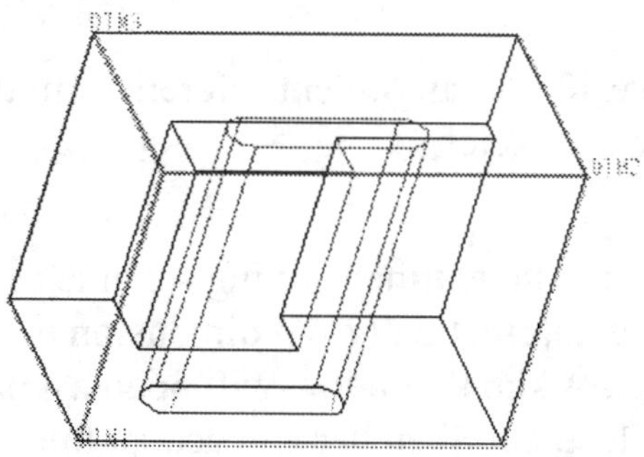

Let's change both the shape and depth of the top
cut at the same time. Select

> *Feature > Redefine*

Figure 15 Block width increased to 15

and click on the cut. Starting in the elements window, select

> *Section > Define > Sketch*

Using the Sketcher tools, change the shape of the cut to a simple L-shape as shown in Figure 16.
With the Intent Manager, you should be able to do this very quickly.

> **Helpful Hint**:
> When you select the *Modify* command in Sketcher, you can left click on entities (lines or
> vertices) in the graphics window and drag them to a new location. Dimension values will
> automatically update.

Don't forget to constrain (align) the right end of the cut with the surface of the block. Also, note
that the cut dimensions are different. When you have a successful regeneration, select the "Done"
button from the Sketcher menu.

To change the depth of the cut, starting in the element window, select (you may have to scroll
down the list)

Depth > Define > Thru All | Done

Preview the part, and if it looks all right, select *OK*. The modified part is shown in Figure 17.

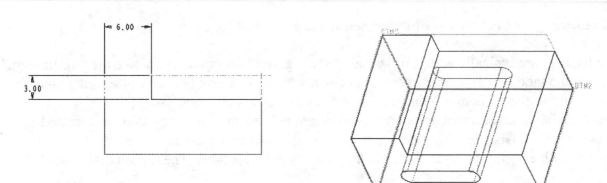

Figure 16 New sketch for the cut

Figure 17 Part with redefined cut

⑥ Changing the Regeneration Sequence using REORDER

This is the last of the 3 R's! It is sometimes convenient or necessary to change the order of the features in the regeneration sequence. For example, an advanced technique involves grouping adjacent features in the regeneration sequence so that the group can be patterned or copied. The major restrictions on reordering features are:

- ♦ a child feature can never be placed before its parent(s)
- ♦ a parent feature can never be placed after any of its children

The reasons for these restrictions should be pretty self-evident. Fortunately, Pro/E is able to keep track of the parent/child relations and can tell you what the legal reordering positions are. To see how it works, in the **Feature** menu select

Reorder

and click on the inside cut, then *Done*. This cut (feature #6) was originally a child of the top cut (#5), but that relation was modified above. Thus, we should be able to create the cuts in any order, after the block (#4). This is what Pro/E tells you in the message window. In a more complicated part, Pro/E would tell you where the legal positions in the regeneration sequence are, and you could specify a *Before* or *After* placement for the reordered feature. In this simple part, there is only one legal possibility, that is, reorder the selected cut (currently #6) before the top cut (currently #5). Go ahead and complete the reorder: select *Confirm* and then call up the model tree. Note that the feature numbers of the cut and slot have now changed, but the internal ID's are still the same.

With Release 2000i², Pro/E has gone a step farther with the Reorder command. You can now drag and drop features in the model tree. Try that now by reordering the top cut. Click on the feature in the model tree and drag it upwards. The mouse icon changes slightly as you move back up the list to show you where legal reordered positions are. In this part, of course, there is only one valid position. You might try out this mode of reordering sometime when you get a more complicated part.

⑦ **Creating New Features Within the Sequence using *INSERT***

New features are typically added at the end of the regeneration sequence (notice the "Insert Here" arrow in the model tree). Sometimes it is necessary to create a new feature whose order you want to be earlier in the sequence. You could do this by creating it and then using the reorder command, being careful that you don't set up parent references to features after the targeted reorder position. Also, you would have to be careful not to create any new features that could interfere with existing features (like cutting off a reference surface). There is an easier way!

In the **Feature** menu, just select

Insert Mode > Activate

You will be asked to select which feature to insert after. Pick on an original surface of the block (not one created by either of the cuts) or pick the block in the model tree.. The part will automatically roll back by suppressing all features created after the block. Notice the new position of the "Insert Here" arrow in the model tree.

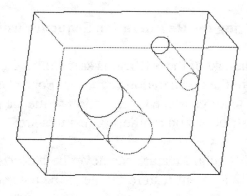

Create two circular holes in the part as shown in the figure (the diameters are 2 and 5; placement is approximately as shown).

Figure 18 Two holes inserted after block feature

Insert mode will stay on until you turn it off by selecting

Insert Mode > Cancel

You will be asked about resuming the features; accept the default [Y]. Call up the **Feature List** or model tree to see that the two holes have been added to the model after the block and before the cuts.

Conclusion

The modeling utilities described in this lesson are indispensable when dealing with complex parts. You will invariably come across situations where you need to redefine, reroute, or reorder features. The information utilities are useful for digging out the existing parent/child relations, and discovering how features are referenced by other features. The more practice you get with these tools, the better you will be able to manage your model. As a side benefit, having a better understanding of how Pro/E organizes features will cause you to do more careful planning prior to creating the model, with fewer corrections to be made later. This will save you a lot of time!

In the next lesson, we will investigate the use of datum planes and axes, including creating temporary datums called "make datums".

Questions for Review

1.   How can you find out the order in which features were created? What is this called?
2.   How can you find which are the parent features of a given feature?
3.   How can you find the references used to create a feature?
4.   How can you find any or all other features that use a given feature as a reference?
5.   What is the difference between the Feature # and the internal ID?
6.   What is the command to exclude a feature temporarily from the model?
7.   What happens to the parents of a suppressed feature? To the children?
8.   Is it possible, via a convoluted chain of parent/child relations, for a feature to reference itself?
9.   What happens to suppressed features when the model is saved and you leave Pro/E?
10.   If you are given a part file that you have never seen before, how can you determine if it contains any suppressed features?
11.   In Sketcher, how many variations of the right mouse pop-up menu can you find? In what modes are these active (Sketch, Modify, Dimension, etc.)
12.   How can you restore previously suppressed features?
13.   How can you change the sketch references when you are in Sketcher?
14.   How many features can you suppress at once?
15.   Is there any aspect of a feature that cannot be modified using *Redefine*?
16.   When you select *Redefine > Section > Define*, what options do you have?
17.   What is the difference between redefining and rerouting?
18.   What is meant by "rolling back the part?"
19.   How can you remove unwanted alignments in a feature?
20.   What symbol in the model tree indicates suppressed features?
21.   What are the two fundamental rules of reordering?
22.   Are there any restrictions on the insertion point in *Insert Mode*?
23.   What happens if Insert Mode is on when you save a part and then later retrieve it?
24.   How do you get out of insert mode?

Exercises

Here are some simple parts to model using the features we have covered up to here. Before you start creating these, think about where you will place them relative to the datum planes, what type and order you should select for the features, and how you should set up parent/child references and dimensioning schemes.

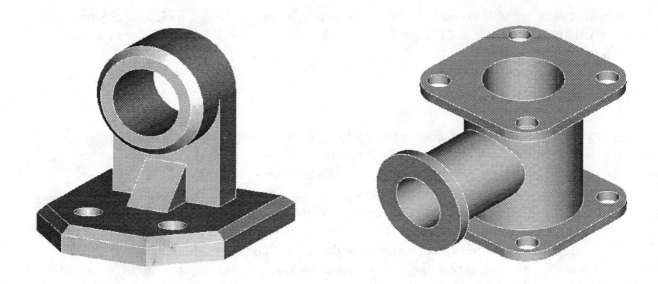

Project

Here are three small parts for the project. All dimensions in millimeters. For the acorn nut, you might like to investigate alternate Sketcher environments (see *Utililities > Sketcher Preferences* when you are in Sketcher), including a polar grid, and the use of centerlines as construction aides (straight lines and/or circles). Note that the hexagon on the nut requires only one dimension to give its size.

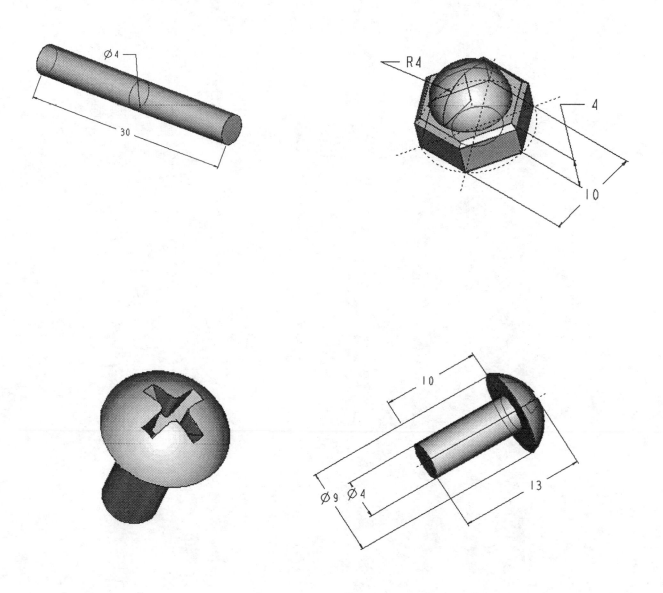

NOTES:

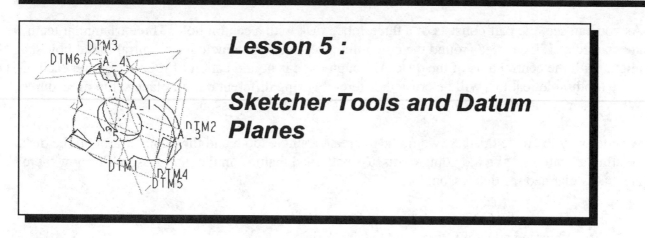

Lesson 5 :

Sketcher Tools and Datum Planes

Synopsis

More tools in Sketcher are introduced, including sketching relations. The mysteries of datum planes and make datums are revealed! What are they, how are they created? How are they used to implement design intent?

Overview of this Lesson

In this lesson we are going to look at some new commands in Sketcher for creating sections. We will also use relations within Sketcher to control the geometry. Our primary objective, though, is to look at the commands used to set up and use datum planes. Some of these will result in permanent datum planes added to the model, like the default ones we usually create (**RIGHT**, **TOP**, and **FRONT**), while others will be temporary (called *make datums*), created "on-the-fly" when needed. Along the way, we will discuss some model design issues and explore some options in feature creation we have not seen before. The part we are going to create is shown in the figure below.

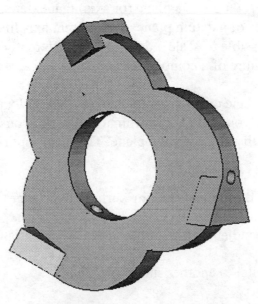

Figure 1 Final part - three tooth cutter

As you can see, the part consists of a three-lobed disk with a central hole. Three triangular teeth are spaced at 120 degrees around the circumference. Each tooth includes a central radial hole that aligns with the central axis of the disk. Although there is no indication of it in the figure, each of these tooth/hole features will be created differently using different datum plane setup procedures. We will see what effect this has on the model at the end of the lesson.

A better way to create this part would be to create a single tooth and then copy it around the disk, creating a "pattern." We are going to discuss patterned features in the next lesson. For now, here is what is planned for this lesson:

1. Overview of Datum Planes and Datum Axes
2. Creating a Datum Plane and Datum Axis
3. Create the Disk with Hole
4. First Tooth - Offset
5. Second Tooth - Normal and Tangent
6. Third Tooth - Make Datums
7. Effects on the Model
8. Things to Consider about Design Intent

As usual there are some Questions for Review, Exercises, and a Project part at the end of the lesson.

Overview of Datum Planes and Axes

Datum planes and axes are features used to provide references for other features, like sketching planes, dimensioning references, view references, assembly references, and so on. Datum planes and axes are not physical (solid) parts of the model, but are used to aid in model creation (or, eventually, in an assembly). A datum is a plane (or axis) that extends off to infinity. By default, Pro/E will show visible edges of a datum plane or the datum axis line so that they encompass the part being displayed. It is possible to scale a datum plane differently so that, for example, it will extend only over a single feature of a complex part.

Let's consider how a datum plane can be constructed. In order to locate the position and orientation of a datum plane, you will choose from a number of constraint options. These work alone or in combination to fully constrain the plane. The major options for datum planes are:

Through
       the datum passes through an existing surface, axis, edge, vertex, or cylinder axis
Normal
       the datum is perpendicular to a surface, axis, or other datum
Parallel
       the datum is parallel to another surface or plane
Offset
       the datum is parallel to another surface or plane and a specified distance away

Angle

the datum is at a specified angle from another plane or surface

Tangent

the datum is tangent to a curved surface or edge

Some of these constraints are sufficient by themselves to define a new datum plane (for example, the **Offset** option). Other constraints must be used in combinations in order to fully constrain the new datum. When you are constructing a new datum, Pro/E will tell you when it is fully constrained.

Construction of a datum axis is similar, with the following constraint options:

Thru Edge

the axis is along an existing edge

Normal Pln

the axis is located using linear dimensions and is normal to a selected plane

Pnt Norm Pln

the axis passes through a datum point and is normal to a selected plane

Thru Cyl

the axis of a surface of revolution

Two Planes

the axis is placed at the intersection of two planes

Two Pnt/Vtx

the axis is defined by two separate points or vertices

Pnt on Surf

the axis is on a surface through a specified point

Tan Curv

the axis is tangent to a specified curve

Let's see how this all works. Start Pro/E in the usual way, and clear the session of any other parts. Start a new part called *cutter* using the default template. The default datum planes are created for you as the first features in the part (see Lesson #1). You can delete the datum coordinate system feature for this part since we won't need it and it just clutters up our view (or just turn off its display).

After the default datums are created, new datum planes and axes are created using either the shortcut buttons on the right of the graphics window or using the *Datum* pull-down menu at the top. A new development in Pro/E 2000i^2 is that datums can be created more-or-less at any time - even during the creation of another feature.

Creating a Datum Plane and Datum Axis

First, we will define a datum axis that will be the central axis of the cutter. This will be at the intersection of the existing datums **RIGHT** and **TOP**. Starting in the pull-down menu, select

Datum > Axis > Two Planes

Pick on datums **RIGHT** and **TOP.** An axis **A_1** will appear.

Now we will create a datum that will be used in the sketch for the disk and later on to create one of the teeth. Select (again starting from the pull-down menu)

Datum > Plane

A menu opens that contains all the possible placement constraints for defining the new datum. Once we have picked a sufficient number and type of constraint, the option portion of the menu will gray out. If you make a mistake or want to change the datum references, select *Restart*.

We want our new datum to pass through the axis **A_1** and be inclined at an angle of 30° to the vertical datum **RIGHT.** Select

Through

and pick on axis **A_1.** You may have to use *Query Select* to ensure you have picked the correct entity. Then select

Angle

and pick on **RIGHT.** All the options should now be grayed out, indicating that we have selected enough constraints to locate the new datum. Select

Done > Enter Value

and observe the direction of the curved green arrow on the screen (see Figure 2).

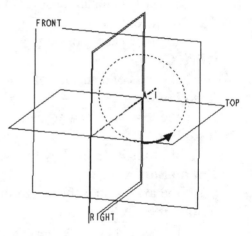

Figure 2 Angle direction arrow

Enter the value *60.* The result is a new datum plane **DTM1.** Of course, this angle value becomes a parameter of the model. Select *Modify*, click on **DTM1,** change the value of the angle to **30,** then *Regenerate*. The result is shown in Figure 3.

We will leave datum planes for a bit now, so that we can create the base feature of the cutter.

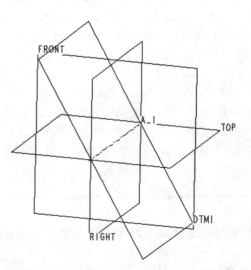

Figure 3 DTM1 created at 30° to **RIGHT**

Creating the *Cutter* Base Feature

Our base feature is a solid protrusion that will eventually look like the figure shown below. Just for practice, we will first create the sketch using "manual" mode. Then we'll come back and use Intent Manager. Go to

> *Utilities > Environment*

and turn off the check mark beside Sketcher Intent Manager. Then select *OK*. (What happens if you select *Close* on this window by mistake?)

To create the feature, select the following:

> *Feature > Create*
> *Solid > Protrusion*
> *Extrude | Solid | Done*
> *Both Sides | Done*

Select **FRONT** as the sketching plane, and **TOP** as the *Top* reference plane. The following description assumes that you are creating the feature in "manual" mode. We're going to discover some new Sketcher tools. Before we accept the sketch, we'll erase it and create it again using Intent Manager. The same sketcher tools are in the Intent Manager interface, but they are in slightly different places.

Sketch three circles as shown in Figure 5. Try to get these to have the same radius (we want the implicit rule to fire when we regenerate).

Note:
> Starting from the circle on the right, going in a counterclockwise order, we will call these the first, second, and third circles.

Use the command

> *Line > Centerline | 2 Points*

to sketch a construction line from the origin of the datum planes to the center of the third circle.

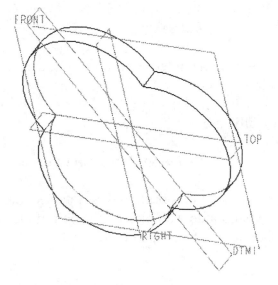

Figure 4 Both-Sides solid protrusion

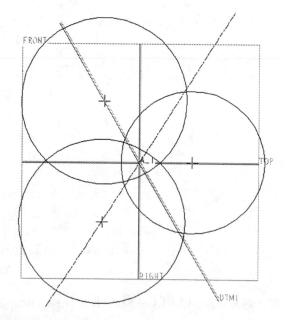

Figure 5 First circles and construction line sketched

Now use

Geom Tools > Divide

and pick on the circles at the 6 points indicated with X's in Figure 6 (Step #1). This will cut the circles at the pick points and place new vertices there. Then we can use

Delete

to remove the interior portions of the circles (Step #2).

Finally, use

Geom Tools > Trim | Corner

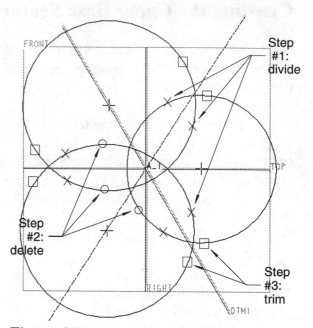

Figure 6 Trimming back the circles

to cut the circles back to their intersection points (Step #3). Notice that when using *Trim* in manual mode, you pick on the part of the line you want to keep in the sketch. Your sketch should now look like Figure 7.

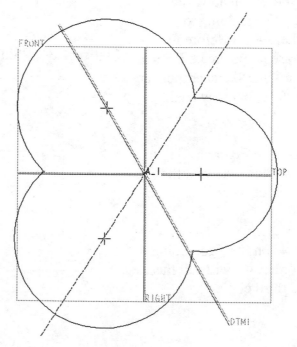

Figure 7 Circles divided and trimmed

The drawing part of the sketch is now complete.

Align the first circle to **TOP** and the second circle to **DTM1** (this was our reason for making this datum). Remember that circle alignment refers to the circle center, but you can pick anywhere on the circle to select it. There are a couple of other vertices that you can align to **TOP** and **DTM1**.

Now *Dimension* the sketch as shown here. To dimension the construction line angle, click on the line and the datum then place the dimension with the middle mouse button.

Take note of the dimension labels for the centers of the circles (labeled **sd2**, **sd4**, and **sd6** in the figure - **yours may be different!**). *Regenerate* the sketch and *Modify* the values to those shown in Figure 9.

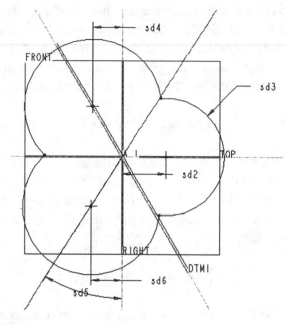

Figure 8 Sketch dimensions

Using Intent Manager

It is strongly suggested that you try to create this sketch using Intent Manager. It is surprisingly easy. To do that, select

> *Delete > Delete All*

and *Repaint* the screen. Turn Intent Manager on with

> *Sketch > Intent Manager*

and start again, paying attention to the constraints created on the fly. Use **TOP**, **RIGHT**, and **DTM1** as references in Intent Manager.

As you sketch the three circles, adjust the radius so that the "same radius" constraint R_1 fires as you sketch.

In the new Sketcher in 2000i^2 we don't have to divide the circles before trimming, as we did above. There is a nifty tool on the "Trim/Divide" button that looks like this ![icon]. As the icon

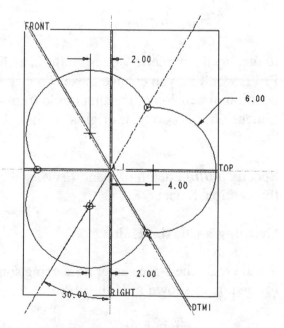

Figure 9 Actual dimensions

implies, all you have to do is swipe the mouse pointer across the edge segments you want to remove. The edge will be trimmed back at both ends to the nearest intersection point or vertex.

Try it!

When the arcs are created, use the "Constraints" button to set up any desired constraints that Sketcher didn't place automatically if your sketch was not really precise. Then set up the dimensioning scheme shown in Figure 9. Finally modify the dimension values to those desired. Recall that to change a single dimension, just double-click on it. To modify a group of dimensions, shift-click on each one and change the values in the *Modify* window.

Creating Sketcher Relations

We would like to control this geometry with as few dimensions as possible. We will add a couple of relations to control the placement of circles 2 and 3, based on the dimension to the center of circle 1. Relations are another way of implementing design intent. The centers of the three circles should be the same distance away from axis A_1. Starting in the pull-down menu at the top, select

> *Sketch > Relation > Add*

The dimensions on the sketch change to symbolic form. Type in the following relations (**NOTE: your symbolic names may be slightly different - refer to Figure 8 above**):

> $sd4 = sd2 * sin(sd5)$
> $sd6 = sd2 * sin(sd5)$

Hit the enter key on a blank line to end data entry. Select **Show Rel** to see the relations and the values they are currently computing. Close this window and select

> **Switch Dim**

to display the numeric values on the sketch. Try to change either of the controlled dimensions. Pro/E won't let you change these. To make sure the relations are working properly, change the position dimension of the first circle from 4 to **6**. Change the circle radius to **8**. Change both dimensions back to their original values. Assuming your regeneration is successful, select "Done".

Specify a **Blind** depth of **2** and **Preview** the feature, that should look like the figure at the top of this section. Select **OK**.

Creating a Coaxial Hole

We'll create the large center hole using some new options in the hole dialog window. Select the following, as shown in Figure 10:

- Straight hole
- Diameter = 8.0
- Depth One = Thru All, Depth Two = Thru All
- Primary Reference = FRONT (this is the placement plane for the hole center)

- Placement Type = Coaxial
- Axial Reference = A_1 (this field appears when you select Coaxial)

As you fill in the dialog box, observe the prompts in the message window and the indicated directions for depth one (single red arrow) and depth two (double yellow arrow). When you are asked to pick the hole placement references, notice that the selection button in the dialog box is depressed. You can come back to any of these buttons to change the chosen reference. The completed hole dialog window is shown at the right. Preview the feature and if it is acceptable, select the **Build Feature** button (with the check mark).

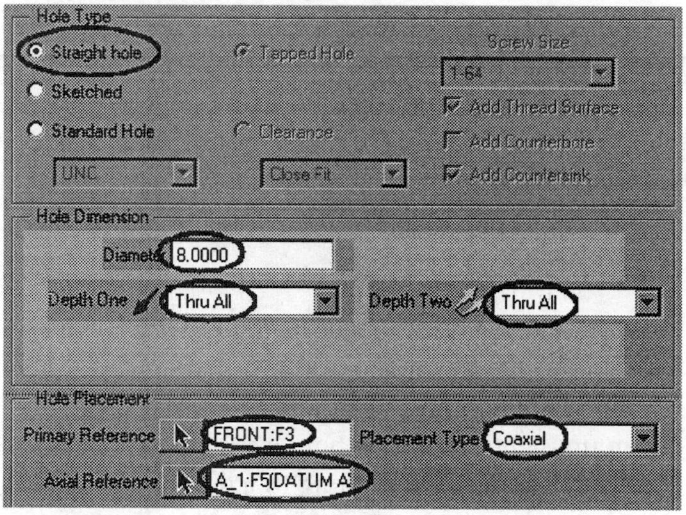

Figure 10 Dialog window for central hole

First Tooth - Offset Datum

The first tooth will be the one at the right (3 o'clock position). The design intent for this tooth is that the inner extent of the tooth will be a specified distance away from the disk axis. We will create a datum plane at the desired distance that we can use as a sketching plane and extrude the tooth outward to the outer edge of the disk. Then we will place a hole, also on the new datum plane, using the both sides option to go radially inward and outward. Start by creating the new datum plane. This time, select the "Datum Plane" button on the right of the graphics window. Then select

Offset

Click on **RIGHT** then select *Enter Value*. A green arrow will appear and you will be prompted for an offset distance in the direction of the arrow. If you wanted to go to the other side of **RIGHT**, you could enter a negative offset. For now, enter a value of *8*. You have given enough information to create the datum, indicated by Pro/E graying out all the options in the **DATUM** menu. Select *Done* and the new datum **DTM2** should appear as shown here.

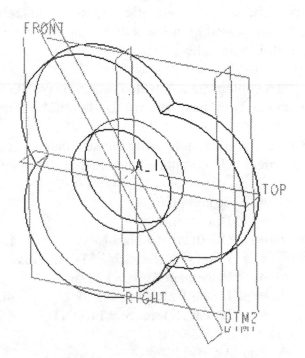

Figure 11 Disk with datum plane, **DTM2** for first tooth sketch

Now we can create the tooth:

> *Feature > Create > Solid > Protrusion*
> *Extrude | Solid | Done > One Side | Done*

and pick **DTM2** as the sketching plane
(you may have to use *Query Select*).
Observe the feature creation direction (use
Flip if required) and select **TOP** as the
Top reference plane.

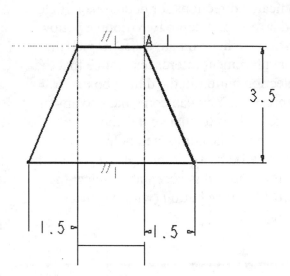

You are now looking at the sketching
plane. For the following, turn off the
datum plane display. This will not only
clean up the visual view, but also prevent
us from accidentally aligning to a datum.
You may also want to turn off the grid. If
you are using Intent Manager, then two
references have been selected for you
already (**TOP** and **FRONT** datums).
Create two new references for the two
sides of the disk.

Figure 12 Sketch of first tooth

Make the sketch shown in Figure 12. Align the top line in the sketch to axis **A_1.** Note the
width of the tooth is determined by the extension or overhang beyond the side of the disk. When
you have a successful regeneration, add a relation so that the extension of the tooth to the left is
the same as to the right. Be sure to test this relation out before leaving Sketcher. Note that the
sdx labels used in this sketch may appear to be numbered the same as in the previous sketch, but
Pro/E is able to keep them sorted out.

When you have a completed sketch, leave Sketcher, select a *Blind* depth of *2*, and accept the
feature. Turn the display of the datums back on.

Create the small hole using the new datum plane as a placement surface. Use the following
information to complete the hole dialog window:

- Straight hole
- Diameter = 1.0
- Depth One = Thru Next   Depth Two = Thru Next
- Primary Reference = DTM2 (this is the placement plane for the hole center)
- Placement Type = Linear
- Linear Reference = TOP   dimension = 0
- Linear Reference = FRONT   dimension = 0

Note that in one direction, a *Thru All* depth would have gone completely through the other side of the disk, which we don't want. *Thru Next* extends the hole until it passes through the next part surface.

The tooth should now be complete and look like Figure 13

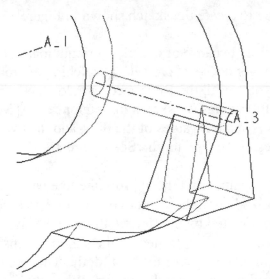

Figure 13 First tooth and hole complete

Second Tooth - Normal and Tangent Datum

The second tooth is the one at the top left of the part (on circle #2). The intent demonstrated here is to have the planar outer surface of the tooth tangent to the circle of the disk and to extrude the tooth inwards towards the center of the disk. So, we will create a datum to give us a flat sketching surface at the outer edge and tangent to the disk. We can make use of our existing datum **DTM1** which passes through the center of the disk and the second circle.

Select (or use the "Datum Plane" button)

> ### *Datum > Plane*

Select *Normal* and click on **DTM1**. Then select *Tangent* and click on the outer surface of the disk at about where DTM1 intersects the surface (you may want to spin the object to make this easier). The new datum should be fully constrained (menu grayed out) so just select *Done*. The new datum **DTM3** appears, Figure 14.

Create a one-sided solid protrusion on the new datum plane. Note that the extrusion direction is inwards towards the axis A_1 of the disk (use *Flip* if necessary). Select **DTM3** as the sketching plane, and choose *Top > DTM1*. In what direction are you facing the sketching plane? When you get into Sketcher, give the part a little 3D spin to orient yourself. To return to the initial orientation, select *View > Sketch View*. We're

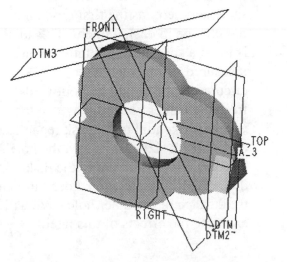

Figure 14 Tangent datum plane for second tooth

going to create the sketch shown in Figure 15.

Possibly because of our view orientation, Intent Manager does not pre-select sketching references for you. With the References window open, pick the following five sketching references: DTM1 (or axis A_1), both sides of the disk, and the two outer edges of the first tooth. See Figure 15.

Once again, align the appropriate line with axis **A_1**, and align the corner vertices to the vertical edges created by the first tooth. In this way, the width will be controlled by the single dimension driving the width of the first tooth. This sketch only needs one new dimension. When the sketch is complete, leave Sketcher and choose a **Blind** depth specification and enter the value **2**.

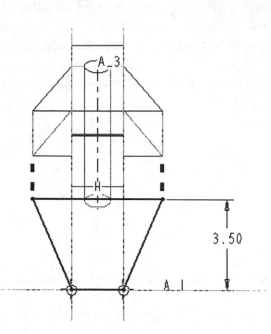

Figure 15 Sketch for second tooth

Create a **Straight Linear** hole using the outer planar surface of the tooth as the primary reference (placement plane). The hole has a diameter of **1**. For Depth One, specify **Variable** (this used to be called a blind hole) and enter a value of **8.0**. Leave Depth Two unspecified - this makes the hole one-sided off the placement plane. Use the datums **FRONT** and **DTM1** for placement references (giving a dimension of **0** to each). The complete tooth looks like Figure 16.

IMPORTANT NOTE:

Although this results in exactly the same geometry as the first tooth, notice our change in design intent. This tooth is to go a specific depth into the disk measured inwards from the circumference rather than outwards from the center. In this way, the tooth will be tangential to the disk regardless of the disk's size. Similarly, the hole's depth is a fixed value into the disk. At the present time, the hole goes through the surface of the inner hole. We will examine the effects of this later.

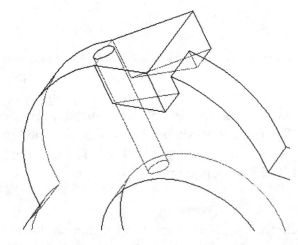

Figure 16 Second tooth completed

Third Tooth - Using Make Datums

The model is getting pretty cluttered up with datum planes. This makes the screen very hard to look at. Furthermore, if a datum is only going to be used once to create another feature, it seems wasteful to create one that will be permanent. A *Make Datum* is a datum that is created on-the-fly when needed, and then *disappears after you're done with it*. The rules and methods for constraining a Make Datum are the same as if it was permanent. Make datums can be constructed at almost any time that Pro/E asks you to select a planar surface (for example, for a sketching plane or a reference plane).

The third tooth is on the lower side of the part so you might like to reorient your view. We are going to do things in a slightly different order here, by creating the hole first. However, a hole requires a planar surface for its placement plane. We don't have such a plane at the desired angle. So, we will create the hole using an extruded cut (circular), using a make datum to act as the sketching plane for the cut.

Proceed as if we were going to create the small hole as a thru-all circular cut outward from the center of the disk.

> *Create > Solid > Cut > Extrude | Solid | Done > One Side | Done*

You are asked to select a sketching plane - but there isn't one in a suitable orientation (**DTM1** is at the wrong angle). Here is where we will make a datum on-the-fly:

> *Make Datum > Through > [click on the axis A_1 of the disk]*
> *Angle > [click on TOP] > Done > Enter Value*

Note that after clicking on **TOP**, all the datum creation options are grayed out - this means the datum is fully constrained. Observe the creation arrow direction and type in *-30*. The temporary datum **DTM4** should now appear - it will be our sketching plane. Note the red arrow indicating direction of feature creation (we are still working on creating the small hole using an extruded cut, so the direction should point in the direction we want the cut to go). For the sketching reference plane, select

> *Left > [click on FRONT]*

What orientation is your view relative to the part? Spin the view a bit to get oriented. Select *View > Sketch View* to return to the normal sketch orientation. Remember that all one-sided cuts are created away from you as you look at the sketch.

For the Intent Manager sketching references, select axis **A_1** and **FRONT**. Sketch a circle where these cross. Set the diameter of the circle to *1*. Spin the model to see the sketch floating in space. After a

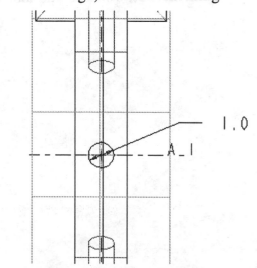

Figure 17 Sketch for tooth #3 hole

successful regeneration, observe the material removal direction (inside the circle), and select ***Thru All*** for the depth. When the hole appears, there is no sign of the *Make Datum* we just created, although the extruded cut does have an axis.

Now create the tooth.

> ***Create > Solid > Protrusion > Extrude | Solid | Done > One Side | Done***

For the sketching plane, we will create a *Make Datum* tangent to the disk and normal to the axis of the circular cut:

> ***Make Datum > Normal***
> ***[click on the axis of the small hole we just made. Use Query Select.]***
> ***Tangent***
> ***[click on the outer cylindrical surface of the disk]***

This will make the tangent datum **DTM5** that will serve as our sketching plane. Observe the direction of the feature creation, and make sure it is into the disk. Use **FRONT** as the *Left* reference plane for the sketch. Once again, check your view orientation relative to the part. Sketch, align, and regenerate the tooth as shown in the figure. Note that, in order not to fill in half the hole through the tooth, we must sketch around the circumference of the hole. The "Use Edge" button ▢ is handy for this.

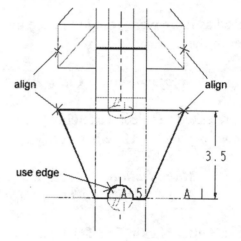

Figure 18 Sketch of third tooth

When you are finished with the sketch, select a ***Blind*** depth of *2*. We have now finished constructing the part, which should look like Figures 19 and 20 below.

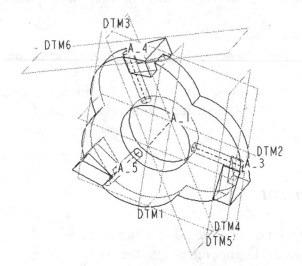

Figure 19 Finished part - wireframe showing datums

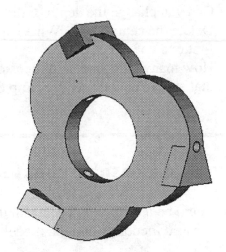

Figure 20 Completed part

Effects on the Model

We have created three geometrically identical teeth using three different modeling strategies. Let's see what happens when we start to play with the dimensions of the features. Try the following and see if you can explain what is going on. In each case, change the geometry back to the original before making a new modification. Before you try any of this, save the part so that you can recover from any future disasters!

1. Using the *Modify* command in the **Part** menu, change the radius dimension of the first circle of the disk (currently 6.0) to values of **4.0**, **5.0**, and **8.0**. What happens to each of the tooth/hole features? Why?
2. Using *Modify*, change the location dimension to the center of the first circle (currently 4.0) to values of **2.0**, **3.0**, and **6.0**. What happened? Why?
3. Using *Modify*, change the diameter of the large central hole to 0.5. What happened? Why?
4. What happens if you try to *delete* the datum **DTM1**? (Try *Feature > Delete*) Don't actually delete the datum.
5. What happens if you try to change the angle of the datum **DTM1**?
6. Examine the parent/child relationships in the model. It is likely that, rather than being related only through the width alignment, some of the tooth/holes refer to other features in ways that were not intended. A possible reason for this is when you were aligning features or selecting references, the alignments were made to axes or edges of previously created features rather than the datum planes. How you can be more selective in choosing alignment references?
7. Can you modify the offset of **DTM2**? What happens if you specify an offset of *6.0* or *12.0*?
8. Can you modify the diameter of the "hole" going through the third tooth? Where does the dimension appear for this extruded cut?

9. Can you modify the angle of the Make Datum used to create the third hole? What happens if you change this angle to 60°?
10. Can you change the depth of the second and third teeth easily?
11. Delete the central hole. What happens to the small radial holes? How far through does the first one go?
12. How many independent dimensions are there in this model? What is the minimum number that should be required? Set up the model so that only these dimensions can be modified.

Things to Consider about *Design Intent*

You should be able to see once again that capturing the design intent is an important part of feature-based modeling and the model creation strategy. Design intent involves the following:

- ▸   What is the design function of the feature?
- ▸   How does this influence the modeling strategy?
- ▸   How does the design function of a feature relate to other features?
- ▸   Which features should be unrelated in the part?
- ▸   How can you set up references and dimensioning schemes so that the parent/child relations reflect the above?
- ▸   How can you create the model so that it is driven by as few as possible critical design dimensions? Will this necessarily always be desirable?
- ▸   When should you use relations internally in the part to drive the geometry automatically, depending on the critical design dimensions?

Design changes are inevitable. Therefore, you should try to design the features so that it will be easy to make the kinds of changes you expect later on in as direct a manner as possible. This is possibly the hardest part, since if you know only a few methods to create new features, your choices will be limited. You can often create the correct geometry, but it may be very difficult to modify or change later. Furthermore, it is often difficult to foresee exactly how you might want the model to change later. One thing is for sure, if you just slap-dash your features together, sooner or later you will run into a serious modeling problem. This can then become a nightmare for making design changes.

In the next lesson we will look at more feature creation commands for revolved protrusions and patterned features (a flexible form of copying), including some new Sketcher tricks.

Questions for Review

1.   What are the six constraint types for creating datum planes and make datums?
2.   What are the constraint types for creating datum axes?
3.   Using the six constraint types, what combinations will lead to a completely constrained datum plane? Draw some freehand sketches to illustrate these.
4.   What references are required to create a coaxial hole?
5.   For a **Blind**, **Both Sides** solid protrusion, do you specify the depth in each direction, or the total depth? What about for a **Blind**, **Both Sides** cut?
6.   What is the easiest way to create a datum plane parallel to a previous one at a specified distance away?
7.   Suppose you want to create a datum plane at an angle to another datum. You want to use the **Through** placement option, but there is currently no part edge or axis to use as a reference. How can you create the desired datum?
8.   Does the order of selection of **Through** and **Angle** matter?
9.   What is the difference between **Thru All**, **Thru Next**, and **Up to Surf** when specifying an extruded feature's depth? For the last two, what happens if the extruded sketch does not completely intersect the specified surface?
10. Compare the advantages and disadvantages of using permanent datums and make datums.
11. If you want to **Modify** a feature created using a make datum as a sketching plane, where does the sketch show up (since there is no permanent sketching plane in the model for that feature - or is there?)?
12. When the model starts to get cluttered up with surfaces, edges, datums, and axes, how can you make sure that you are making an alignment to the desired entity? What might happen if you align to the wrong entity?
13. Can the elements of a make datum (placement, orientation) be controlled using relations?
14. Are other feature dimensions available for use in Sketcher relations?
15. Think of an example of a simple part where different design intents would lead to different feature creation schemes.
16. Do make datums show up in the model tree?

Exercises

Here are some objects for you to make. Don't worry about exact dimensions, but datums and make datums will come in handy for these!

Project

Here is another part for the project. More pictures with dimensions are shown on the next page (all dimensions in millimeters). As usual, study the geometry carefully, and plan your modeling strategy before starting to create anything!

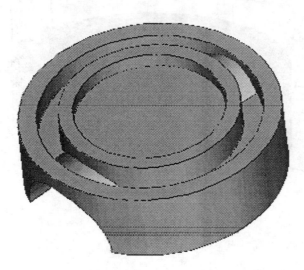

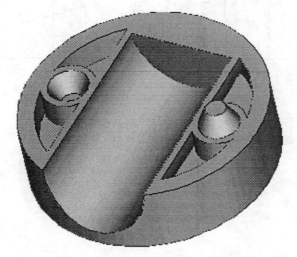

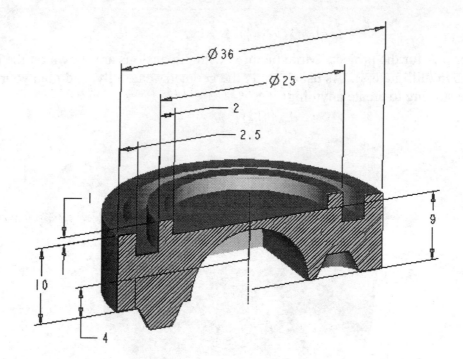

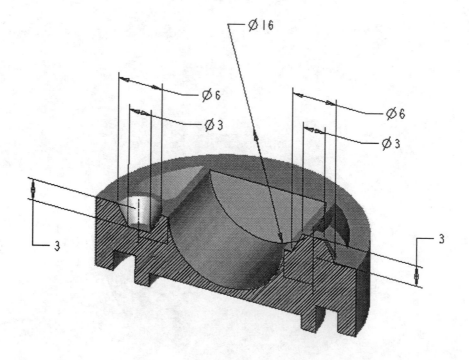

Lesson 6 :

Revolved Features, Patterns, and Copies

Synopsis

Revolved features are created by revolving a sketch around an axis - very useful for axisymmetric shapes. Creating a counterbored hole. Patterns are groups of features based on a pattern leader and arranged in a one-dimensional or two-dimensional array; each member of the group can be parametrically modified. A simple copy is a duplicated feature created by translation, rotation, or mirroring.

Overview of this Lesson

This lesson will introduce you to the following operations:

Creating Revolved Features
made by creating an open or closed edge and revolving it around an axis. Can be used for protrusions, cuts, or slots. Since we have seen a simple revolved protrusion before (Lesson #3), we'll take this opportunity to present a method of creating complex geometry in Sketcher.

Creating Patterns
generates multiple parametrically-related instances of any type of feature or group of features. We'll see how to create and pattern a counterbored hole.

Copying Features
copying a single feature or group of features by translation, rotation, and mirroring

To demonstrate these features, we will be creating several different parts. The parts are totally independent of each other, so you can jump ahead to any one of these:

1. Revolved Features
    ▸   A Revolved Protrusion
    ▸   A Revolved Cut
2. Patterned Features
    ▸   A Radial Pattern of Holes
    ▸   A Patterned Array of Grouped Features
3. Copied Features

> ▸   Copying with the Same References
> ▸   A Translated Copy
> ▸   A Rotated Copy
> ▸   A Mirrored Copy
4.   Design Considerations
> ▸   Some things to think about when designing with complex features

As usual, there will be some Questions for Review, Exercises, and a Project part at the end.

Revolved Features

A revolved feature is an axisymmetric shape that is created by revolving an open or closed section by a specified angle around a central axis. The section can be used to produce a protrusion or a cut. That is, it can either add material or take it away. We are going to create the part shown in Figure 1.

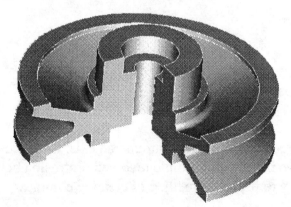

This is a V-pulley that has been cut away to show the cross sectional shape. The finished part will have only three features: a revolved protrusion, a revolved cut, and some rounds.

Figure 1 Cut-away view of V-pulley

Start up Pro/E as usual. Create a part called *v_pulley* using the default template.

Revolved Protrusion

To illustrate a concept in feature-based modeling, we are going to create most of the geometry of the pulley with a single revolved feature. This is an extreme example for illustrating what is normally a compromise between the number of features in a part and their complexity. For the pulley, we will use a single, very complex feature to define most of the geometry. We could also use a number of simpler features (probably five or six) to create the same geometry (see Lesson #8). Your modeling approach will generally be somewhere between these two extremes, depending on the part geometry and your familiarity with the feature creation tools. Although the geometry is complex, we will see how a skillful use of Sketcher functions will make it not too difficult to construct the feature.

The major part feature will be a revolved protrusion:

> *Feature > Create > Solid > Protrusion*
> *Revolve | Solid | Done*
> *One Side | Done*

Pick **FRONT** as the sketching plane, and **TOP** as the *Top* reference plane. Let the feature creation arrow come towards the front.

The most difficult operation for this feature is generating the sketch for the cross section. We are going to revolve this sketch 360° around the central axis. Creating this sketch will give you lots of practice with Sketcher! For reference, Figure 2 shows the dimensioned cut-away view of the revolved protrusion. (DO NOT try to create this sketch until you have read the BIG HINT below!):

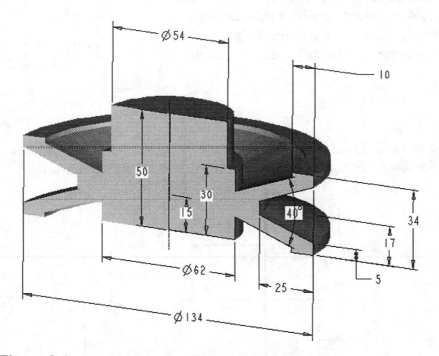

Figure 2 Cross section view of revolved protrusion

Study this carefully. Several dimensions have been implicitly determined by the Sketcher rules and these constraints are not shown on the figure.

BIG HINT : There is no law that says you have to produce the final sketch all at once! Using Sketcher functions, we will produce this section in three stages. At each stage, make sure you get a successful regeneration. You may have to alternate between Intent Manager and "manual" sketching. You will also find the commands *Trim*, *Intersect* (in manual mode), and *Divide* useful. Watch out for strong and weak dimensions. The dimensions shown in Figure 2 should all be strong by the time you are finished. Note the following:

- In the figures following, new entities are added and dimensioned/constrained at each stage; the previous dimensions should still be on the sketch.
- To dimension the section, remember this trick: **To dimension a diameter**, click first on the outer edge, second on the axis, third on the outer edge again, and fourth (middle button) to place the dimension.
- Explore the menu available with Utilities > Sketcher Preferences to control the display of vertices, constraints, the grid, number of dimension decimal places, grid type and spacing, and so on.

Stage 1

Sketch the hub as shown at the right. Create a centerline on the vertical reference (**RIGHT** datum). The horizontal reference (**TOP** datum) will go through the midpoint of the V on the pulley. The sketch should be closed (ie with a line down the center). Apply appropriate constraints, set up the dimension scheme, and modify values to match the figure.

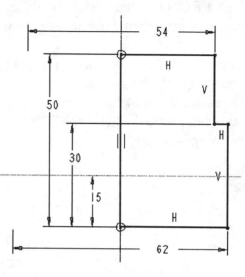

Stage 2

Sketch the rim added to the hub as shown below. Beware of the constraints (which are not shown). Some will be automatic; some you will have to create yourself.

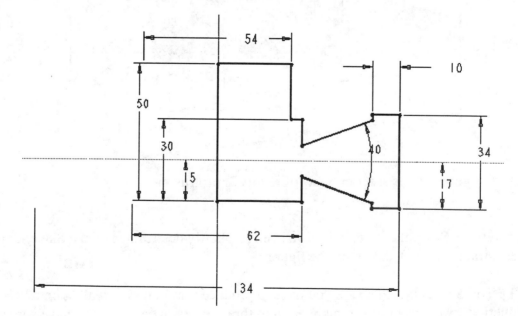

Stage 3
Sketch the pulley groove. Again, the constraints are not shown here.

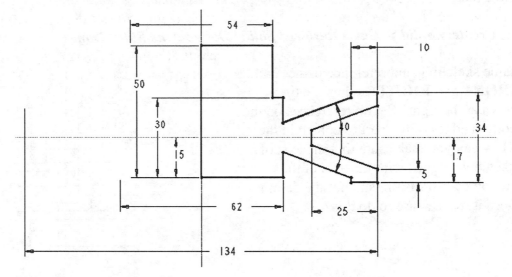

When you get a successful regeneration of the final sketch, select **Done**.

Now we specify the angle for the revolved section. In the **REV TO** menu, select

> *360 | Done*

to specify a 360° rotation of the sketch around the axis. Your part should look like Figure 4.

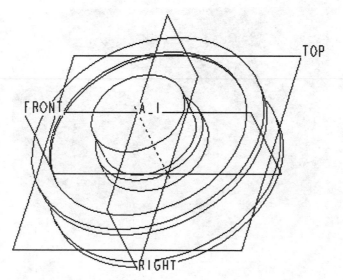

Figure 4 The revolved protrusion

Now we will add the central hole (including the counterbores) as a revolved cut.

Revolved Cut

To create the cut:

Create > Solid > Cut > Revolve | Solid | Done > One Side | Done

Use the same sketching and reference planes as before (**FRONT** and **RIGHT**) and create the sketch shown at the right. Set up references on the top and bottom edges of the part to constrain the cut line. How can you make sure that the axis of the new sketch is aligned with the axis of the previous revolved protrusion, and not the datum plane? Does it make sense to do this?

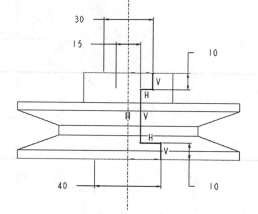

When the sketch regenerates successfully, select *Done.* Make sure the material removal arrow points inwards. Then select

Figure 5 Sketch for the revolved cut

360 | Done

The last job to do for this part is to create some *rounds*. There are four of them, all with a radius of *3*, shown in Figure 6.

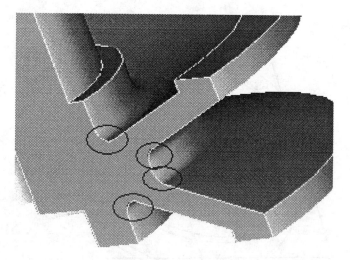

Figure 6 Four round locations

All the rounds *can* be created at the same time, provided that you want them to always have a common radius. If you want to change the radius of one or two of them, you'd have to create them separately. It may be necessary when you are selecting the edges to reorient the part to see the edges clearly. It is also easier to pick out the edges using a shaded display. Don't forget to use *Tangent Edge*.

You will note that we could have created this part using a single revolved feature that would include the central counter-bored hole and the rounds into the revolved solid we made here. That is, we could have made this entire part from a single revolved feature. We will discuss the consequences of this at the end of the lesson.

Save the part.

Patterned Features

Creating a feature pattern is similar to a multiple-copy. The pattern is based on a single instance of the feature - called the *pattern leader*. The pattern is created in one (or two) directions by incrementing one (or two) locational dimensions of the pattern leader. Each increment of the pattern dimension produces a new *instance* of the feature. A pattern is even more powerful than just creating multiple instances: it is possible to change the geometry parametrically of each instance in the pattern set. While the locational dimension is incremented, other dimensions of the pattern leader can be incremented so that the instances change size and/or shape. All instances in the pattern can be modified simultaneously, if set up to do so.

In the examples below, we will explore basic pattern techniques. There are many advanced uses of patterns which are not covered here[1].

Creating a Radial Pattern - A Bolted Flange

A common element in piping systems and pressure vessels is a bolted flange. Here is how to create a pattern of bolt holes. To demonstrate this, we'll explore the new Hole menu to create a standard counterbored hole. In addition, we will set up a couple of relations to control the geometry based on the specified number of holes.

Start a new part called *flange* using the default template. Create the circular disk with central hole shown in Figure 7. We will need a central axis A_1 for the counterbored hole placement so you have a number of options: a) create a solid protrusion of two concentric circles, b) create a solid circular disk and add a coaxial hole, or c) revolve a rectangle around a central axis aligned with the datums. Each of these options will create the axis automatically. The outer diameter is *16*, the hole diameter is *8*, and the disk is *3* thick. Note that the disk is constructed on **TOP**.

---

[1]See the on-line help for pattern tables, pattern relations, *Identical*, *Varying*, and *General* patterns. These are presented in the *Pro/E Advanced Tutorial* from SDC.

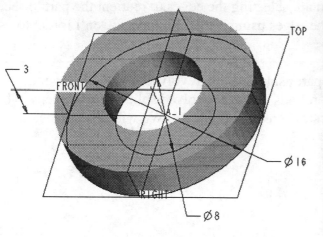

Figure 7 Base feature of flange

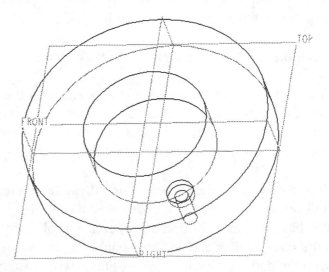

Figure 8 Creating the hole pattern leader

Now we'll create a single counterbored hole in the disk. This will be the pattern leader. In order to specify the pattern using an angular dimension, we choose a *radial* placement scheme (requiring an angle from a reference plane, and a distance radially outward from an axis):

Create > Solid > Hole

See Figure 8 for the hole parameters. The hole is for a 1" bolt with 8 threads per inch (UNC). Both the hole and thread are *Thru All*. The counterbore is 1.75 diameter and 0.5 deep. When selecting the upper surface of the disk as the placement plane, click at about the 5-o'clock position. See the figure at the right. The initial dimensions will be at the pick point. For Placement Type, select *Radial*. Then select the axis of the disk for the axial reference, and datum **RIGHT** for the angular reference. The radial distance from the axis is **6** and the angular dimension is *30* degrees. *Preview* the hole and if everything is satisfactory, select the "Build Feature" button.

Figure 9 Pattern leader for bolt circle

The hole appears with a descriptive note, as might appear in a drawing. Open the model tree and select

View > Model Tree Setup > Item Display

and make sure that **Notes** is checked. Select *OK*. Now in the model tree, expand the line containing the hole feature. The note is listed there. This is called, in Pro/E language, a *3D Note*. Hold down the right mouse button on the note entry. This brings up a pop-up menu that let's you do things with the note. For example, select *Move*. You can drag the note around on the screen to a convenient location (notice it stays attached to the hole), then left click to drop it. To remove the note from the screen, rather than erasing it just turn off its display using

Utilities > Environment

and remove the check beside **3D Notes**. Select *OK*. These notes can contain any text and are useful ways to attach documentation to the model. In the model tree, select a feature, right-click and in the pop-up menu, see *Note Create > Feature*. Try it! Follow the message prompts.

Now, back to our pattern of holes. This first hole becomes the pattern leader. We are going to make a pattern of 8 instances of the hole spaced equally around the flange. That is, to create each instance, we will increment the angular placement of each hole. This is another example of the importance of planning ahead: if you are going to use a pattern, you have to have a dimension to increment! For example, we could not create the bolt circle if we had used a linear placement for the pattern leader. As we create the pattern, follow the prompts in the message window. Starting in the FEAT menu, select

Pattern > [click on the hole] > Identical | Done

To create a pattern, you first select a dimension associated with the leader that will be incremented to create new instances in the pattern. The dimension can be linear or angular and usually describes a feature location. More than one dimension can be incremented simultaneously for each subsequent copy in the pattern (for example, the bolt holes could get larger as they are copied around the flange).

For the bolt circle, we want to increment the angular position, so click on the 30 that shows the angle between the hole and the **RIGHT** datum plane. Now enter the increment to be used in the chosen direction, that is, *45* degrees. Since this is all we want to increment, select *Done*, and enter the total number of instances of the hole, *8* (this includes the leader!). If you want to make an array pattern (like a double row of bolt holes), you could now select a second dimension (like the radial dimension). We'll do something similar to this in the next exercise. We don't want to now, so select *Done*. The part should now regenerate and show you the bolt pattern in Figure 10.

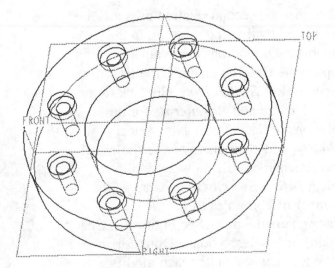

Figure 10 Completed bolt circle using a pattern

Controlling a Pattern using Relations

This bolt pattern is not symmetric about the vertical datums. Also, suppose we wanted to change the number of bolts on the flange - this would change all the angular dimensions. Do we have to recreate this pattern from scratch? The answer is no - we can use relations! In the **PART** menu, select

Relations

and click on the 2nd hole in the bolt pattern (the one at about 3-o'clock). You should see all the dimensions that control the pattern as in Figure 11.

Take note of the symbols for the following dimensions (your symbols might be different): angular dimension between bolts (*d9*), the angle of the first bolt from RIGHT (*d8*), and the number of holes (*p10*).

We can *Add* a couple of relations for these by entering the following:

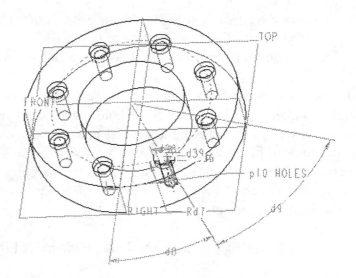

Figure 11 Dimensions involved in bolt circle relations

        /* angular separation of holes
        d9 = 360 / p10
        /* location of first hole
        d8 = d9 / 2

Note that the second relation uses a value computed by the first relation. In the database, all relations are evaluated top-down. Before you leave the **Relations** menu, select *Switch Dim*. Go back to the **PART** menu and *Regenerate* for the relations to take effect. Now select *Modify*, and click on any of the holes. If the dimensions still show as symbols, select *Info > Switch Dims*. Change the number of bolt holes to *12*, then *Regenerate* the part. See Figure 12. Check again for 6 holes, 5 holes. Don't forget you have to regenerate after each modify. In each case, the correct number, separation, and pattern leader placement are automatically determined.

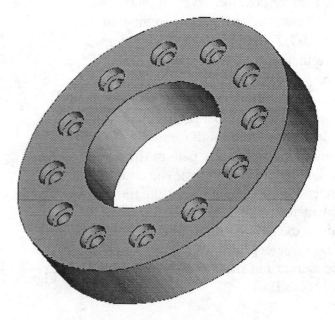

Figure 12 Bolt circle modified for 12 bolts

Use *Modify* to change the diameter of the counterbore to *2*. *Regenerate* the model. With the diameter of 2, try to create a pattern of *16* holes, then *20* holes. What happens? Remember that we specified a pattern of *identical* features. This does not allow the instances to intersect; other options would allow it (*varying, general*). To recover from this error, select

> *Undo Changes > Confirm*

Try to directly modify the separation angle between holes or the placement of the pattern leader. What message does Pro/E give you?

If you want to play with this part later, then *Save* it now. Otherwise, select *File > Erase*.

A Bi-directional Pattern of Grouped Features

The bolt circle pattern was pretty straight forward - we only duplicated a single feature in a single direction, and its size/shape stayed the same for each copy. We can go much farther than that by using grouped features.

We are going to create the part shown in Figure 13. The pattern leader is the cylindrical boss on the left in the front row. Each instance in the pattern actually consists of three features: a protrusion, a hole, and a round. We will use a pattern to set up two rows with the dimensions of the features incrementing along each row, and between rows.

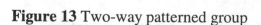

Figure 13 Two-way patterned group

Figure 14 Pattern leader composed of circular protrusion, hole, and round

Start a new part called **plate1** using the default template. Create the base (**rectangular solid protrusion 20 x 30 x 3 thick**). Align the left face of this base plate with the **RIGHT** datum and the rear face of the plate with **FRONT**. Now create a **circular solid protrusion** (diameter *2*, up *3* from the lower edge of the plate, over *5* from the left edge, and with a height of *2*). Create a *thru-all coaxial hole* (diameter *1.0*) on the circular protrusion. Finally, add a *0.25 round* on the circular edge where the protrusion meets the plate. The protrusion should look like Figure 14.

Before we can create the pattern, we have to group all the features (circular protrusion + hole +

round) on the circular protrusion. Note that grouped features must be adjacent to each other in the model tree. In the **FEAT** menu, select

Group > Create > Local Group > [holder]

where *holder* is the name we supply for the group. Now pick on the hole, the protrusion, and the round. You may want to zoom in on the protrusion to make sure you select the right features, and you may find *Query Sel* useful here as well. Or, you can select the features in the model tree; each will highlight in red when selected. Then select *Done Sel > Done*

You should be informed that the group *holder* has been created. Now, still in the **GROUP** menu, select *Pattern* and pick on the protrusion.

NOTE:

> The *Pattern* command in the **FEAT** menu is only for single features. If you want to pattern a group, you must use the command in the **GROUP** menu.

You should see all the dimensions associated with the group as shown in Figure 15.

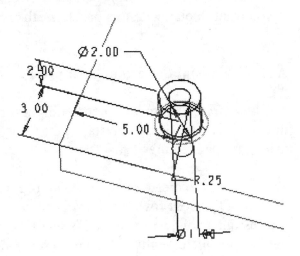

Figure 15 Features in group "holder"

First Pattern Direction
1. pick on the 5.00 dimension, and enter the increment *10*. This will increment the location of the group along the plate.
2. pick on the diameter of the protrusion 2.00, and enter the increment *1*
3. pick on the diameter of the hole 1.00, and enter the increment *1*
4. select *Done*
5. enter the number of instances *3*

Second Pattern Direction
1. pick on the 3.00 dimension, and enter the increment *12*. This will increment the location of the group to the next row.
2. pick on the height of the protrusion 2.00, and enter the increment *3*
3. pick on the protrusion diameter 2.00, and enter the increment *3*
4. pick on the hole diameter 1.00, and enter the increment *2*
5. select *Done*
6. enter the number of instances *2*

All the patterned pockets should now be added to the part. Go back to the **PART** menu, and experiment with the *Modify* command. What dimensions are available for modification (this may depend on what feature you pick on)?

What happens here if you try to create a group off the end of the plate by extending the pattern (4 instances instead of 3)? How do you recover from this?

Open up the model tree to see how a group pattern is represented.

This concludes our discussion of patterns. There are many more things you can do with patterns, and some more advanced techniques. For example, instead of simply incrementing dimensions between instances, you can use pattern relations to develop formulas that will control the instance placement and geometry. Another tool called a pattern table allows you to place instances at non-uniformly spaced locations driven by dimension values stored in a table like a spreadsheet. These advanced pattern functions are presented in the *Pro/E Advanced Tutorial* from SDC.

Copying Features

In the previous section, we saw how to create a multiple-instance pattern of a single feature or a group of features. The pattern could only be created by incrementing one or more of the feature's existing dimensions. The **Copy** command allows more flexibility in terms of placement and geometric variation (you aren't restricted to the references used to create a pattern leader, for example), but only creates one copy at a time. There are several options available with Copy, and we will create several different simple parts to illustrate these.

A Same Ref Copy

We are going to create the part shown in Figure 16. The bracket on the left is the original, and the one on the right will be the copy.

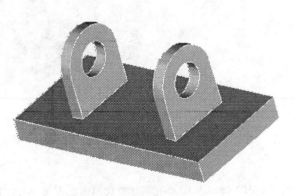

Start by creating a new part **plate2** with the default template[2]. Create a rectangular solid protrusion on **TOP** that is **10 x 20 x 2 thick**. *Align* the left face with the **RIGHT** datum.

Figure 16 Part with copied feature

For the vertical bracket on the left, the sketching plane is a *Make Datum* that is *offset* from **RIGHT** by **5**. Thus:

Create > Solid > Protrusion > Extrude | Solid | Done

---

[2]Or, if **plate1** from the previous exercise is still in session, use *File > Save As > [plate2]*. Then open up the new file, open the model tree, delete the pattern, and modify the dimensions of the plate.

One Side | Done
Make Datum > Offset > Sel By Menu
Datum > Name > RIGHT
Enter Value > [5] > Done

Select the top of the rectangular base as the
Top reference plane. Then sketch the
protrusion as shown in Figure 17. Note the
sketching references. The hole is included
in the protrusion - Pro/E will know where
to add material, and where to leave the
hole. Also, the sketch must close across
the bottom since you can't have a mix of
open and closed curves (Try it!).

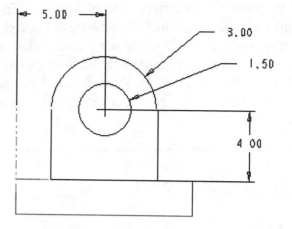

When you get a successful regeneration,
select a *Blind* depth of *1*. The part should
look like this:

Figure 17 Sketch for original feature

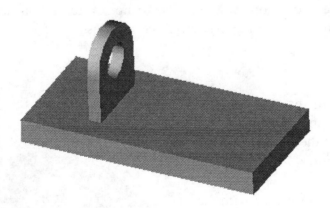

Figure 18 First feature completed

Now, we are ready to copy the feature. We want the copy to be 10 units to the right of the first. If
the geometry of the first feature changes, we want the copy to change too - it will be *dependent*.
As you encounter these new menus, watch the message window and command description at the
bottom of the screen.

Copy > Same Refs | Select | Dependent | Done

Pick on the bracket and select *Done Sel > Done*.

The **GP VAR DIMS** window will open up. This is giving us the opportunity to select which
dimensions in the copy we want to vary from the original. At this time, we will only change the
distance from the left end. Move the cursor up and down the listed dimensions. As you do this,

the dimension will highlight on the model. Find the dimension *5* that locates the protrusion from the left end (this was the offset dimension for the make datum), and check it. Then select **Done**. You are prompted for a new value for this dimension; enter *15*, then select **OK** from the elements window. The new protrusion should appear at the right.

What happens if you try to **Modify** the hole diameter on the first protrusion? Or the height dimension on the copy? What happens if you suppress the original? The copy?

Delete the copy and create a new *independent* copy. Try the same modifications.

A Translated Copy

We will make the part shown at the right. The original feature is again in the lower left corner.

You can keep the same base plate as the previous part (10 x 20 x 2 thick, on TOP). You will have to delete the two vertical protrusions (or suppress them). Create a circular solid protrusion near the lower left corner of the plate (dimension *4* from left surface, *3* from lower surface, diameter *3*, *blind* depth *5*). See Figure 19.

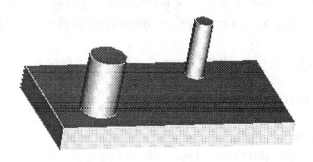

Figure 19 Part with a Translated copy

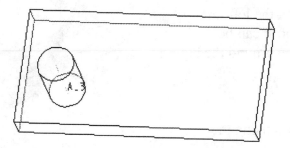

Figure 20 Original feature to translate/copy

Now we will copy the feature and change its diameter at the same time:

Copy > Move | Select | Dependent | Done

Click on the protrusion, then **Done**.

Translate > Plane > Sel By Menu > Datum > Name > RIGHT

Check the direction of the translation arrow. It should be pointing towards the right end (off the yellow side of **RIGHT**). Enter the distance *10*. The new feature won't show up just yet. To move it again:

> *Translate > Plane*

Pick on the front vertical surface of the plate. The default direction is the outward normal to a solid surface, so *Flip* the direction arrow. Enter the distance *5*. Then select:

> *Done Move*

In the **GP VAR DIMS** menu, select the diameter of the protrusion as variable, then *Done*. Enter the new value *1.5*. Then select *OK*.

Select *Modify* and pick on the copied cylinder. Spin the part and observe the dimensions. The translation dimensions are displayed slightly differently - this is an easy way to pick them out.

You can now either *Save* this part or *Erase* it.

A Rotated Copy

Now, we will use a rotated copy to create the part shown in Figure 21 - a large circular pipe with two pipes joining it off-axis. At the same time, we will see a situation where feature creation order can be used to advantage (or foul you up!).

The original side pipe is on the left, the rotated copy is on the right. It can be obtained by a 180° rotation around the big pipe axis.

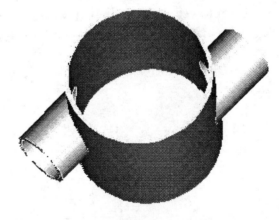

Create a new part **sidepipes** using the default template.

Figure 21 Part with Rotated copy

Start by creating a circular solid *both-sides* protrusion from the sketching plane **TOP**. Use **RIGHT** and **FRONT** as sketching references. Sketch a circle with a diameter of *20* and set *blind* depth of *20*.

Do not add the inner surface of the pipe at this time - we will do that later. This is not an obvious thing to do but we have a situation where feature creation order is important as discussed below.

For the side branch, create another solid protrusion. Use **FRONT** as the sketching plane (**Top** reference **TOP**) and sketch an *8* diameter circle *aligned* with TOP and with a center *5* from RIGHT. Check the feature creation direction arrow. Make the protrusion *one-sided* with a *blind* depth of *15.* This will extend it outside the circumference of the major pipe.

Create a *Straight, Thru-all, Coaxial hole* on the axis of the branch pipe. The hole diameter is *7.* Use the placement plane **FRONT**. Observe the direction arrows for Depth One and Depth Two. In one direction, we want no depth; in the other we want *Thru All.* The part should look like Figure 22.

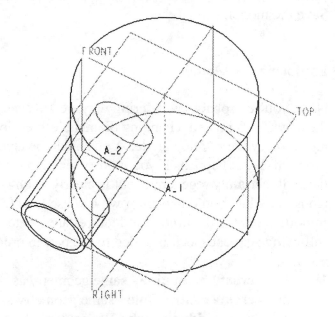

Figure 22 First pipe (Note the vertical pipe is still solid)

Now we are ready to copy the branch pipe (protrusion plus hole). We may want to change the size of the copied branch pipe, so we will make an *independent* copy:

> *Copy > Move | Select | Independent | Done*

Pick on the branch protrusion and hole, then select *Done.* Now we specify the rotation:

> *Rotate > Crv/Edg/Axis*

and pick on the axis of the main pipe. The red arrow shows the direction of rotation (right hand rule). Enter the angle of rotation *180.* Then select:

> *Done Move > Done*

to keep all the existing dimensions. However, we have created an independent copy, so we could come back and change any dimensions of the copied pipe. All the elements of the copy have been defined, so click *OK.* The model should now look like Figure 23.

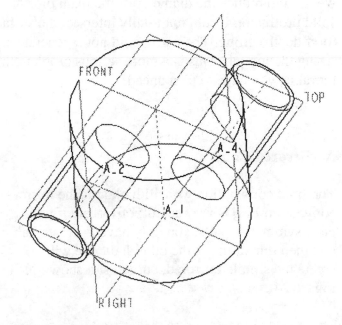

Figure 23 Rotated copy completed

Now we can add the central *hole* of the main pipe. Make it a *straight, coaxial* hole from the placement plane **TOP**. Make it *Thru All* in both directions, with a diameter of *19*.

Save the model.

Exploring the Model

Now, you're probably wondering why we left the central hole until last. Let's experiment with the *Modify* command, changing diameter dimensions of both the original and the copy. You can also modify the rotation angle. You should be able to modify both branch pipes with no problem. What happens if you modify the diameter of the main pipe to *12* and hole to *11?* The part will certainly regenerate, but is clearly wrong. However, the error is relatively easy to fix. Consider what would happen if we had used the following "obvious" sequence (what is important here is the order that features are created - you might like to sketch each feature in the following sequence as it is added to the part in order to visualize the problem that would arise):

1.   **create main pipe** - same geometry as before.
2.   **create central hole** - same geometry as before.
3.   **create side branch** - We couldn't do this from **FRONT** since that would be inside the pipe (that now has the inner hole in it). We would have to create a **Make Datum** outside the pipe using an offset of 15 from **FRONT** and create the branch towards the main pipe using an **Up To Surf** depth.
4.   **create the side branch hole** - We could use the planar face of the branch as the placement plane for a coaxial hole with a depth specified as **Thru Next** (through the next part surface encountered).

These steps would create the same original geometry. However, we would have a big problem if we tried to reduce the diameter of the main pipe to 12, as we did above. Why? The side branch solid protrusion would not totally intersect the surface of the main pipe as required by the **Up To Surf** depth setting. The part would not regenerate at all, and we would have to spend some time fixing the model. This is a more serious problem than we have with the current model. The moral is, you have to plan ahead!

A Mirrored Copy

The final copy option we will look at is the mirror copy. Mirroring is very useful; obviously if you have symmetric parts, you only have to create half and then mirror to get the other half. We will create the simple mirrored, curved slot shown in Figure 24.

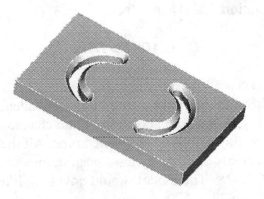

Figure 24 Part with Mirror copy

Start with a rectangular base plate (12 x 20 x 2), sketched on **TOP** so that the datum planes **RIGHT** and **FRONT** are on the centerline of the plate. Create a single *Thru-All* cut using the dimensions shown in Figure 25. Make sure in your sketch that all the arcs are tangential.

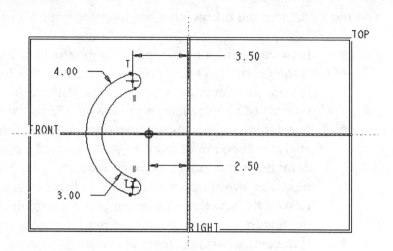

Figure 25 Sketch of original slot

Add a *45 x 0.5 Chamfer* to the upper and lower edges of the slot. The mirror copy is easy:

Copy > Mirror | Select | Dependent | Done

Pick on the slot and the chamfers, then select *Done*. To specify the mirror plane:

Plane > Sel By Menu > Datum > Name > RIGHT

That's all there is to it! Try to *Modify* the mirrored copy. You should investigate to see what happens if you make an *independent* mirror copy of the same slot, and what happens if you try to make a mirror copy that intersects the original feature.

Here is a word of warning about *Mirror*. When you select this command, the *All Feat* option becomes available. Be aware that this grabs every current feature in the part and mirrors them. This includes all solid features, datum planes, datum axes, notes, etc....EVERYTHING! This is a "great" way to clutter up your model with useless and redundant features. This command has its uses, but must be used with discretion.

Design Considerations

We have covered a lot of ground rather quickly in this lesson, and hopefully added a lot of ammunition to your modeling arsenal! We have also seen how the feature creation options can control the behavior of the model. So, now is a good time to say a few more words about part design.

The first part created in this lesson, the *V-pulley*, consisted of only three features (the revolved protrusion, the revolved cut, and the rounds). It was mentioned that it would be possible to create the pulley completely from a single feature (a revolved section that included the inner bore and the rounds).

You must consider the following when trying to put a lot of geometry into a single feature:

- ♦ How easy will it be to modify the part/feature later?
- ♦ If the geometry is very complex, it may take a lot of work to get the sketch of a single feature to regenerate without errors. Perhaps it would be more efficient to create a number of simpler features that would have the same resulting geometry.
- ♦ If you plan to do some engineering analysis of the part, for example a finite element analysis, then minor features such as rounds, chamfers, small holes, etc., will only complicate the model, perhaps unnecessarily. They will also lead to increased modeling effort downstream. These features are normally added last. We saw in Lesson #4 how they can be temporarily excluded from the model (called *suppressing* the feature), as long as they are not references (parents) of other features.
- ♦ If the entire part is contained in a single feature, some major changes to the part may not be feasible using that feature.
- ♦ What is the design intent of each feature? How should each feature be related to other features (via the parent/child relations)? Don't set up unnecessary interdependencies between features that will restrict your freedom of modification later.
- ♦ You must be very careful with alignments. Sometimes an alignment is an essential element of the design intent; sometimes you will fall into the trap of using alignment as a "convenience" when setting up a sketch, where this alignment is not in the design intent. If you try to modify the feature later, you may find that the alignment will get in the way.

When creating the patterns and copies, we discovered the ways that duplicated features could be modified, either during feature creation or after the fact. We also saw some of the ramifications of feature order in the model.

These considerations should be kept in mind as you plan the creation of each new part. It is likely that there are many ways in which to set up the part, and each will have different advantages and disadvantages depending on your goals. The more you know about the Pro/E tools, and the more practice you get, the better you will be able to make good decisions about part design. Good planning will lead to an easier task of part creation and make it easier to modify the geometry of the part later. Like most design tasks, the model design is subject to some iteration. We discussed in Lesson #4 some of the tools that Pro/E provides (the three R's) to allow you to change the structure of your model if it becomes necessary or to recover from modeling errors.

Most importantly, since design is increasingly becoming a group activity, make sure your model will be easy for someone else on your design team to understand. They may have to make modifications while you are away on vacation!

In the next lesson we will discuss the final two main feature types for creating geometry: sweeps and blends. These are very complex features that can be used to create a very wide variety of shapes.

Questions for Review

1.   When creating a revolved protrusion, does the sketch have to be open or closed or either?
2.   When creating a revolved cut, does the sketch have to be open or closed or either?
3.   What essential element is common to all revolved features?
4.   Suppose you are creating a revolved protrusion and you align a vertex of the sketch with an existing feature surface. What happens if you try to create a 360 degree revolve and the aligning surface doesn't exist for the full revolution?
5.   What limitation arises if you create a number of simple rounds at the same time?
6.   What is the first feature in a pattern called?
7.   What is meant by a "radial" hole?
8.   What dimensions are available for patterning a feature?
9.   How could you create a spiral pattern of holes?
10. How could you create a circular pattern of rectangular slots so that the orientation of the slots (a) changes with each instance to stay aligned with the pattern axis or (b) stays constant?
11. What is the difference between independent and dependent copies?
12. What is the easiest way to create a pattern of several related features?
13. Is it possible to create a copy that is translated and rotated at the same time?
14. Comment on the rule of thumb in solid modeling: "Add material first, subtract material last."
15. What happens if you try to mirror one instance in a patterned feature?
16. What happens if you try to pattern a feature created using a make datum as a sketching plane?

Exercises

Here are some parts to practice the features you have learned in this lesson.

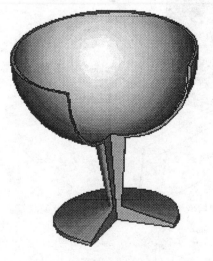
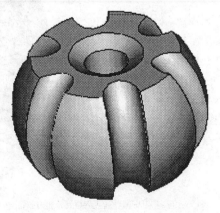

(More exercise parts on the next page!)

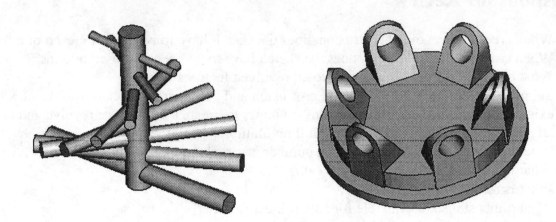

Project

This is the most complex project part. All dimensions are in millimeters. Some dimensions may be missing (because of implicit Sketcher rules or because the figures get too busy!) - make a reasonable estimate for these. The important thing is that the assembly should fit together. If the geometry is confusing, visit the SDC web site for a VRML model of this part.

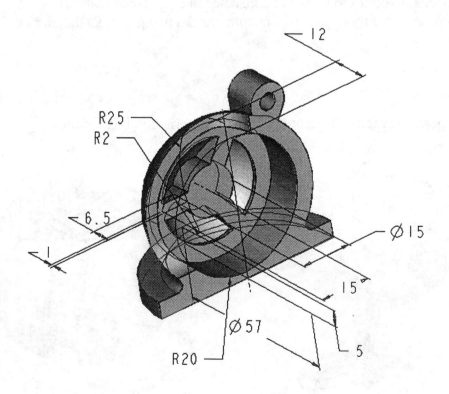

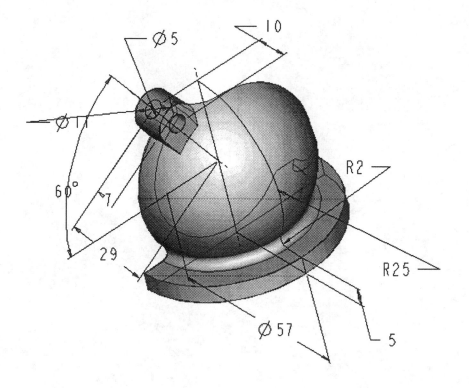

NOTES:

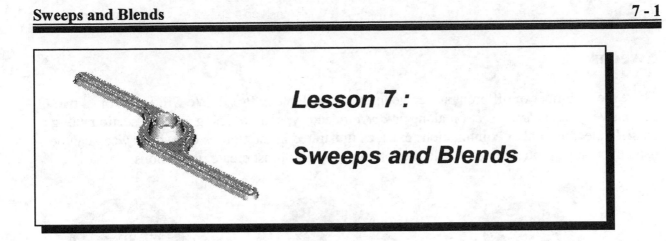

Lesson 7 :

Sweeps and Blends

Synopsis

Sweeps and *blends* are the most complicated (ie. flexible and powerful) features that we will cover in this tutorial. They are both types of solids and can be used to create protrusions and cuts. We will look at the simpler versions of these features. We'll also look at *Sketched* holes and the *Shell* command.

Overview of this Lesson

This lesson will introduce you to the last part design features covered in this series. These are:

Sweeps
> a feature that sweeps an open or closed sketch along a specified trajectory

Blends
> a feature that allows smooth transitions between specified cross sections (like an extrusion with a varying cross section)

These are very advanced modeling features with many options. In this lesson, we will only look at the simplest versions. We will create several different parts that are totally independent of each other, so you can jump ahead to any one of these:

1.   Sweeps
      ‣   Sweeping a Closed Section
      ‣   Sweeping an Open Section
2.   Blends
      ‣   A Straight Parallel Blend
      ‣   A Smooth Rotational Blend

As usual, there are some Questions for Review, Exercises, and a Project part at the end of the lesson.

Sweeps

There are a number of different sweep geometries available in Pro/E. We will look at just two of them: sweeping a *closed* section along an *open* trajectory, and sweeping an *open* section along a *closed* trajectory. Other combinations exist, as illustrated in the figures below. A sweep can be used to create a protrusion or cut. In the following, we will just create protrusions.

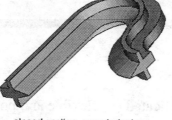
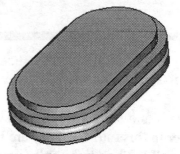

closed section, open trajectory

closed section, closed trajectory

open section, closed trajectory
(inner faces added)

Closed Section, Open Trajectory - The S-Bracket

The first part we are going to create is shown in Figure 1 below.

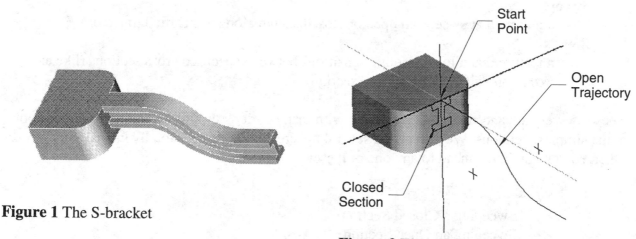

Figure 1 The S-bracket

Figure 2 Elements of a simple sweep

The part consists of two features: the solid protrusion block at the left, and the S-shaped sweep coming off to the right. The elements of the sweep feature are shown in Figure 2. These are the *trajectory* and the *section*. The cross section of this sweep is like an I-beam. It is created on a sketching plane located at the *start point* of the trajectory.

Start a new part called **s_brack** using the default template. First create the block as a **solid protrusion, one-sided**, with a **blind** depth of **60** using **TOP** as the sketching plane and **RIGHT** as the **Right** reference. The right edge of the sketch **aligns** with **RIGHT** and the sketch is symmetric about **FRONT**. The sketch for this protrusion is shown in Figure 3.

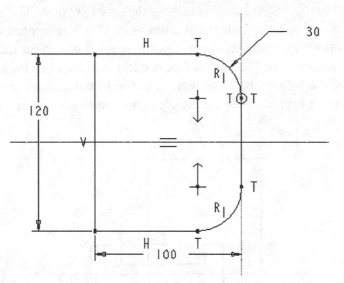

Figure 3 Sketch of the S-bracket base feature

Now we will create the sweep. This is done in two steps: creating the *sweep trajectory*, then creating the *cross section*. The trajectory is the path followed by the section as it is swept. For simple sweeps, the section stays perpendicular to the trajectory. The trajectory can be either an existing edge or datum curve, or it can be sketched as we will do here. To start, select

> *Create > Solid > Protrusion > Sweep | Solid | Done*

In the **SWEEP TRAJ** menu select

> *Sketch Traj*

and use **FRONT** for the sketching plane, and the top surface of the block as the **Top** reference plane. Sketch the S-shaped line shown in Figure 4. Note the sketch references are the right side and top of the block. Start the sketch at the left end.

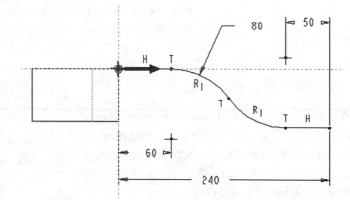

Figure 4 Sketch of the trajectory of the sweep

Notice the arrow starting at the left end of the trajectory. This shows the starting point and direction of the sweep (this might be clearer if you spin the view). If the start point is not at this vertex, select the vertex with a left click. Then hold down the right mouse button and in the pop-up menu select *Start Point*.

When the trajectory is completed, select *Done*. The next menu has to do with the end conditions of the sweep. These options determine how Pro/E will joint the ends of the sweep to other features. For now, select

> *Free Ends | Done*

Now you will move on to the second step - creating the cross section. The screen should show you a light blue cross hair that automatically defines your sketch references. This is centered on the *start point* of the trajectory with the sweep coming toward you. You might like to rotate the view a bit to see the orientation of the sketch that is determined automatically by Pro/E. Use the Sketcher tools to create the following cross section of the I-beam (don't forget alignment). The constraint display has been turned off in the figure - can you figure out what constraints are active?

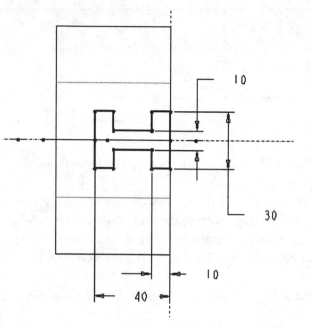

Figure 5 Sketch of closed cross section to be swept

When this successfully regenerates, you can select **Done** from the Sketcher menu, and then **Preview** the sweep. If everything is satisfactory, select **OK**. The part should now look like Figure 6.

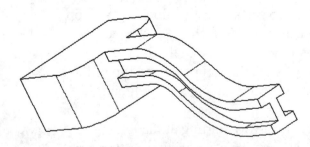

Figure 6 Sweep completed

Use the **Modify** command to experiment with changes you can make to the sweep. A menu opens for you to select the dimensions of the sweep trajectory and/or section. Not all combinations of dimensions are guaranteed to work, however. For example, if you increase the height of the section from 40 to 60, then 80, then 100, the feature will eventually not regenerate. Try to figure out why. (A hint is given in the next paragraph!)

Before we leave this sweep, you should note the following:

- It is not strictly necessary for the cross section to lie exactly on the trajectory. If the section is offset from the trajectory, then the sweep will be offset.
- You have to be careful that during the sweep, the cross section doesn't pass through itself - this can occur when the radius of a trajectory corner is very small (relative to the section size), and the section is on the inside of the curve.
- You can sweep a closed section around a closed trajectory.
- The trajectory need not be formed of tangent edges. If there are corners in the trajectory, the Pro/E will produce mitered corners in the solid, as shown at the right.
- The trajectory can also be formed as a three-dimensional spline.
- It is possible to do more advanced sweeps - like a helical sweep that might be used to create a spring, or cut the threads in a bolt.

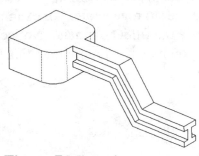

Figure 7 Mitered corners

Open Section, Closed Trajectory - The Lawn Sprinkler

This version of the sweep command will be used to create the part shown in Figure 8. This part has only three features: the sweep used to create the base with two arms, a revolved protrusion to create the hub, and a sketched hole to create the bore. A detailed view of the arm cross section is shown in Figure 9.

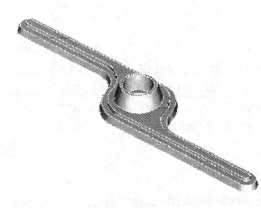

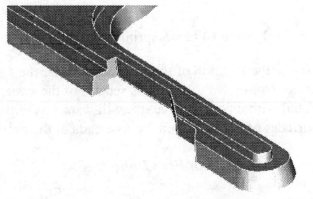

Figure 8 The Lawn Sprinkler

Figure 9 Close-up of lawn sprinkler cross section

Start a new part called *sprinkler* using the default template. The first feature we will create is the base, with two extending arms, using a sweep. As before, we do this in two steps: first the sweep trajectory (a closed curve around the outer edge), then the cross section. For the section we only need to create an open curve showing the edge detail. We will use a special command to fill in the surfaces between the open swept edges at the top and bottom of our sketch.

> *Feature > Create > Solid > Protrusion*
> *Sweep | Solid | Done*

Sketch Traj

Using **TOP** as the sketching plane, and **RIGHT** as the **Right** reference plane, sketch the trajectory shown below. This trajectory is for the outer edge on the bottom surface of the part. The swept section will be inside and above this trajectory. Unless you are very good with Sketcher, don't try to sketch this all at once. Sketcher allows you to cycle through the draw - dimension - regenerate - modify - draw sequence as often as you wish. As we did for the pulley in the previous lesson, build the sketch up in stages. Creating the sketch this way will make it easier to regenerate. For example, start with a central circle, add one arm, add the other, and then use the fillet command. Notice how few dimensions are actually required to define the sketch (you may need more than this initially, but can remove unnecessary ones using constraints):

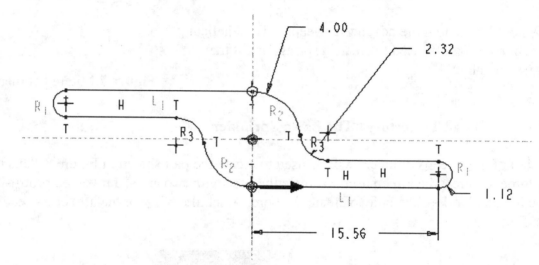

Figure 10 Lawn sprinkler sweep - trajectory

Notice the location of the start point. After the successful regeneration of the trajectory sketch, select *Done*. On to the cross section of the sweep. Since we are only going to sketch the edge detail with an open curve, we will want Pro/E to completely fill in the top and bottom inner surfaces of the part from the free ends of the sketch. Therefore, select

Add Inn Fcs | Done

Again, you are presented with an edge view of the trajectory, with the light blue cross hairs to show where you will create the section (its sketching plane). You might have to spin the view a little to get a better idea about the orientation of the part. Sketch (including alignment and dimensioning) the open line shown in Figure 11. Compare this sketch to the cutaway view of the sprinkler back in Figure 9. You can see where the inner faces are required.

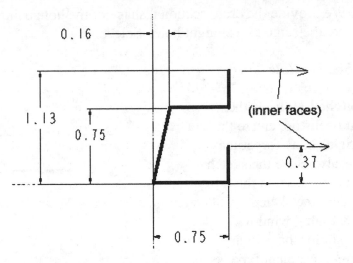

Figure 11 Lawn sprinkler sweep - cross section

The purpose of the cross hair is to show you the relative position of your sketch and the trajectory. As stated above, the cross section does not necessarily have to touch the trajectory. The free ends of the cross section will be closed in by the inner faces of the sweep. When you get a successful regeneration, select *Done*. You can ignore the WARNING about the open ends. Finally, you can *Preview* the feature. Select *OK* if it is satisfactory. The part should look like Figure 12.

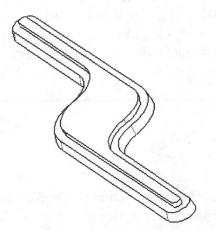

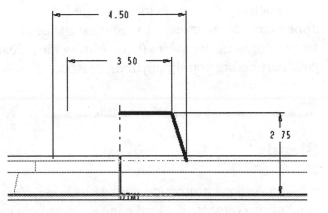

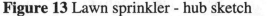

Figure 12 Lawn sprinkler completed sweep   **Figure 13** Lawn sprinkler - hub sketch

Add the hub as a revolved protrusion using the sketch in Figure 13 for dimensioning details. Note that the height of the hub is measured from the bottom surface of the sweep.

Finally, create a hole for the central shaft. This time, instead of a straight or standard hole, we will specify a cross sectional shape for the hole, including the counterbore. This is called a *sketched hole*. This type of hole is essentially a revolved cut that it is automatically revolved through 360 degrees. We provide the cross sectional shape of the hole using Sketcher. The placement references are the same as a straight hole. Select:

Create > Solid > Hole

Check the option **Sketched Hole**. In the Sketcher window that opens up, create the sketch shown at the right (don't forget the centerline). You must also close the sketch down the centerline (note shown in the figure). When you accept the sketch, you're back in the hole dialog window. Select the axis of the hub for the primary reference. The **Coaxial** placement type is then automatic.

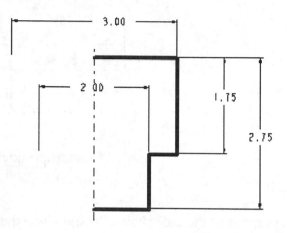

The placement plane is the top surface of the hub. Pro/E will take the top edge of the sketched hole and align it automatically with the axis of the hole coinciding with the axis of the

Figure 14 Lawn sprinkler - sketched hole profile

hub. We also could have used a linear placement using the datum planes but this means that if the hub moved, the hole would not go with it. Try it!

So, that's the end of sweeps! As you can see, these are quite complicated features, packing a lot of geometric information into a single feature. You might like to go back and modify any of the dimensions of the sweeps to see what happens. You can modify either the trajectory, or the section, or both! Be aware that arbitrary modifications might make the sweep illegal, so save your part before you try anything drastic.

Blends

A blend is like a protrusion with a changing cross section. The cross section is specified using a number of sketches. A blend can be used to create a protrusion or a cut. Some restrictions apply:
   ♦   At least two sections are required.
   ♦   The section planes must either be parallel to each other (a *parallel* blend), or they must all intersect on a common axis (a *rotational* blend)
   ♦   Each section must be created separately and constrained to either the existing geometry, or a previous blend section.
   ♦   Each section must have the same number of vertices; normally this means the same number of line (or arc) segments. This rule can be overridden using a *blend* vertex (see the on-line help for information on this).
   ♦   Each section has a starting point (one vertex on the sketch) - these must be defined properly on all the sections or else the resulting geometry will be twisted.

♦   For a rotational blend, the section planes can be no more than 120 degrees apart.
♦   For a rotational blend, a coordinate system is needed in the sketch of each section, whose Y-axis will be the axis of rotation of the blend.

The sections of the blend can be connected either with *straight* (ie. ruled) surfaces, or with *smooth* surfaces. In the following, we will create two parts that illustrate the basic features of blends.

Straight, Parallel Blend

This is the simplest form of a blend. We will create the part shown in Figures 15 and 16. This blend has three sections: a square, a rounded rectangle, and a final thin rectangle. These are seen best in the wireframe view.

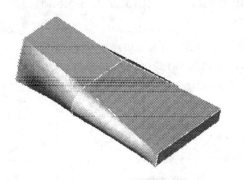

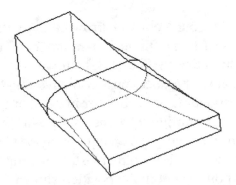

Figure 15 A straight, parallel blend   **Figure 16** Straight, parallel blend - wireframe

Start up a new part called **blend1** using the default template. To create the blend:

> *Feature > Create*
> *Solid > Protrusion*
> *Blend | Solid | Done*
> *Parallel | Regular Sec | Sketch Sec | Done*
> *Straight | Done*

Select **FRONT** as the sketching plane, and **RIGHT** as the *Right* reference plane.

Each section of the blend is sketched separately, although all sections appear in the same sketch. This includes dimensioning, aligning, regenerating, and so on. When each section is completed, we will move on to the next section with a special command. Do NOT select *Done* in Sketcher until all sections have been defined. When we move on to the next section, the previous section will remain displayed on the screen in gray. The new sections can use the old ones for constraint references, or they can be defined with respect to other part features. The first section is a 10 X 10 square centered on the datum planes, as shown in Figure 17.

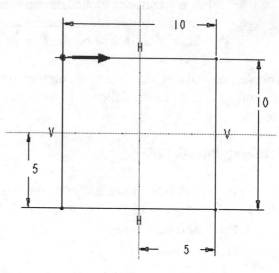

Figure 17 Straight Parallel blend - section 1

Note the round dot and arrow on one of the four vertices (on the figure, it is in the upper left corner). This is called the *start point* and shows the direction that vertices will be traversed in the section. Since the square has four vertices, each section we produce must also have four, corresponding to each other in number and in sequence starting from the start point. If you make an error with the start point on any of the sections, your blend will become twisted. If your sketch's start point is not in the position shown, left click on the desired vertex, then hold down the right mouse button and select:

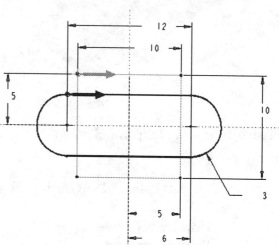

Figure 18 Straight parallel blend - section 2

> *Start Point*

from the pop-up menu.

When you have a successful regeneration, **DO NOT SELECT *DONE*** since this indicates that *all* the blend sections have been created[1]. Instead, select

> *Sketch > Feature Tools > Toggle Section*

or hold down the right mouse button and select the command from the pop-up menu. This will take us to the next section (the rounded rectangle). The previous section is grayed out, and Sketcher is now used to create the second section. The sketch is shown in Figure 18. When that one is regenerated successfully, toggle to the third section (the thin rectangle). The dimensions

---

[1] If you accidentally leave Sketcher too early, in the Elements window, select Section in the elements list, then click the *Define* button and select *Sketch*.

and placement of all the sections are shown in Figure 19. Make sure all your start points are located correctly. (Use the right mouse button to get the pop-up menu.)

If you need to go back to a previous section, use the right mouse pop-up menu to select *Toggle Section*. You can then cycle through each of the sections to make corrections using Sketcher. The active sketch is shown in light blue. When the third section is complete, select *Done*.

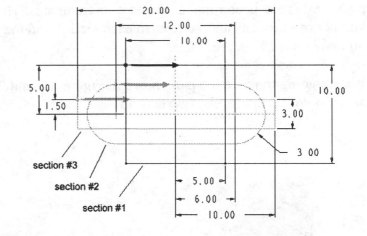

Figure 19 Straight parallel blend - all sections

Now you will be asked for the distance between each planar section. The distance from the first section (the square) to the middle section is *15*. The distance to the next section is *20*. This should complete the specification of the blend. *Preview* the part, and select *OK* when you are satisfied with the part.

You might like to try to *Modify* the dimensions of the cross sections. When you select the feature, you will see all the section shapes with their dimensions displayed on the original sketching plane, and the distances between planes shown normal to the sketch.

The *Shell* Command

Just for fun, here is a feature creation command we haven't mentioned before. Select

> *Create > Solid > Shell*

and pick on the front and back surfaces (you may have to use *Query Select*) as shown in the Figure 20. Then select *Done Sel > Done Refs* and enter a thickness *0.5*. This will shell out the part, removing the designated surfaces, and leaving a uniform thickness of 0.5 everywhere else.

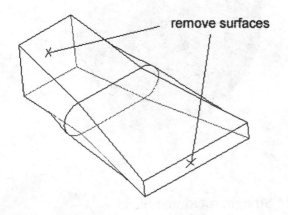

Figure 20 Surfaces to be removed

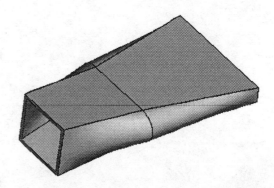

Figure 21 The *Shell*ed part

Smooth, Rotational Blend

A rotational blend is set up by specifying the cross sectional shape on a number of sketching planes that have been rotated around a common axis. The usual restrictions apply as to the number of segments and vertices in each section and the start point. Consecutive sections can be no more than 120 degrees apart.

We are going to make the part shown in Figures 22 and 23. Note that the surfaces on the blend are smooth, except for the two end surfaces.

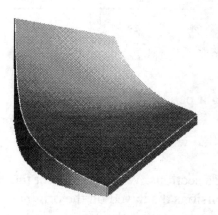

Figure 22 Smooth rotational blend - front isometric

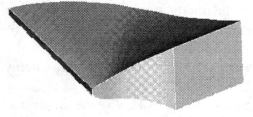

Figure 23 Smooth rotational blend - rear isometric

If we select straight surfaces, we will get the shape shown in Figure 24.

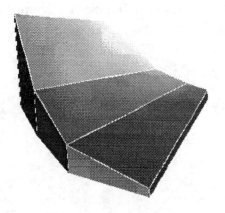

Figure 24 Straight rotational blend

Start a new part called *blend2* using the default template. For this part we will need the **default datum coordinate system** - this is necessary to define the rotation axis of the blend. Then start the blend creation:

> *Feature > Create > Solid > Protrusion*
> *Blend | Solid | Done*
> *Rotational | Regular Sec | Sketch Sec | Done*
> *Smooth | Open | Done*

Now select **FRONT** as the first sketching plane (the view direction is okay), and **RIGHT** as the *Right* reference plane. We are going to create four cross sections, with a separation of 30 degrees between each section. Therefore, the total angle of rotation of the blend will be 90 degrees. Each section must include a coordinate system in the sketch (discussed below). The rotation will occur around the Y-axis of this system.

The first section will be sketched directly on **FRONT**. The dimensions of the section, and its position on the blend, are shown in Figure 25.

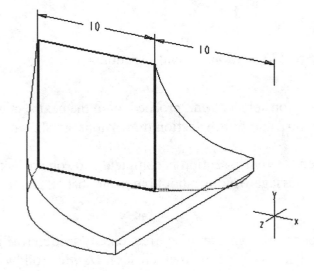

Figure 25 Rotational blend - section 1

Draw and dimension the sketch, aligning the lower edge on **TOP**. If you try to leave Sketcher, you may get a message about a missing coordinate system. Select the coordinate system toolbar icon and place the sketched coordinate system to coincide with the model coordinate system at the origin.

Take note of the start point of the sketch and correct it if necessary (we want the top left corner). Since we are moving on to a different sketch plane for the next section, select *Done.* You will be asked for the angle to the next section. Enter *30*.

A new sketcher window opens up. In this window, you need to sketch the second section and supply a coordinate system to allow alignment with the first section. Dimension the sketch to the coordinate system and make sure the start point is on the correct vertex (top left corner). The second section has the dimensions shown in Figure 26.

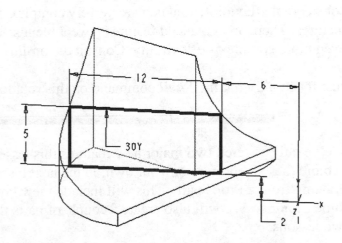

Figure 26 Rotational blend - section 2

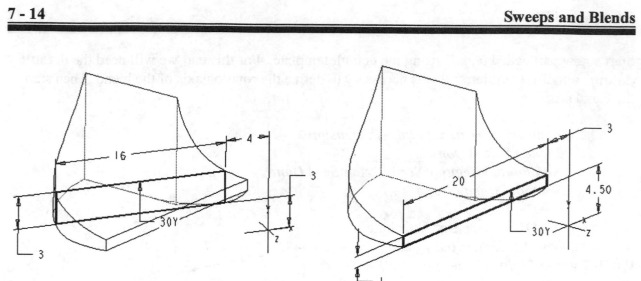

Figure 27 Rotational blend - section 3

Figure 28 Rotational blend - section 4

When you select **Done**, proceed on to the next section. The separation angle is again 30 degrees. The third and fourth section dimensions are shown in Figures 27 and 28 above.

When the fourth section is complete and you are asked to continue to the next section, type in **n**. The message window should indicate that all elements are complete, and you can **Preview** the part.

If your start points aren't correct on any section (the blend will be twisted), highlight **Section** in the Elements window, then click on **Define**. Follow the message window instructions. Eventually you will get to the Sketcher menu. Select the desired vertex and use the right mouse pop-up menu to set the start point.

Leave Sketcher and select **OK** in the elements window when you are satisfied. Try to **Modify** dimensions in the blend. Where do the dimensions show up on the screen?

That completes our limited presentation of blends. As you can see, blends contain a lot of geometric information and are therefore a bit more difficult to set up. However, they offer considerable flexibility and can create very complex shapes not attainable with the simpler features. There are advanced features (swept blends and helical blends, for example) that offer even more complexity/flexibility. Consult the on-line help for information about these.

Just for fun, try out the **Shell** command on this rotational blend using a negative shell thickness!

We've only covered two major new features this lesson. Hopefully, you have some time to explore these a bit more on your own. In the next lesson we will see how to create an engineering drawing from a Pro/E part. This will include view layout, section and detail views, and dimensioning. We will also create a couple of parts that we will need in our assembly in the last two lessons.

Questions for Review

1. Draw a 3D sketch of an example of each of the following sweeps:
    ▸   closed section, open trajectory
    ▸   closed section, closed trajectory
    ▸   open section, open trajectory
    ▸   open section, closed trajectory
    What additional information will be required to create each (or any!) of these features?
2. Does at least one of the vertices of the swept section have to align with or be on the sweep trajectory?
3. What problem may arise if the swept section is "large" and the sweep trajectory has a "small" radius arc in it?
4. What happens if the sweep trajectory has discontinuities (kinks) in it rather than being composed of smooth "tangential" transitions?
5. Which gets created first: the sweep trajectory or the sweep section?
6. When first entering the Sketcher window to define the section for a sweep, it is often difficult to understand the orientation of the view. How can you determine the location and orientation of the section with respect to the trajectory?
7. Find out what happens if you put the start point in the middle of an open trajectory.
8. In the exercises above, the swept section was normal to the trajectory. Is it possible to create a sweep where the section is oriented at an angle to the trajectory?
9. One of the sweep options is *Free Ends*. What does this do? What is the alternative, and what does it do?
10. Can you change the geometry of the trajectory independent of the geometry of the section?
11. What is meant by "inner faces" of a sweep?
12. Can a closed section have any inner faces?
13. Can you have several non-overlapping closed sections in a single sketch for a sweep?
14. Can a sweep trajectory intersect itself (like a figure-8)?
15. What are the essential common characteristics of all sections in a parallel blend?
16. When creating a blend, what is meant by the "start point" of the sketch?
17. What is meant by a ruled surface?
18. Does a straight, parallel blend have to have a common centerline normal to each sketch?
19. Are all parallel blends symmetrical?
20. In a parallel blend, do the sections have to overlap in the sketch?
21. What are the essential common characteristics of all sections in a revolved blend?
22. What feature do you have to remember to create before starting to create a revolved blend?
23. What happens if you try to delete one of the sections in a blend?

Exercises

Here are some parts to try out using the commands in this lesson.

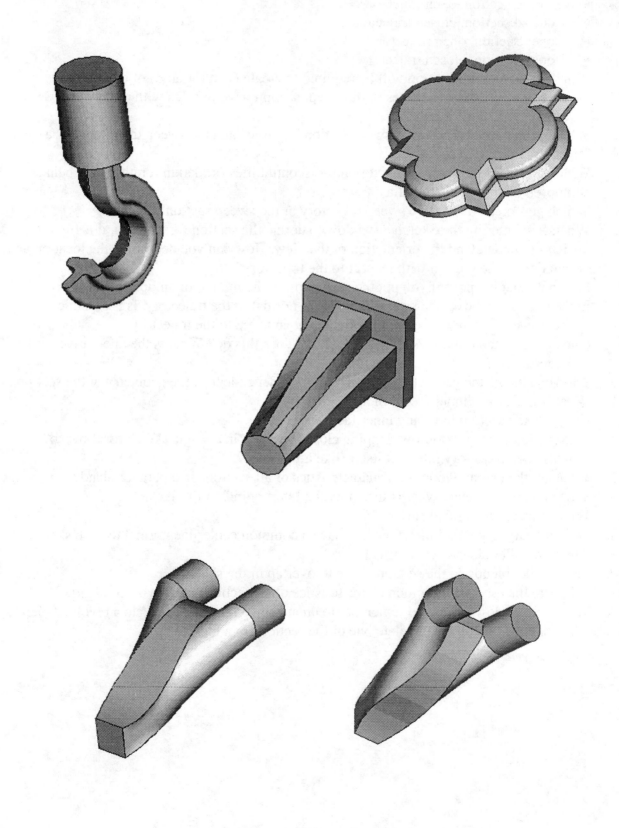

Project

Here is a cut-away view of the final major part of the project. All dimensions in millimeters. Some dimensions will have to be inferred - use a reasonable estimate. See the VRML model on the SDC web site if required. Some careful planning for this part will pay off in reduced modeling time.

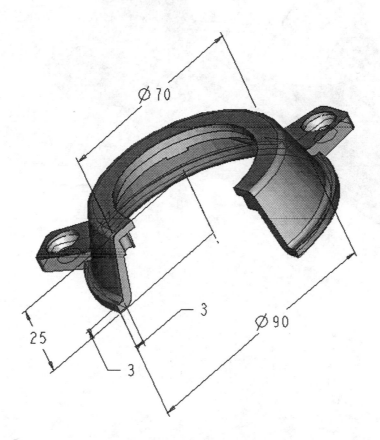

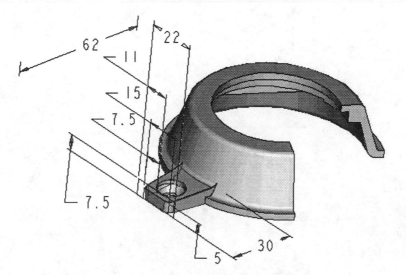

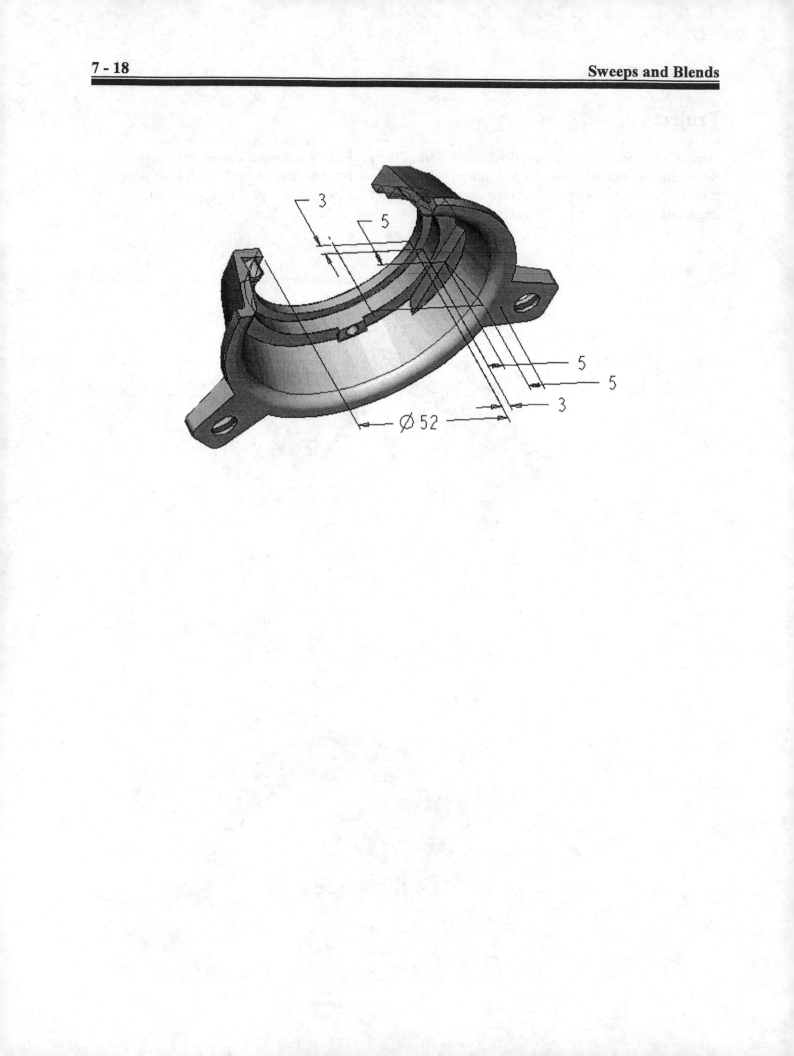

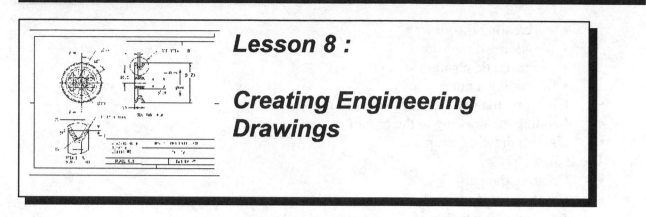

Lesson 8 :

Creating Engineering Drawings

Synopsis

Creating dimensioned engineering drawings of two parts. Changing model units. View selection, orientation, and layout, section and detail views, dimensioning and detailing. Using a drawing template. Notes and parameters.

Overview of this Lesson

The primary form of design documentation is the engineering drawing. The drawing must contain complete and unambiguous information about the part geometry and size. Over the years, the layout and practices used in engineering drawings have become standardized. This makes it easier for anyone to read the drawing, once they know what the standards are. Fortunately, Pro/E makes creating drawings relatively easy. First of all, it is virtually impossible for Pro/E to create a part that is not physically realizable - we don't have to worry about any 3-pronged blivots (see the introduction to this series of lessons). The Pro/E solid model contains all necessary and sufficient information in order to define the part geometry. Therefore, by getting all this information into the drawing, it is very difficult to create a drawing with insufficient or inaccurate information. However, remember that when, for example, Pro/E interprets a sketch it fires a number of internal rules to solve the geometry. These rules are not indicated on the final drawing, and it may be necessary to augment the dimensions placed by Pro/E in order to complete the drawing. When Pro/E is used to create a drawing, you will find that all the standard practices are basically built-in - if you accept the default action for commands, by and large the drawing will be satisfactory. There are a number of commands we will see that will improve the "cosmetics" of the drawing.

In this lesson, we are going to create drawings of two parts: an L-bracket support and a pulley. We will first create these parts and then produce the drawings. At the end, we will create hard copy of each of the drawings. Both parts will be used in a subsequent lesson on creating assemblies, so don't forget to save the part files. We will also discover the power of bidirectional associativity, mentioned in the tutorial series introduction.

1.   The L-Bracket
  ‣   Creating the part
  ‣   Creating the drawing
    •   selecting the sheet

- • creating the views
- • adding dimensions
- • cosmetic changes
- • adding a note
  ‣ Changing the part/drawing - exploring associativity
  ‣ Sending the drawing to the printer
  ‣ Using a drawing template
2. The Pulley
  ‣ Creating the part
  ‣ Creating the drawing
    - • selecting the sheet
    - • creating a section view
    - • creating a detailed view
    - • adding dimensions
    - • cosmetic changes
    - • using parameters in notes

As usual, there are some Questions for Review, Exercises, and some Project parts at the end of the lesson.

The L-Bracket

Creating the Part

Create the part shown in the figure at the right. Call this part **lbrack** and use the default template for a solid part. Study this figure carefully. When you create the part, make sure that the back surface of the vertical leg is aligned with **FRONT**, the lower surface of the horizontal leg is aligned with **TOP**, and the plane of symmetry is **RIGHT**. An obvious choice for the base feature is a both-sides solid protrusion in the shape of an L sketched on **RIGHT**. Observe the dimensioning scheme for the holes.

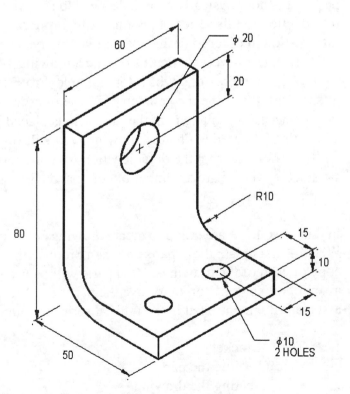

Figure 1 The L-bracket part

In Pro/E, the part should look like this in default orientation:

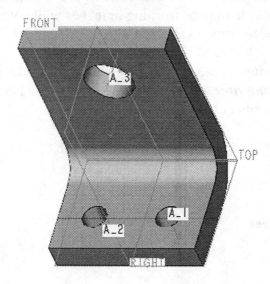

Figure 2 The Pro/E part

Changing Part Units

Note that the units are given in millimeters, whereas in a standard Pro/E installation, the default template contains units of inches. This is a common "oops" when creating a model, since the units are not topmost in our mind when we first start the part (or when you inherit a model from another source). Here's how to change the part units. Select (from the **PART** menu)

Set Up > Units

The **Units Manager** window opens, as shown in Figure 2. This lists the common unit systems in Pro/E (and its companion Pro/MECHANICA used for finite element analysis). The current units are indicated by the arrow pointer. Select the line containing the unit system

millimeter Newton Second

and then *Set*. A warning dialog opens. When you change the units of a model, you have two options that will affect all linear dimensions:

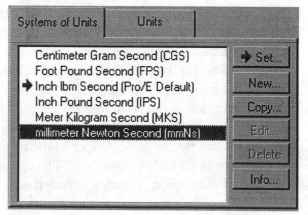

Figure 3 The Units Manager window

Convert existing numbers - This leaves the model the same real size as the original. For example, a 10 inch long bar will be converted to a 254mm long bar. The dimension number changes.

Interpret existing numbers - This keeps the dimension numbers the same, but interprets them in the new units. In our example, the 10 inch long bar becomes a 10mm long bar.

Managing units is especially important if you are going to produce an assembly of parts, as we will do in the last two lessons. It is also critical to be aware of units when you are working in a design group, since some people may be working in inches while others are in millimeters. Parts downloaded from the web also come in all varieties.

If you have used the dimension values in the figure above, then you want to pick the second option here (***Interpret existing numbers***). When this is applied, use the *Modify* command to verify that the dimension numbers haven't change.

Don't forget to save the part! We are now ready to create the drawing.

Creating the Drawing of the L-Bracket

① **Create the Drawing Sheet**

Select the following:

>   *File > New > Drawing | [lbrack]*

Deselect the option **Use default template**. We will deal with drawing templates a bit later.

The New Drawing menu will open up as shown at the right. Note the currently active part is automatically selected as the drawing model. Keep the defaults for the template (**Empty**) and orientation (**Landscape**), but change the Standard Size option to **A** (8-1/2" by 11" in landscape mode). When this window is complete, accept the entries with *OK*.

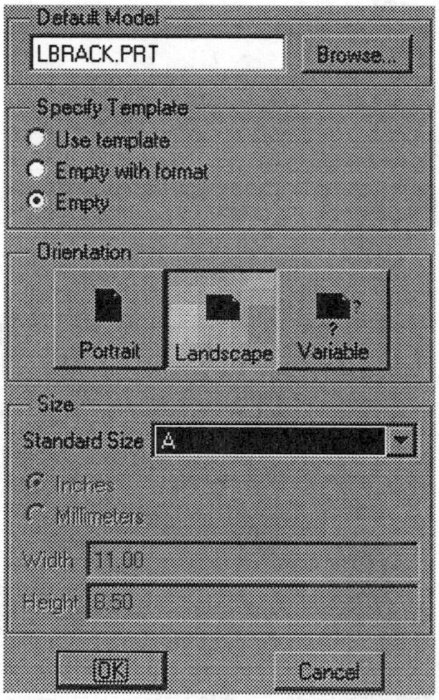

A new window will open up with the title *LBRACK (Active)*. This overlaps the part window, which is still open but hidden. You can switch back and forth between the part and drawing windows using *Window* (in the pull-down menu). Current windows are listed at the bottom of the menu. Clicking on any listed object

Figure 4 The New Drawing menu

window brings it to the front and makes it active. You can minimize any window and/or resize it by dragging on its border. If several windows are in view, only one of them will be active at a time (indicated by the word Active in the title). On the drawing window, some new short-cut buttons have been added at the top. The top menu on the right is the DRAWING menu, and some new information is shown across the bottom of the graphics area.

As usual when confronted with new menus for the first time, browse through the menu choices, paying attention to the message line at the bottom of the screen and the menu pop-ups.

② **Adding Views**

In the **DRAWING** menu, select (most of these selections are defaults)

Views > Add View
General | Full View | No Xsec | No Scale | Done

Read the message window. The view we will place first will be our primary view. It will be the front view of the part, so select a **CENTER POINT** a bit left and below the center of the sheet, as shown in Figure 5.

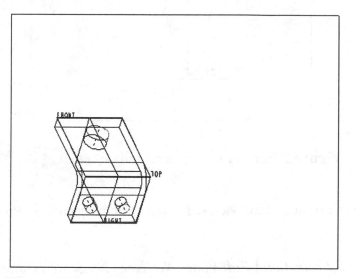

Figure 5 Placing the primary view

A drawing scale is set automatically, in this case it is 1.0 as shown in the bottom line in the graphics window. We can change that to a better value if required. So far, we have just selected the placement of the view. Now we want to reorient the part to get the proper front view. We do this by telling which surfaces or references in the model face which directions on the drawing. We will use the datum planes, although planar surfaces of the part could also be used. Select the following in the **ORIENTATION** window (Figure 6):

For Reference 1:
       Front | Sel by Menu | Datum | Name | FRONT
For Reference 2:
       Right | Sel by Menu | Datum | Name | RIGHT
       OK

We used *Sel by Menu* because it might be difficult to pick out just the datum planes from the clutter of lines in the small image on the screen (although you could have zoomed in on the display using CTRL-left) and/or use *Query Select*. *Repaint* the screen.

Observe the appearance of the tangent lines in the rounded corner. Turn off the datum plane display. In the Environment (*Utilities > Environment*) select *Tangent Edges (No Display) > OK*, then *View > Repaint*. Your drawing should look like Figure 7.

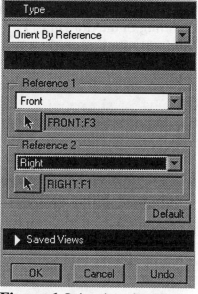

Figure 6 Orienting the view

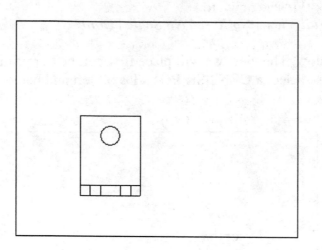

Figure 7 Primary view placed and oriented

Now we want to add the right and top views. These can be projected by Pro/E off the front view as follows:

Add View > Projection | Full View | No Xsec | No Scale | Done

then click on the drawing to the right of the front view. Voilà! The right side view appears. Repeat the command and click above the front view to get the top view. This is too easy! (But it gets even easier later.)

In the **VIEWS** menu, select *Done/Return*, or just middle click.

If you don't like the spacing of your views, you can easily move them. Pro/E will ensure that your views stay aligned. With the **Right**-mouse button, click anywhere in the graphics window, and read the message window. (Using the Right-mouse button will allow us to change practically anything in the drawing.) Left-click on the right side view - it will be surrounded by a magenta border. Left-click on the view again and drag the view. Try to move the right view up, down, left, and right on the screen (you can't move up or down since the view must align with the front view). Left-click again to drop the view at a new location and middle click to accept.

Try moving the top view. Finally, try moving the front view. You should see the other views move to maintain the correct orthographic alignment.

Click the **middle**-mouse button when you are finished moving the views. The same view movement control is available by selecting

Views > Move View

from the main **DRAWING** menu.

Let's add a fourth view that shows the part in 3D. Note that this is not a projected view but a general one. We'll scale this one down to half size. Select

Add View > General | Full View | No Xsec | Scale | Done

and click in the upper right area of the drawing. Enter the scale factor *0.5*. Leave the part in the default orientation by selecting *Default > OK* in the **Orientation** window. In the **VIEWS** menu, select *Done/Return*. Your screen should look like Figure 8.

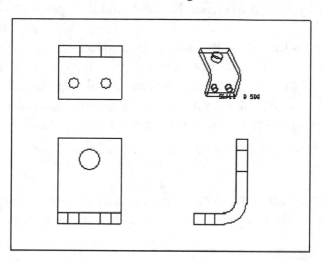

Figure 8 All views placed for L-brack

③ **Adding Dimensioning Detail**

In the **DETAIL** menu select

Show/Erase

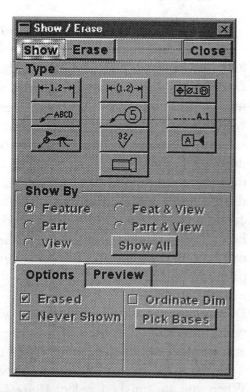

A new window opens with a number of detailing types and options as shown in Figure 9. Move the mouse cursor over each of the buttons in the **Type** area - the message window (and a pop-up) will show you what the button does. Select

> *Dimension* (the top left button)
> *Show By (Part)*
> *Preview > With Preview*
> *Show All*

Confirmation will be requested (select *Yes*) and all of the part dimensions used to create the model will be put up on the display in light blue. We have several options for dealing with these: erase them all, keep them all, or just select the individual ones we want to keep. There aren't too many dimensions in this drawing so select

Figure 9 The *Detail > Show/Erase* menu

Accept All > Close

in the **Show/Erase** window. The dimensions will change to yellow.

Take a moment to think back to how you created the part. The dimensions shown are exactly the ones you used to create the features. **The lesson here is to use the dimensions in feature creation that you want to appear on the drawing.** So, you should know something about drawing standards before you start to create the solid model - a point often missed by many.

Another thing to consider is the **Show By** button selected above. We chose to show all the part dimensions at once. This was all right for this simple part since there were not too many dimensions to deal with. For more complicated parts, you might like to show the dimensions by individual feature, all dimensions in a given view, or a specific feature in a chosen view. Some experience with these options is necessary to make good choices here.

④ **Dimension Cosmetics**

Although all the dimensions are now on the drawing, there is a lot we may need to do to their placement and appearance. For example, some of the dimensions may be a little bit crowded. To fix this, select

Tools > Clean Dims

This opens the window shown in Figure 10. We have to identify which dimensions we want cleaned. Select

Pick Many > Pick Box > Inside Box

and draw a rectangular box around the entire drawing. Then select *Done Sel*. All the linear dimensions will show in red, and the number of dimensions affected will appear at the top of the window. Accept the default distances for the offsets (the 0.5 is the spacing in real inches from the edge of the part to the first dimension, the 0.375 is the offset between parallel dimensions - these are drawing standards). Then pick on the *Apply* button. All the dimensions should spread out. The dashed gray lines are called the snap lines. As you proceed to modify the drawing layout, the dimensions will snap to these locations to help you maintain the spacings set in *Clean Dims*. These snap lines are a convenience and will not be printed with the drawing.

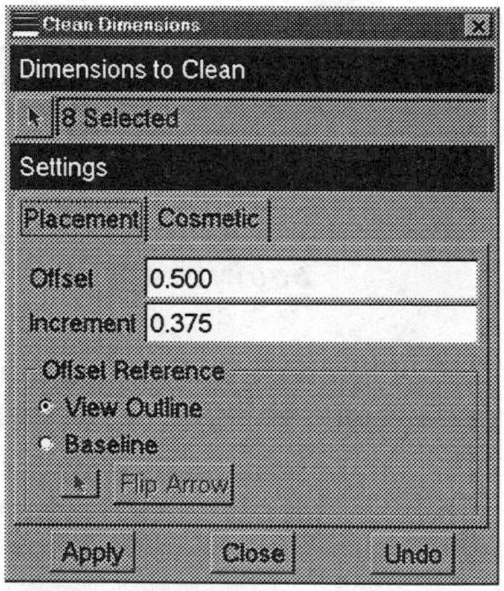

Figure 10 The Settings window for *Clean Dims*

Depending on your view placement and dimensioning scheme, Pro/E might have some trouble with dimension placement (for example, too little room between views). Move the views to accommodate the detail items. *Close* the Clean Dimensions window.

When you are finished, select *Done/Return* in the **TOOLS** menu.

The drawing should now look like Figure 11 (your dimensioning scheme may be slightly different from this, depending on how you created your model):

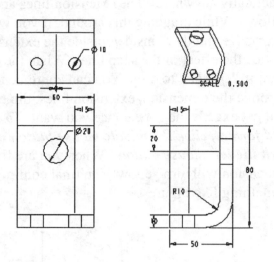

Figure 11 Dimensions placed and cleaned

There is a lot more we can do to modify the display "esthetics" of the dimensioning detail. Some of the dimension placement locations chosen by Pro/E may need to be touched up a little. It is probably necessary to switch some of the dimensions to a different view, and you may want to modify spacing and location of dimensions on views, direction of dimension arrows, and so on. For example, the location dimensions for all the holes should be on the view that shows the circular shape of the hole. For the two small holes, this is the top view. For the large hole, this is the front view. Most of these cosmetic modifications can be made using the **Right**-mouse button as follows.

Right-click in the graphics window. A **START EDIT** menu will open. Pick (left click) on one of the dimensions you want to modify. For example, you might select the dimension giving the thickness of the plate as shown in the right view. (See Figure 12). Once you have selected an entity, the **EDIT ACTIONS** menu appears (Figure 13).

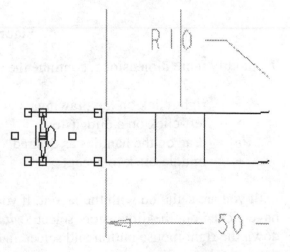

Figure 12 "Handles" for modifying dimension cosmetics

| Mod Attach |
| Default Wit Line |
| Switch View |
| Make Jog |
| Nominal Val |
| Toggle Type |
| Values / Text |
| Flip Arrows |
| Arrow Style |
| Break |
| Del Breaks |
| Erase Wit Line |
| Show Wit Line |
| Erase |
| Unerase |
| Delete |
| Undelete |

Note the small square "handles" on the dimension components. Left-click on any handle in order to drag it to the desired position. If you select the handle directly under the dimension value, you can move it practically anywhere. The extension lines and arrows will automatically follow. While dragging this around, if you want to flip the dimension arrows (ie. put them inside/outside the extension lines), just *Right-click*. Notice the effect of the snap lines. When the dimension is where you want it, *left-click* to drop. You can continue to left-click on the handles to move the dimension, extension lines, dimension line, and arrows until you get exactly the appearance you want. *To accept the final placement and format, click the middle mouse button or select another detail item with the left mouse button.* When you are finished, middle click. The dimension will turn yellow. The final configuration might look something like Figure 14.

Figure 13 Menu for editing the drawing obtained by right-clicking the graphics window

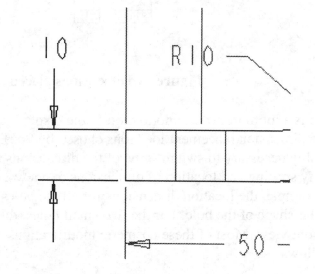

Figure 14 Modified dimension cosmetics

To modify more dimensions, continue the sequence:

- ▸ right-click on the drawing,
- ▸ left-click on a dimension,
- ▸ drag on the handles as desired,
- ▸ middle-click to accept

until you are satisfied with the layout. If you want to move a dimension to another view, after you have picked out the dimension, select *Switch View* in the **EDIT ACTIONS** window (or hold down the right mouse button and select *Switch View* from the pop-up menu), then left-click on the desired new view.

All of these cosmetic modification commands are also available in the **DETAIL** menu. Try these out to see how they work:

Erase

(available under *Show/Erase* and with the pop-up menu on the right mouse button) removes detail items from the drawing. Note that this is not the same as *Delete*. With erase, the dimension still stays with the model, it just isn't displayed. A dimension that is part of the model cannot be deleted. However, you can create "cosmetic dimensions" that can be deleted, since they are not necessary parts of the model.

Move

moves the dimension and extension lines

Move Text

moves the dimension text only

Mod Attach

changes the attachment point of a leader or radius/diameter dimension

Flip Arrow

changes the dimension arrows from inside the extension lines to outside, and vice versa

Align

aligns dimension lines vertically or horizontally in different views

Try to lay out all the dimensions so that your drawing looks similar to Figure 14. The dashed offset (snap) lines created when we did *Clean Dims* can be removed with *Delete*. A snap line under a dimension line can be safely picked because Pro/E will never delete a dimension!

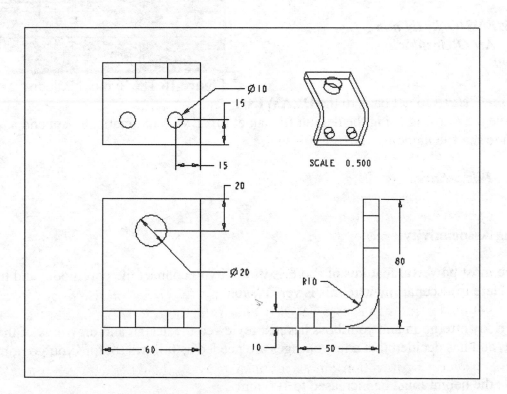

Figure 15 L-bracket final drawing

Do not be concerned at this time if the yellow extension lines are touching or crossing the model. As you probably know, this is a "no-no" in engineering drawings. Pro/E will clean up the extension lines when a hard copy is generated. Pro/E will also look after all the line weights and line styles (for visible and hidden lines, center lines, dimension and extension lines, and so on) according to standard engineering drawing practice.

⑤ **Creating a Note**

Let's add a short note on the drawing (we will talk about title blocks in the next section). You may have to move the other views up a bit to fit this in (you can do that after the note is created, if necessary). Select

> *Detail > Create > Note*
> *No Leader | Enter | Horizontal | Standard | Default | Make Note*

Select a location a little below the right side view. A small **Symbol Palette** Window opens from which you can select special characters to insert in the note. Normal characters are just typed in (see the message window). Pressing the enter key will advance you to the next line of text in the note. Pressing the enter key on a blank line will complete the note. Type in something like the following:

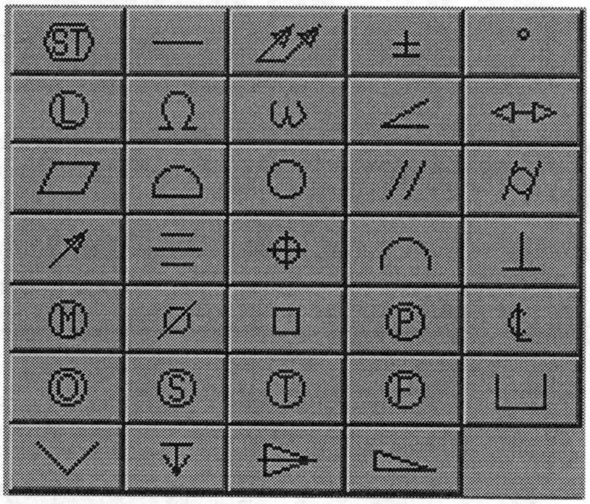

ALL DIMENSIONS IN mm
Drawn by Art O'Graphic
17 May 00

Figure 16 The Symbol Palette

Select *Done/Return* to get back to the **DRAWING** menu. Save the drawing using the default filename; Pro/E will automatically append a *drw* extension to the file name.

> *File > Save*

Exploring Associativity

One of the most powerful features of Pro/E is its ability to connect the part model and the drawing. Here is a scenario where this is very useful.

It's late Friday afternoon and your boss has just reviewed the design and drawings of the L-bracket, and has decided that a few changes are needed as follows (before you go home!)

- ♦ the height must be increased to 100 mm
- ♦ the diameter of the large hole must be changed to 30 mm

♦   the top of the bracket must be rounded in an arc concentric with the large hole
♦   the manufacturing group wants the drawing to show the height of the large hole off
   the bottom of the part, which should be 70mm

Hmmmm... You could do this by going back to the part and modifying/changing. BUT..there is
an easier way! To really see the power of what you are about to do, resize the drawing and part
windows so that both are visible.

Make sure the **DRAWING** window is active. If not, click on the drawing window and select
Window > Activate in the pull-down menu (or use CTRL-A). In the **DETAIL** menu, select

> *Modify > Value*

Click on the diameter dimension of the large hole. Enter a new value of *30*. The dimension will
show in white. Click on the height dimension and change it to *100*. Now, click on the head of the
DRAWING menu to open it and select

> *Regenerate > Model*

The drawing should change to show the new geometry. Even better, click on the title bar of the
part window and activate it. You may have to repaint, or Ctrl-click on the window (this is a quick
way of getting a repaint!). It also shows the new geometry. In the **PART** window, change the
width of the bracket from 60 to *80*, then *Regenerate*. Change back to the drawing window and
activate it - it shows the new shape too. These actions show that there is a *bidirectional* link
between the drawing and the part. If changes are made to any item, the other is automatically
updated. The same holds true when you deal with assemblies of parts, and drawings of those
assemblies. Before we forget, change the width of the bracket back to *60*.

One thing we can't do with *Modify* in the
DRAWING window is change the basic
features of the part (like creating new
features, or changing feature references).
For that you have to go back to the **PART**
window. Do that now, so that we can add
the cut to round off the top of the bracket.

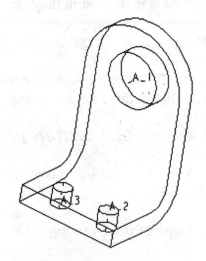

First, if necessary, *Reroute* the large hole
(select it using the model tree) so that the
horizontal dimension reference is **TOP**
instead of the top surface of the bracket.
The distance above this reference should
be *70*. If the hole disappears off the bottom
of the part (the axis is still visible), modify
its dimension value to -70. If you scroll
back a few lines in the message window,
you will see a warning that was produced
when the hole was regenerated.

Figure 17 The modified L-bracket

Now create a circular arc cut, concentric with the large hole and aligned with the left and right sides of the bracket. The part should look like Figure 16 when you are finished. Don't forget to save the new part.

Now we have to touch up the drawing a little. Change back over to the drawing window.

First, the drawing scale is a little too big for the sheet. Select *Modify* and click on the *Scale* value shown on the bottom line of the graphics window. Change the value to *0.8*. You might like to reposition the views.

Next, you may note that the large arc isn't dimensioned. Actually, a dimension isn't needed for the arc since we know the block width. And anyway, because of the way the feature was created, it has no dimensions in the model! We will provide a reference dimension in the drawing. Select (in the **DETAIL** menu)

Create > Ref Dim > Standard | New Ref | On Entity

and then left click on the arc. Use the middle mouse button to place the dimension. You might like to clean up the dimension cosmetics a bit.

Let's add the axis lines for the holes:

Show/Erase > Axis (middle button in right column)
Part > Show All > Accept All > Close

You can get rid of the axis labels **A_1**, **A_2**, etc. by turning off the axis display using one of the short-cut buttons, then *Repaint*. This leaves the axes but removes the labels when you are in drawing mode.

You should also change the text in the note:

Modify > Text > Text Line

and click on the first line of the note. The text will appear in the message window. Use the cursor keys to move around in this line, and change it to something like

SCALE 0.8, DIMENSIONS IN mm

Press the enter key when you are finished and don't forget to save the drawing.

Getting Hard Copy of the Drawing

Obtaining hard copy depends on the details of your local installation. See your system administrator for information on this. However, there are two possible ways that might work.

If you are running under Windows with an attached printer, try this:

File > Print

or use the "Print" shortcut button. In the **Destination** field of the new window, select *MS Printer Manager*, then

Configure > Model > Plot (Full Plot) > OK
OK

This should bring up your normal Windows print control dialog. Use it as you usually would to select the printer and printer properties (quality, speed, color, page size, etc). Some experimentation may be required here to get margins, orientation, and so on set just right.

If you do not have a plotter attached directly (or wish to archive the drawing file for use in another program), obtaining a hard copy of the drawing is a two-step process. First, we create a postscript-format file of the drawing, then copy the file to a postscript-capable printer. Try this:

File > Print

In the **Destination** field of the new window, select *Generic Postscript*, then

Configure > Model > Plot (Full Plot) > OK
To File (and deselect *To Printer*)
OK

A dialog box will open asking you for the name and path of the file. The default will be *lbrack.plt* in the current working directory (unless this has been over-ridden by your system administrator). Click *OK* to generate the file. Once you have a postscript file of the drawing, there are a number of ways to obtain hard copy. You will need access to a postscript-capable printer and you may have to find out how to transfer the file from your Pro/E computer/directory to the printer. Generally, once you have the file on a computer connected directly to a postscript-capable printer, you only need to copy the file directly to the printer. See your system administrator for further information.

Using Drawing Templates

For our first drawing, we did a number of operations manually. Many of these are common to all part drawings. In Pro/E 2000i^2 there are now tools to do much of this tedious drawing creation automatically.

First, erase the current drawing with *File > Erase > Current*. Note that this does not erase the drawing from your hard disk but just removes it from the current session (takes it out of memory). You should be back in the part window.

Create a new drawing called *lbrack2*. This time, use the default template for an A sized drawing by selecting *a_drawing* in the **Template** area of the **New Drawing** dialog window (Figure 4). This does the following:

- creates the drawing sheet (A size)
- orients the model
- places the standard views (top, front, right) for a multiview drawing
- scales the views to give you room for detailing

When you enter the drawing window, everything should be set up for you as shown below.

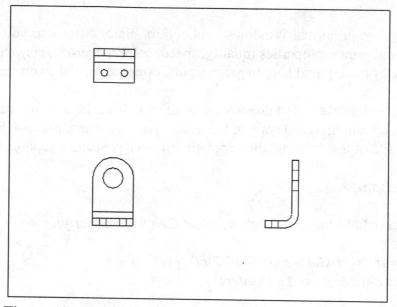

Figure 18 Drawing created using the template

How does Pro/E know what standard views you wanted? The answer is that these are views embedded in the part model, that was created with the part template. The views are based on the default datum planes TOP, FRONT, and RIGHT and the associated Saved Views. The orientation of the part in the drawing is therefore determined by how we orient the geometry of the part relative to the datums. If your part is upside down in the model, then the drawing views will be upside down too. Another good reason to plan ahead!

Now, there may be a good reason to have the orientation of the part different in the model than in the drawing. If you still want to use the part and drawing templates, here is how to reorient the drawing views created automatically. In the **DRAWING** menu, select

Views > Modify View > Reorient

and pick on the current front view in the drawing. The other views will be surrounded by magenta boxes, and in the message window you are asked whether you want these reoriented as well (to maintain projection). Select the *Yes* button or type in a "*y*". The Orientation menu appears. In the **Saved Views** region, select the *Left* view and then the *Set* button. The primary view reorients to the predefined **LEFT** view of the model, and the other views also reorient to suit. Change back to the original **FRONT** view and then use *OK* to close this dialog window.

With the views created, go ahead and finish detailing the drawing for practice. Try to do this on your own, but refer back to our previous procedures if necessary.

Now, on to the second part. This will require creating a section view, and controlling the display of hidden lines.

The Pulley

We're going to use this part in the next lesson (on assembly). We will create it now so that we can see how to create a drawing with a section view. We'll also look at some other things we can do when creating drawings, like setting up a title block and border. First, let's get on with the pulley model.

Creating the Pulley

The pulley we are going to create looks like Figure 19. The main interest in this part is the cross sectional shape. The key dimensions of this shape are illustrated in Figure 20.

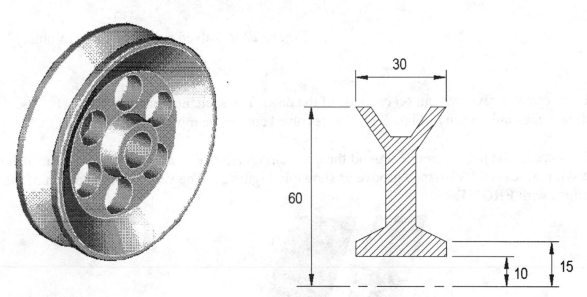

Figure 19 The pulley   **Figure 20** Pulley cross section

We could create the base feature as a single revolved protrusion. However, this single feature would be difficult to set up in the sketcher. Instead, we'll create the pulley using a number of features (we'll use about 12 in all, including the holes and rounds).

Start by creating a new part called *pulley* using the **mmns_solid_part** template. In the appropriate data fields, enter [pulley] for the *Description* and your initials for *Modeled_by* parameters.

Create a circular disk (both sided protrusion off **FRONT**) aligned with the origin. Look ahead to Figure 31 to see why we want this orientation. The disk has a diameter of *120* and a thickness of *30*. The disk should look like Figure 21.

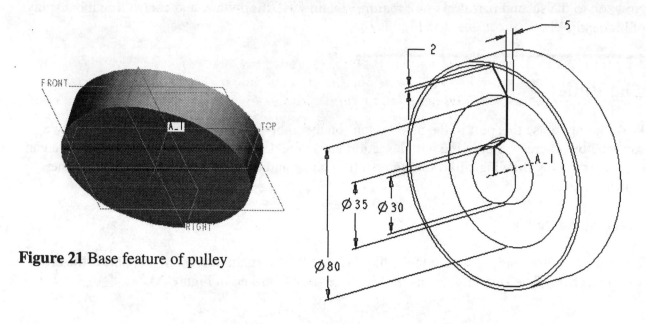

Figure 21 Base feature of pulley

Figure 22 Revolved cut on one side of pulley

Now, create a revolved cut on one side of the disk. The sketching plane is **RIGHT**. The dimensions are shown in Figure 22. The revolved cut can be mirrored through **FRONT**.

Now create the pulley groove around the outer circumference as another revolved cut. Just make a symmetrical 60° V-shaped groove as shown in Figure 23. The vertex at the bottom of the V aligns with **FRONT**.

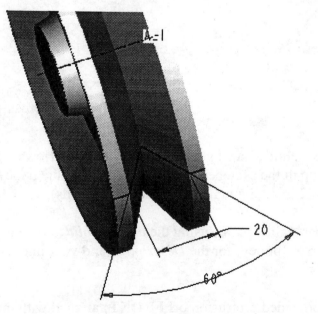

Figure 23 Revolved cut to make pulley groove

Add a round at the bottom of the groove with a radius of *3*. Now add the central hole for the pulley axle. This can be created as a *coaxial hole* off **FRONT** with a diameter of *20*. The depth is *Thru All* in both directions. See Figure 24.

Now we'll start putting the pattern of holes arranged around the pulley. We start by creating the pattern leader. Again, use **FRONT** as the placement plane and go *Thru All* in both directions. Create the hole using the *radial* option (*28.5* from pulley axis). Measure the angle *30* from **TOP**. This is the angle that we will increment to make the pattern. See Figure 25.

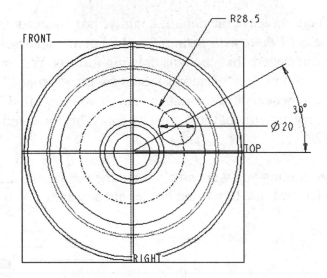

Figure 25 Hole Pattern leader

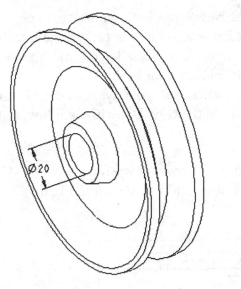

Figure 24 Central hole added to pulley

Now create the pattern using the first hole as the leader. Increment the angular dimension by *60* and make a total of *6* holes.

As a final touch, add some *rounds* (radius *1*) to the outer edges as shown here. All four edges are in the same feature - don't create four separate rounds!

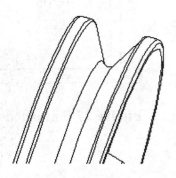

That completes the creation of the pulley. Before we go on to the drawing, don't forget to save the part!

Figure 26 Rounds added to outer edges

Creating the Drawing

① Selecting a Formatted Sheet

For this drawing, we will use a pre-formatted sheet with a title block. Start a new drawing with

File > New > Drawing > [pulley]

You can leave the default template box checked. In the **New Drawing** window that opens up, select *Empty with format*. In the **Format** area, select *Browse* to find the path to the directory on your system that contains drawing formats. We are looking for a file called **a.frm**. The default location is (for Windows systems with a "generic" Pro/E installation) **/ptc/proe2000i2/formats/a.frm**. If you can't find it, either consult your system administrator, or carry on without the format by canceling the command. In the **New Drawing** window, select *OK*.

Assuming you were able to load the format, the drawing window will open with an ANSI standard title block and border already drawn on the A-sized sheet as shown in Figure 27.

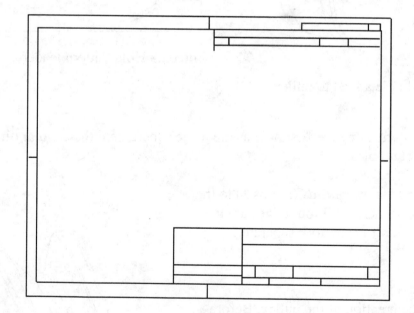

Figure 27 Formatted drawing sheet (A size)

② Creating the Primary View

Create a front view of the pulley showing its circular profile:

Views > Add View
General | Full View | No Xsec | No Scale | Done

Click to the left of center of the sheet. In the Orientation window near the bottom click on the region labelled Saved Views. This opens a list of the views saved in the part template. Select

FRONT > Set > OK

Return to the **DETAIL** menu and change the sheet scale to *0.5* using *Modify*. Your screen should now look like Figure 28.

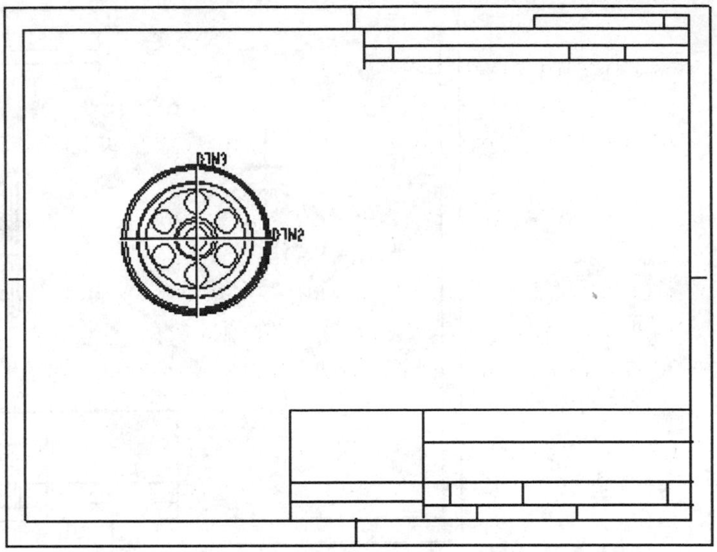

Figure 28 Primary view placed and oriented

③ **Add a Full Section View**

We will create a full section to the right of the primary view. To do this, we have to specify the type of view, the location of the view, where the section is to be taken, and on what view to indicate the section line. Select the following (follow the prompts in the message window while you do this):

Views > Add View
Projection | Full View | Section | No Scale | Done

Then in the **XSEC TYPE** menu, select

Full | Total Xsec | Done

Pick a location of the view off to the right. Now we have to tell Pro/E what to call the view and where we want the section taken. In the **XSEC ENTER** menu select:

Create > Planar | Single | Done > [A]

Our section will be identified as *Section A-A*. We want to use a vertical line through the pulley. If a datum plane doesn't exist for this, you can create a Make Datum. In our case, **RIGHT** will do just fine:

Sel By Menu > Datum > Name > RIGHT

Read the message window. Pro/E is asking you on which view to put the cutting line ("arrows"). Pick on the front view. We are finished with the datum planes, so you can turn them off now. Your drawing should look like Figure 29.

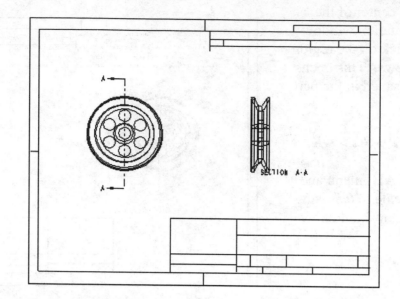

Figure 29 Section view placed

④ Modify the Section View Display

Section views generally do not show any hidden edges. Let's turn them off.

> *Views > Disp Mode > View Disp*

Pick on the section view, then select

> *Done Sel > No Hidden | Tan Default | Done*

⑤ Adding a Detail View

We'll add a broken out detail view of the pulley groove. This will be useful for dimensioning and showing the rounds. We'll also draw this at twice the scale of the drawing. Select

> *Add View > Detailed | Full View | No Xsec | Scale | Done*

Pick a point on the drawing where there will be enough space for the view (we can always move the view later if this point doesn't work out). At the prompt for the Scale, enter *1.0*. Now pick a point near the bottom of the pulley groove. We now want to indicate the area around the previous pick point to be included within the detailed view. As you click with the left mouse button, a spline curve will be drawn. Make sure this encloses the groove. When you have fully enclosed the area to be drawn, click with the middle mouse button. Enter the name of the view, *B* and select the *Circle* boundary type. A circle will appear roughly around the area you identified, and you can pick (left click) a location for a note to identify the circle. This can be moved later if required. You should now have a scaled-up detailed view something like Figure 28. You can move the views around using *Move View* if desired.

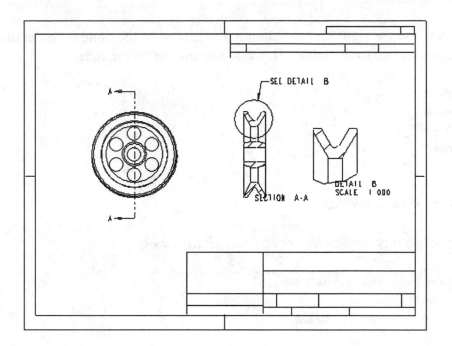

Figure 30 Detail view of section added

⑥ Adding Dimension Details

Instead of getting Pro/E to show us all the dimensions at once using *Show All*, we will be a little more selective since this part has quite a few dimensions. This will give us more control about initial placement of dimensions, which means fewer changes later (hopefully!). In the **DETAIL** menu, select

> *Show/Erase > Dimension | Feat_View | Preview | With Preview*

and click on one of the features in the model. *Query Select* will come in very handy here to make sure you are selecting the desired feature, otherwise you can zoom in on the drawing to help make your selections. Or, you can open the model tree to select the features there. It helps in this case if the features are all named. Pro/E will place the dimensions associated with the selected feature in that view. Pro/E will place each necessary dimension only once, so if you want a dimension in a particular view you must either first create it there, or use *Switch View* later.

Examine the function of the *Accept All | Erase All | Select to Keep* options in the **Show/Erase** menu. You might like to clean up the initial dimensioning scheme a bit with

> *Tools > Clean Dims*

Accept the defaults, and select the desired dimensions to clean individually.

⑦ Improving the Esthetics

As we did before, use the right mouse button to modify/move the dimension details.
Alternatively, you can go to the **DETAIL** menu and use the commands
> *Move*
> *Move Text*
> *Mod Attach*
> *Switch View*
> *Flip Arrows*
> *Align*

as required to get a better layout.

Change the crosshatch pattern in the section and detailed views:

> *Detail > Modify > Xhatching*

and pick on the section view, then *Done Sel*. Then select

> *Spacing | Hatch > Overall | Half (click twice)*
> *Angle | Hatch > Overall | 30 > Done*

Add all the centerlines for circular features:

> *Detail > Show/Erase > Axis | Part | Show All*

Use *Select to Remove* to retain only the desired axes (there are a couple on the section view that we don't want shown). Turn off the axis labels.

⑧ Adding Notes with Parameters

Finally, add some text to the title block. You can, of course, use notes to create plain text within the title box. You may want some notes to change if the model changes. You can do this with parameters. In the **DETAIL** menu select:

> *Create > Note*
> *No Leader | Enter | Horizontal | Standard | Default | Make Note*

Do you remember entering a value for the parameter *DESCRIPTION* when creating the part using the template? The text was something like "pulley". Pick a point in the appropriate cell in the title block (see Figure 31). Then type in the following text in the prompt area:

> *[&description]*

Press enter when you are finished. The value of the part parameter will appear at the insertion point - this is what the "&" symbol does when used with parameters. You can move the note to center it in the box. Put a note for the *MODELED_BY* parameter in another box in the title block.

Notice that when you select the insertion point, all the dimensions in view are changed to their symbolic form. Try entering a note with the following text (observe the dimension symbol on your drawing for the diameter of the central hole in the pulley):

[Pulley shaft &d15]

How do you suppose you could enter the note to display the drawing scale?

Your final drawing should look something like Figure 31. Here is a test of your drawing-reading abilities: what is the missing dimension in this drawing?

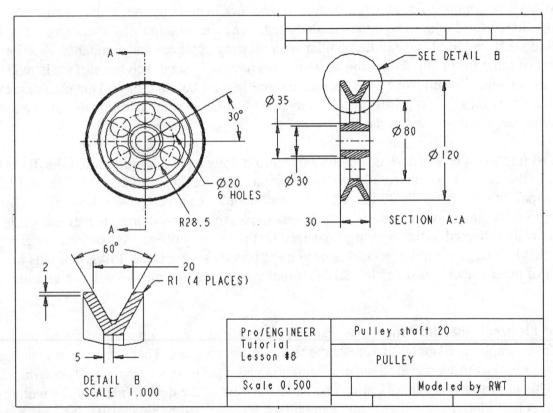

Figure 31 Final pulley drawing

As mentioned earlier, the dimensions placed by Pro/E are the ones used explicitly to construct the model. From time to time, you may have to add some dimensions manually. You can do this using

Create > Dimension

The dimensioning tools available are fairly self-explanatory and will be easy to pick up by anyone who has done 2D CAD. Two things must be remembered however. First, dimensions that you create can be deleted. Second, the dimensions you create cannot be used to drive the geometry - they are strictly lines on the drawing. These are called *"driven"* dimensions and cannot be modified in the drawing (but will change if the geometry changes).

You can also use some Sketcher-like tools to add entities to the drawing such as center-lines and so on.

If you want, make a hard copy of the pulley drawing. If you have zoomed in or out on the drawing, make sure that the plot setup is set to *Full Plot* before creating the plot file.

Don't forget to save your drawing.

Conclusion

As you can see, although Pro/E handles most of the work in creating the geometry of the drawing, there is still a lot to be done manually regarding the esthetics of the drawing. It is for this reason that you need to be quite familiar with drawing practices and standards. Pro/E gives you a lot of tools for manipulating the drawing - we have only scratched the surface here. There is actually an entire volume of Pro/E documentation (several hundred pages) devoted expressly to creating drawings! All this information is available on-line. Some additional drawing tools and techniques are discussed in the *Pro/E Advanced Tutorial* from SDC.

The most important lesson here is that the engineering drawing is a by-product of the 3D solid model. In this respect, we observed how bidirectional associativity works in Pro/ENGINEER. It is this capability that gives Pro/E and all its related modules so much power. If several people are working on a design, any changes done by, for example, the person doing the part modeling, are automatically reflected in the drawings managed by the drafting office. As you can imagine, this means that in a large company, model management becomes a big issue. Pro/E contains a number of other drawing utilities to make that management easier, but we will not go into them here.

A second lesson is that the dimensions that will automatically show up in the drawing are those used (for example, in Sketcher) to create the features of the model. Therefore, when creating features, you must think ahead to what information you want to show in the final drawing (and how). This involves your identification and understanding of the design intent of the features in the part. A part kludged together from disorganized features will be very difficult to present in an acceptable drawing.

We will return to creation of drawings in Lesson 10. There we will see some more tools and techniques to expand on the ones covered here.

In the next lesson, we will see how to create an assembly using the L-bracket and pulley you created in this lesson. We will also have to create a few small parts (washers, shaft, base plate).

Questions for Review

1.   When creating a new drawing, how do you specify which part is going to be drawn?
2.   Is it possible to create a 2D drawing without a part? What advantages/disadvantages might this have?
3.   The first view added to the drawing is called the _____?
4.   How do you set the orientation of a view? Consider both the first view and subsequent views.
5.   What is the easiest way to move a view on the drawing sheet?
6.   Is it possible to delete a view once it has been created?
7.   On a very complex part, do you think that *Show All* is very useful? Why?
8.   When you select *With Preview*, what color do dimension details first appear in?
9.   Explain the functioning of the three mouse buttons as used to modify dimension cosmetics.
10. How do you select a drawing template? What does it create for you automatically?
11. Describe two methods to move a dimension from one view to another. When might you want to do this?
12. How do you create a text note (for example, to put in a title block)?
13. Can you move or delete views created automatically with a drawing template?
14. What happens if you *Modify* the value of a dimension in the drawing?
15. What is the difference between *erasing* and *deleting* a dimension?
16. Is it possible to add new features, or redefine existing features when you are in drawing mode?
17. What does the *Sketch* command in the **DETAIL** menu do?
18. How can you produce hard copy of a drawing?
19. When you want to create a section view, at what point in the command sequence for adding a view do you designate it to be a section view?
20. What four items of information are required in order for Pro/E to generate a section view?
21. How can you turn off hidden lines in a section view?
22. What boundary options are available for creating a detail view?
23. When showing dimensions, what are the available **TYPE** options?
24. How can you change the spacing and angle of a hatch pattern?
25. How is the design intent reflected in a drawing, and how does this relate back to the part?
26. Do you think it would be possible to have a completely automatic system for creating a fully dimensioned drawing?
27. What symbol is used in a note to tell Pro/E to display the value of a parameter?

Exercises

Here is a part to create and produce an detailed engineering drawing. Alternatively, you can use any of the exercise parts in the previous lessons to produce drawings.

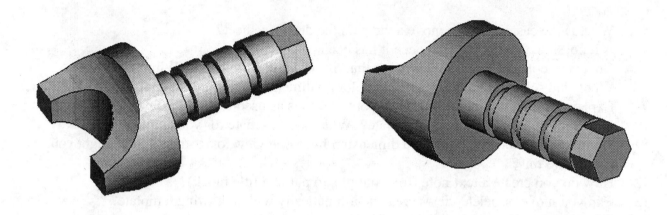

Project

Pick some of the previously created project parts, and produce detailed engineering drawings of each. Find out what information is usually contained in the ANSI standard title block. Use section and detail views where appropriate.

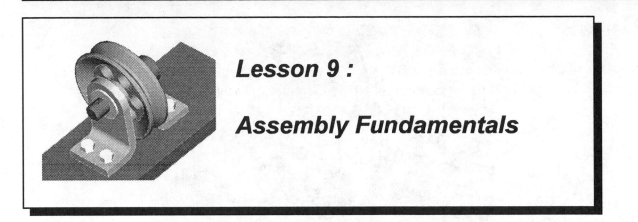

Lesson 9 :

Assembly Fundamentals

Synopsis

Introduces assembly mode, in which previously created parts are put together in an assembly. The assembly constraints are discussed. Two methods of laying out the screen for assembly are presented. Assigning colors to components.

Overview of this Lesson

In this and the next lesson, we are going to look at how you can use Pro/E to create and modify an assembly of parts. You have already created two of the parts involved: the pulley and the support bracket (see Lesson #8). In this lesson, we will first create a number of other parts needed for the assembly exercise. Then we will use Pro/E to combine the component parts into an assembly. When we are finished, we will have created the assembly shown in Figure 1. An exploded view showing all the component parts is shown in Figure 2.

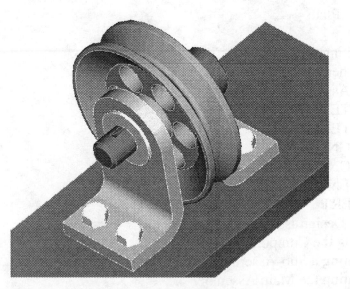

Figure 1 Final assembly containing 14 parts

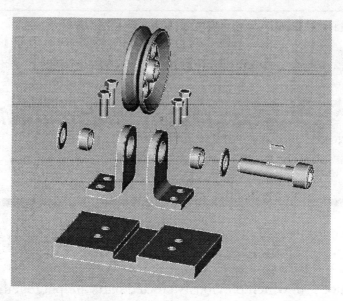

Figure 2 Exploded view of final assembly

We will intentionally create some of the parts with dimensions different from those required in the final assembly so that in the next lesson we can go over some of the part/assembly modification commands.

The lesson is organized as follows:

1. Creating the Assembly Components
    ▸   Pulley
    ▸   Bracket
    ▸   Axle
    ▸   Base Plate
    ▸   Bolt
    ▸   Bushing
    ▸   Washer
2. What are Assembly Constraints?
    ▸   MATE
    ▸   MATE OFFSET
    ▸   ALIGN
    ▸   ALIGN OFFSET
    ▸   ORIENT
    ▸   INSERT
3. Assembly Design Issues
4. Assembling the Components
    ▸   Creating a Sub-Assembly
    ▸   Creating the Main Assembly
5. Assigning Colors

Creating the Assembly Components

IMPORTANT NOTE: Make sure all your parts have units set to millimeters.

The Pulley

As mentioned above, you should have created the pulley in Lesson #8. One thing we forgot to do then was add a keyway to the central hub of the pulley. Do that now: the keyway is *5mm* wide and about *3mm* deep. Create the keyway as a *both sides cut* off **FRONT**. Put the keyway at the 3:00 o'clock position (symmetric about **TOP**). The keyway should look like this

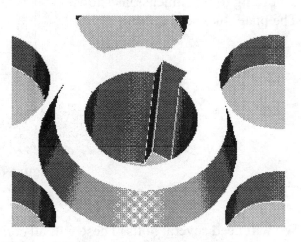

Figure 3 Pulley with keyway added

The Axle

Create this new part and call it **axle**. The part should look like the figure at the right. Use the dimensions shown in the part drawing below (we will change some of these later when we are in assembly mode).

Figure 4 The pulley axle

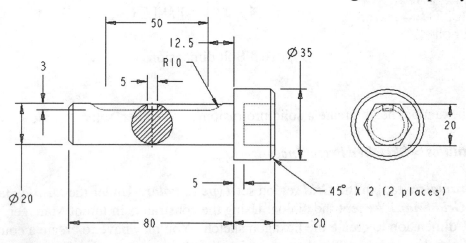

Figure 5 Dimensions for the axle

The Base Plate

Create a part called **bplate** according to the dimensions shown. The plate thickness is *20*.

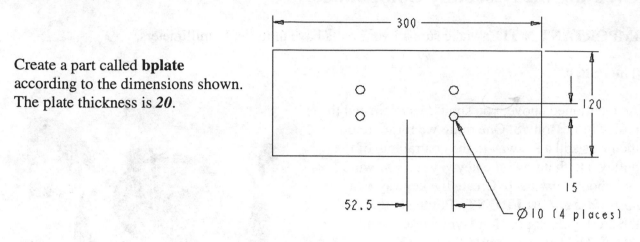

Figure 6 Base plate dimensions

The Bolts

We will need several bolts. These will all come from the same part file **bolt** containing only a single bolt. Note that the threads have not been included for simplicity here. If you wanted to include the thread, you could use a helical cut (making the screen display very slow) or using what is called a *cosmetic thread*. The dimensions of the bolt are shown in the figure.

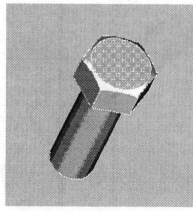

Figure 7 The bolt

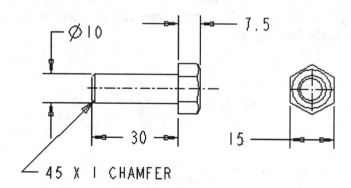

Figure 8 Bolt dimensions

HINT:

To make the hexagonal head, create a solid protrusion. In Sketcher, select

> *Utilities > Sketcher Preferences*

Under the *Parameters* tab, in the *Grid* region set *Type* to *Polar*. Under the *Display* tab, turn on the *Grid* and *Grid Snap*. Accept the dialog. Using the constraints in Intent Manager, you should only require 1 dimension to create the hexagon sketch. You may have to create a couple of construction lines that go across the diameter of the head.

The Bushings

We will need a couple of these too - call the part **bushing**. It is a simple protrusion.

Figure 9 The bushing

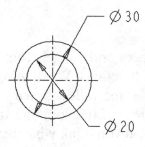

Figure 10 Bushing dimensions

12.5 THICK

The Washers

Our last component part is the washer. It has the dimensions shown in the figure at the right. The easiest way to make this is to do a *Save As* of the bushing part, *File > Open* the new part, then *Modify* the dimensions.

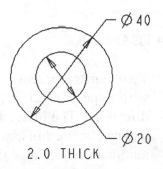

2.0 THICK

Figure 11 Washer dimensions

When you start assembling these components in Section 3 of this lesson, make sure they are all in your start-up directory. And, just a reminder, all these parts should be in millimeters.

Assembly Constraints

Creating an assembly is actually a lot of fun and not too difficult. What we are going to do is to tell Pro/E how the various components fit together. To do this, we specify *assembly constraints*.

The geometric relation between any two parts has six degrees of freedom: 3 translational and 3 rotational. In order to completely define the position of one part relative to another, we must constrain or provide values for all these degrees of freedom. Once we give Pro/E enough information it will be able to tell us when the part is fully constrained and we can assemble the part. We proceed through the assembly process by adding another part, and so on.

There are a number of constraint types that we can specify. In this lesson, we will use six of them. The individual constraints are used with the surfaces, axes, and datum planes of the two parts or with a part and assembly. The constraints usually must be used in combinations in order to fully constrain all 6 degrees of freedom. Here are all the constraint types:

MATE

Two planar surfaces or datums become coplanar and face in opposite directions. When using datums, you must specify either the yellow or red side. This constrains 3 degrees of freedom (one translation and two rotations). Can you think what they are? There are still 3 unconstrained degrees of freedom (what are they?).

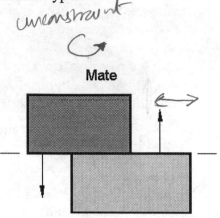

Figure 12 The *MATE* constraint

MATE OFFSET

Two planar surfaces or datums are made parallel, with a specified offset, and face in opposite directions. The offset dimension can be negative, and can be used in assembly relations to automatically change the distance between the surfaces. What degrees of freedom does this constraint fix? Which ones are still free?

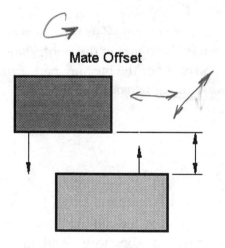

Figure 13 The *MATE OFFSET* constraint

ALIGN

This can be applied to planar surfaces datums, revolved surfaces and axes. Planar surfaces become coplanar and face in the same direction. How many degrees of freedom does this constrain? When aligning datum planes, you will have to specify which side (yellow or red) is to be aligned.

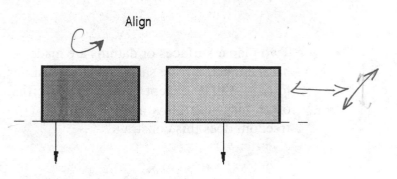

Figure 14 The *ALIGN* constraint with planar surfaces

When Align is used on revolved surfaces or axes, they become coaxial. How many degrees of freedom are constrained? Also, note that there are still two possible positions - you can force one or the other with the Orient constraint described below.

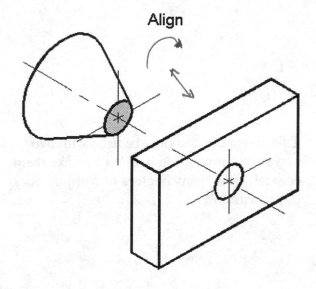

Figure 15 *ALIGN* used with surfaces of revolution aligns the axes

ALIGN OFFSET

This can be used only with planar surfaces: they become parallel with a specified offset and face the same direction.

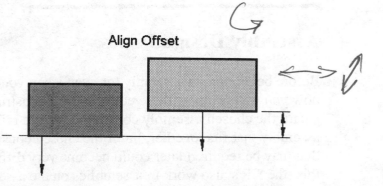

Figure 16 *ALIGN OFFSET* (used with planar surfaces only)

ORIENT

Two planar surfaces or datums are made parallel and face the same direction (similar to Align Offset except without the specified offset distance). How many degrees of freedom does this constrain?

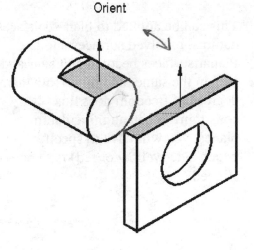

Figure 17 The *ORIENT* constraint

INSERT

This constraint can only be used with two surfaces of revolution in order to make them coaxial. How many degrees of freedom does this constrain?

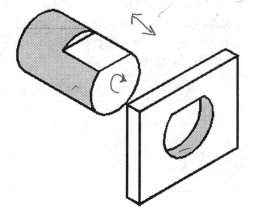

Figure 18 The *INSERT* constraint used with cylindrical surfaces

Assembly Design Issues

Before beginning an assembly (or even when you are creating the parts), you should think about how you will be using these constraints to construct the assembly. Like designing the features of a part, the chosen assembly constraints should reflect the design intent. It is possible to create an assembly that fits together, but if the chosen constraints do not match the design intent, changes that may be required later could become very difficult. Pro/E does provide tools for dealing with this (the 3 R's also work in assemblies on the assembly constraints of components), but you should really try to think it through and do it right the first time!

This is a good time to mention that when you are placing a component into an assembly, it does not matter what order you use to add the placement constraints, since they are applied simultaneously. Pro/E will tell you when you have constrained the component sufficiently for it to be placed. The order you use can be chosen strictly for convenience.

Also, it is possible to create assembly features (like datum planes and axes, and even make datums) that will exist only in the assembly. This would allow you, for example, to use an assembly parameter like an angle or linear dimension between datums, to control the assembly geometry. In this way, if you used the assembly feature as a constraint reference for a number of component parts, you could change the position of all parts simultaneously in the assembly by modifying that parameter. All the parts would still have to assemble according to all the assembly constraints defined between parts.

Assembling the Components

Before you begin, make sure that the parts **lbrack.prt** and **pulley.prt** that you made in Lesson #8 are available in the working directory.

Creating a Subassembly

We will start by assembling the L-bracket, a bushing, and a washer into a subassembly. This will save us some time, since two copies of this subassembly must be inserted into the final assembly. Once created, a subassembly is treated exactly the same way (in regards to subsequent placement constraints) as a single part.

From the **FILE** menu, select

> *New > Assembly | Design > [support]*

Deselect the **Use default template** option and select *OK*. In the **New File Options** window, choose the *Empty* template and again select *OK*. Close the model tree.

In the **ASSEMBLY** menu, select

> *Component > Assemble > lbrack.prt > Open*

You can turn off the datum planes, axes, and spin center if you like. Now we'll add the bushing. In the **COMPONENT** menu, select

> *Assemble > bushing.prt > Open*

The bushing will appear somewhere beside the bracket and the **Component Placement** window (Figure 19) will open up. This window will list the various placement constraints as they are created for this component, and allow us to select constraint types and references on the new component and the existing assembly. Note that the component (ie. the bushing) is not fully constrained - see the **Placement Status** at the bottom of the window.

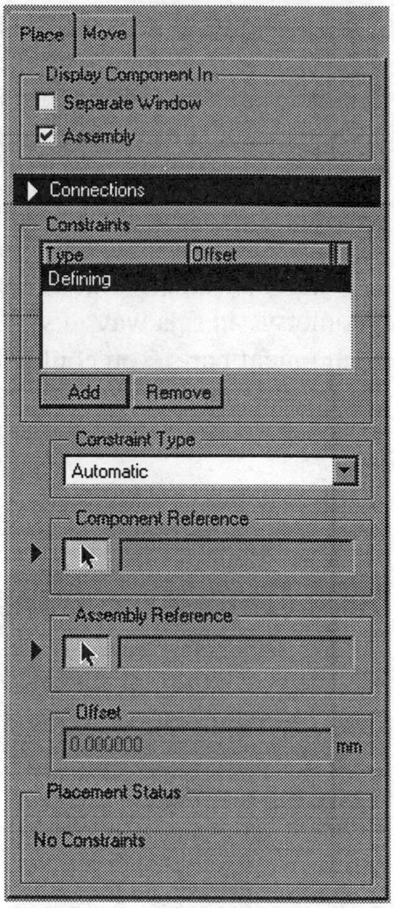

There are two main display modes when you are doing assembly. We will look at both of them. First, make sure that only the **Separate Window** option is checked at the top of the window. We will use the other option shortly. This puts the current assembly in one graphics window (title: *SUPPORT*), and the component being added in another (title: *COMPONENT: BUSHING*). This makes it easy to locate references and gives us independent viewing control over the two windows. We can also independently control the zoom/spin/pan in the two windows. This is useful, for example, when dealing with a small component in a large assembly structure.

Read the following few paragraphs before proceeding:

Placing the component involves three steps:

Figure 19 The **Component Placement** window

1.   With **Defining** highlighted in the **Constraints** box, select the desired **Constraint Type** from the pull-down list.
2.   In the *component window*, select the appropriate component reference surface, datum, or axis for the constraint.
3.   In the *assembly window*, select the matching assembly surface, datum, or axis for the constraint.

As you add constraints, keep your eye on the **Constraints** box, and the **Placement Status** line. You will be told when you have provided enough constraints for the new component to be fixed in the assembly. You have to be a bit careful here, since it will sometimes be possible to include the component at what appears to be the correct position without it being entirely constrained. The **Component Placement** window will let you exit without constraining the component; this is called "packaging" the component. Unless you really want to do this, make sure the **Fully Constrained** status appears before leaving this window. Also, remember that the order of creating the constraints does not matter, nor does the order of picking references on the component or assembly.

If it is difficult to see or select an entity to be used for an assembly constraint in the model's present orientation, either in the **Assembly** window or in the **Component** window, you can use the mouse buttons as usual to spin/zoom/pan the part or assembly as usual, after clicking in the appropriate graphics window. This can be done at any time while specifying a pair of placement constraints. *Query Select* also comes in handy here.

For the bushing, we want to set the constraints shown in Figure 20.

The **Insert** constraint makes the cylindrical outer
surface of the bushing line up with the surface of
the hole; the **Align** constraint keeps the face of the
bushing even with the surface of the bracket.
Before proceeding with applying these constraints,
resize/reorient/move the bracket and bushing
displays so that you will be able to easily pick on
the appropriate entities.

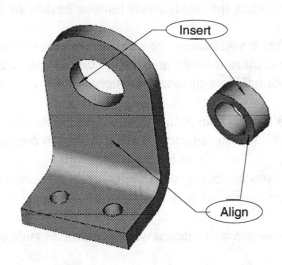

Now we'll proceed with the assembly. Select

Constraint Type > Insert

and pick on the outer surface of the bushing. It
highlights in red. Read the bottom line in the
message window. Pick on the inner surface of the

Figure 20 Constraints for the bushing

large hole in the bracket. In the **Component Placement** window, you should see a new line entry
for the constraint, and the message that the component status is "partially constrained". The
bushing can still slide along, and rotate around, its axis. Now select

Constraint Type > Align

and pick on the flat face of the bushing. Then pick
on the flat surface of the bracket. The message in
the **Component Placement** window will inform
you that the component is fully constrained. Note
that the "Allow Assumptions" box is checked.
What does this do? Is the bushing, in fact, fully
constrained at this time? The answer is no (!),
since the bushing is still free to rotate around its
axis. Pro/E has determined, with an assumption,
that this degree of freedom doesn't matter for this
part. Deselect the **Allow Assumptions** box. Now
Pro/E tells you that, indeed, the bushing is not
fully constrained. What would be required to
complete the constraints? Don't do this now,
since the assumption isn't going to hurt us. Turn
the **Allow Assumptions** box back on.

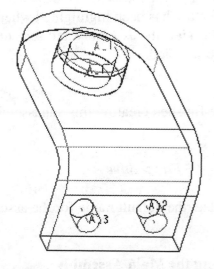

Figure 21 Bushing assembled to L-bracket

You can then select *Preview* to see where Pro/E will put the component. The placement will be
indicated in yellow on the assembly shown in Figure 21. The bushing should be even with one
side of the bracket and protrude slightly from the other (since it is a different thickness than the
bracket).

If you make a mistake in specifying the type or references of a placement constraint, you can select it in the **Constraints** box. The associated references on the component and assembly are shown in magenta and cyan, respectively. Then, either *Remove* the constraint, select a new type, or select the small arrow buttons beside the listed references and pick new ones.

When you create a new constraint, make sure to first select the *Add* button, otherwise you may end up redefining an existing constraint. This button is automatic unless you have interrupted the normal flow of assembly steps.

When all constraints are complete, click on different constraints listed in the **Constraints** box. The various surfaces involved in each constraint will be highlighted.

If you are happy with the bushing placement, select *OK*. The graphics window will now show the L-bracket with the bushing in place.

Now we will place a washer on the outside of the bushing. Select

> *Assemble > washer.prt > Open*

Create the placement constraints shown in the figure at the right. These constraints are *Align* (washer and bushing axes) and *Mate* (washer and bushing faces). You may want to use *Query Sel* to make sure you pick the correct axis on the assembly (the hole and bushing axes are coincident) - the message window will tell you what feature has been highlighted when you pick on it. *Preview* the assembly and select *OK* when you are satisfied.

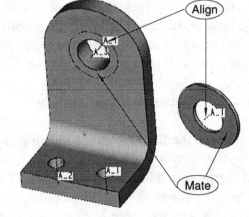

We are finished creating this subassembly, so select

Figure 22 Placement constraints for the washer

> *File > Save*

and select the default name for the assembly (**support.asm**).

Creating the Main Assembly

Leave the subassembly window open, and create a new assembly called **less9** and bring in the base plate as the first part:

> *File > New > Assembly | Design >[less9]*
> *(Use the empty template as before)*
> *Component > Assemble > bplate.prt > Open*

Now bring in the subassembly:

Assemble > support.asm > Open

Keep using the **Separate Window** option for now. We will set up the placement constraints for the subassembly shown in the following figure:

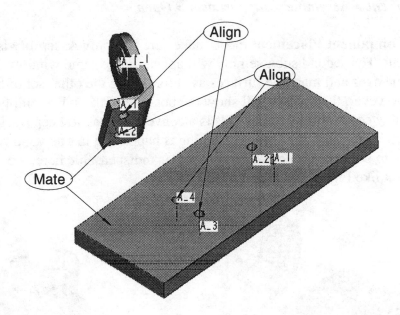

Figure 23 Placement constraints for the subassembly

First, *Mate* the lower surface of the bracket with the upper surface of the base plate. Then *Align* the axis of one of the bolt holes in the bracket with the axis of the appropriate hole in the base plate. If **Allow Assumptions** is turned on, you will get the message that the component is fully constrained, so select *Preview*. You will see the support shown something like Figure 24 (this will depend on which holes you chose to align, and on how you oriented your parts when you created them).

Hmmm... not exactly what we want. The bracket is not actually fully constrained yet, since it can still rotate around the hole. So, (remember to select *Add* first in the **Component Placement** window) *Align* the

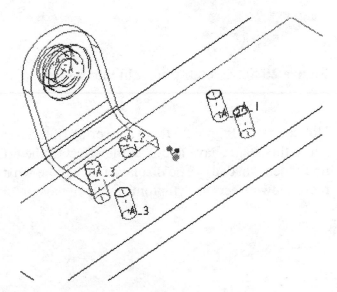
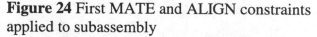

Figure 24 First MATE and ALIGN constraints applied to subassembly

other bolt hole axis in the bracket to the appropriate axis on the base. The sub-assembly is now fully constrained without any assumptions. Select *OK*. You can minimize the *support.asm* window now. You cannot close this window at this time because it is the "base" Pro/E window -

the first one we opened at start-up.

We'll now bring in another copy of the support subassembly using *Assemble*, and attach it to the base plate so that it faces the first one as shown in Figure 28. We will use a slightly different screen display and options. Select

Component > Assemble > support.asm > Open

This time, in the **Component Placement** menu make sure that only **Assembly** is checked under Display Component. The second subassembly will appear in the same window as the total assembly. Align the axes and mate the surfaces as before using the other set of holes in the base plate. This time, however, the display will show the position of the subassembly relative to the assembly as each new constraint is added. This is a convenient way to keep track of the effect of your assembly constraints, however since everything is happening in one window it may be difficult sometimes to select references. *Query Select* is indispensable here. Your assembly sequence might look like Figures 25 through 28.

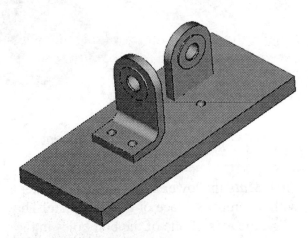

Figure 25 Subassembly brought into session

Figure 26 First hole axes aligned - support buried in base plate!

Notice that in Figure 26 there is overlap (interference) of the bracket and base plate. After you get to this stage, have a look at the effect of the different view options (wireframe, hidden line, no hidden, shaded). The displays may not be what you expect. You should be able to recognize these view effects as symptoms that you have interfering components.

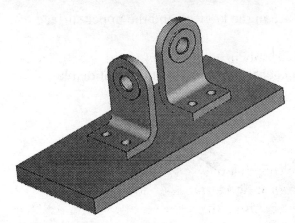

Figure 27 Surfaces mated. Fully constrained with assumptions. No overlap.

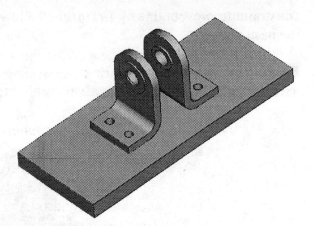

Figure 28 Second bolt axis aligned with other hole on base plate

Save the assembly.

Now we'll assemble the axle using the following constraints. Read ahead through this, since we are going to do something a bit different.

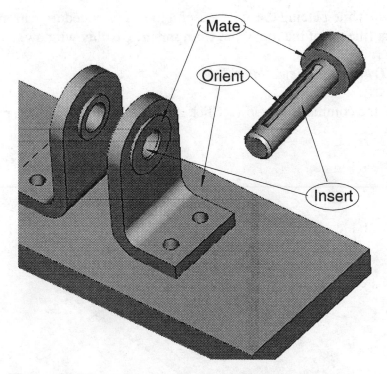

Figure 29 Placement constraints for axle

Before we do the assembly, let's review our constraint design. The *Mate* constraint is between the bottom of the axle head and the outer face of the washer. The *Insert* constraint could be with any of the inner surfaces of the bushings or washers on either support. The design intent will be best served if you pick a surface of a bushing. In either case, this constraint will allow the component to be placed, but it will still be able to rotate around its own axis. We'll add another constraint to prevent this by *Orient*ing the lower surface in the keyway and the upper surface of the base plate.

Bring in the axle and make sure the *Assembly* option is checked for the component display. The axle will appear somewhere, perhaps similar to the figure shown below.

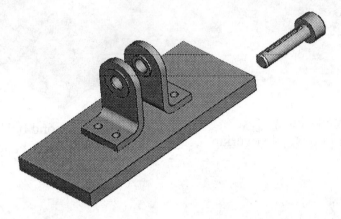

Figure 30 Axle selected for assembly (Note: *Assembly* option checked)

To control the display while placing the axle, a useful tool is provided to rearrange components on the screen. Select (the tab at the top of the **Component Display** window)

Move > Translate | View Plane

Read the message in the command window. Click on the axle and drag it to a position similar to the following:

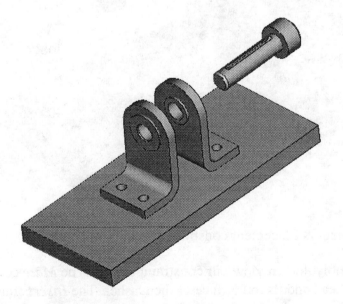

Figure 31 Axle after translating from initial placement position

Now select the ***Rotate*** option, in the **Motion Reference** list select ***Entity/Edge***, click (maybe with ***Query Select***) on the axis of the axle, and spin the axle by dragging with the left mouse button. You should be able to spin it a full 360°. Drop it in the position shown below. Note the new location of the keyway.

Figure 32 Axle after rotating around its axis

At the same time as you are moving the component, you can control your view (spin, zoom, and pan) using the dynamic view controls as usual. This gives you considerable control over what you see on the screen. You can also translate and rotate relative to surfaces and axes in the assembly. Experiment with this so that you will be comfortable with it.

When your display shows you a convenient view of the axle and the assembly together, select the ***Place*** tab and set up the assembly constraints indicated above. Apply the constraints in the order: ***Insert***, ***Orient***, ***Mate***. As mentioned earlier, the order of creating these constraints doesn't matter to the final placement. You will find some sequences easier than others. For example, try to avoid the "buried" phenomenon we encountered earlier that makes it hard to select references.

As you apply the constraints, try to ***Move > Translate*** and ***Move > Rotate*** the part. You will find that these moves are restricted because of the existing constraints at the time.

IMPORTANT NOTE:
  The ***Move*** command (previously called a "Package Move") is used for cosmetic purposes only. Although it may be possible to move a new component into the correct position relative to other parts, you must still specify the geometric constraints in order to assemble it. If you leave the **Component Placement** window without fully constraining the component, it is called "packaged." A special notation will appear in the model tree for such a component. **A new component that is constrained (even fully) to a previously packaged component will itself be considered packaged only.**

The final position of the axle should be as shown in Figure 33. Notice the position of the keyway.

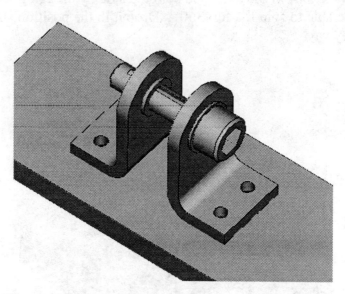

Figure 33 Final placement of axle

If everything is satisfactory, select **OK**. Otherwise, click on a constraint listed in the table, select either the constraint type, component reference, or assembly reference, and make the appropriate corrections.

Now is a good time to save the assembly.

We can now bring in the pulley and attach it using the constraints shown in Figure 34. You might like to experiment with **Separate Window** and **Assembly** component displays, and possibly use shaded views to help identify surfaces. This is useful when the assembly starts to get crowded with visible and hidden edges, datum planes and axes, and so on. At this time, you will also probably find that **Query Sel** is a useful tool.

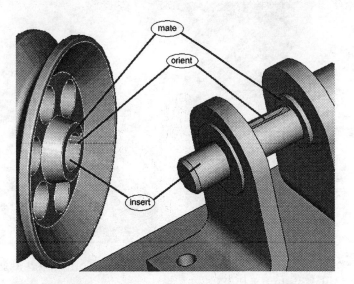

Figure 34 Placement constraints for the pulley

Once again, the pulley could be placed with just the *Insert* and *Mate* constraints. But, we want to make sure the keyway lines up with the axle. The *Orient* constraint can be used with a side surface of the keyway, and a side surface of the keyway on the axle. When the pulley is placed, it should look like Figure 35.

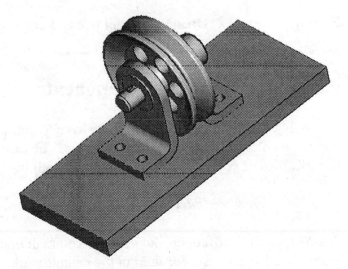

Figure 35 Final position of pulley

Finally, bring in the four bolts to attach the bracket to the base plate. We'll bring these in one at a time for now - there are a number of advanced assembly commands that would allow you to create a pattern of bolts that would match a pattern of bolt holes. This would allow the assembly to automatically adjust, for example, if the pattern of bolt holes in the base plate was changed. To place a single bolt, the placement constraints are shown in Figure 36.

Once again, experiment with the *Separate Window* and *Assembly* options, and try out the *Move* command. You have four bolts to experiment with. Place a bolt in each of the holes available.

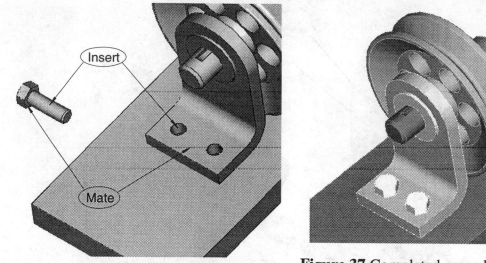

Figure 36 Placement constraints for bolts

Figure 37 Completed assembly

The assembly is now completed and should look like Figure 37.

Save the assembly. Open the model tree and explore the information presented there.

Assigning Colors to Components

We assign colors in two steps: first we have to define the colors we are going to use, then we apply the colors to the desired components. The extent to which you can do this will depend on the specifics of your Pro/E installation and your hardware. Select:

> *View > Model Setup > Color & Appearances*

A small window will open showing the colors defined on your system. The color palette is stored in a file called *color.map* in the default working directory. It is loaded when Pro/E is launched. If it is missing, only one color - white - is defined.

Let's define some more colors:

> *Add*

The Appearance Editor will appear as shown in Figure 38.

This window has three tabs: **Basic**, **Advanced**, and **Detail**.
Colors are defined in the **Basic** sheet. Click on the white
color patch in the top color box. Another window (the **Color
Editor**) will open showing you three sliders that control the
amount of Red, Green, and Blue in the color being defined.
You move the sliders until you get the right mix of RGB for
the new color, or enter integer values in the range 0 - 255 in
the boxes on the right. Once you have the desired color,
select

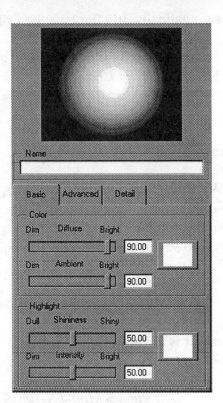

> *OK*

Type in a name for the color and click

> *Add*

at the bottom of the Appearance editor. The new color will
show up in the palette at the top of the Appearances window.

Define the colors in the table below or make up your own
color mix. Color names might correspond, for example, with
different materials (steel, aluminum, plastic, ...) If you have
appropriate hardware, you might experiment with the
Advanced menu to set transparency and other color parameters.

Figure 38 The **Appearance
Editor** window

Color	RGB Composition		
	Red	Green	Blue
Red	255	0	0
Green	0	255	0
Blue	0	0	255
Yellow	255	255	0
Cyan	0	255	255
Magenta	255	0	255

When you have created the palette, *Close* the Appearance Editor. Back in the Appearances
window, you can use

> *File > Save As*

to save your newly created color palette. Remember that if you want this palette loaded automatically, it's file must be called *color.map* and be located in the start-up directory.

To apply color to the axle, select a color in the palette, then in the **Set Object Appearance** pull-down list, select **Components**. Pick on the axle and *Done Sel > Set*. If the axle color doesn't change, make sure that *Colors* is checked under *Utilities > Environment*.

Choose different colors and assign them to the pulley, the base plate, and the four bolts. You might find *Sel by Menu > Name* will come in handy here.

When the total assembly is active, we can't individually color the components in the subassembly **support.asm** - if we tried that now, they would all end up the same color since this is treated as a single component in the current assembly. We will have to have the subassembly in its own window. If it currently isn't in your session (if it is you can do this by *Window > support.asm*), bring it in with

> *File > Open > Assembly > support.asm*

or if it is already loaded, just click on the window containing the subassembly and activate it. Now you can set the colors of the constituent components. Try something different here:

> *View > Model Setup > Color Appearances*
> *[select a color from the palette] > Components*
> *Sel By Menu > [select a listed part] > Done Sel > Set*

Once you have set all the colors, save the **support** subassembly, and change back to the overall assembly window. If you previously colored the support in the main assembly, you will have to *Unset* that color. Colors assigned at the highest level in the assembly tree take precedence. In this regard, you should note that colors can be defined and assigned at the individual part level. These colors are carried with the part into the assembly, where they can be over-ridden. For multiple occurrences of a part (like the bolts), it is easier to assign colors at part level, where you only have to do it once!

See how the display changes for wireframe, hidden line, and shaded displays. In wireframe display the edges of each part are shown in the assigned color. This might be awkward if you want to do any editing of the part, since line color is so important in representing information like highlighted edges, constraint surfaces, parent/child relations, and the like. To turn off the color display, select

> *Utilities > Environment > Colors | OK*

All edges will now be shown in the default colors.

We are finished with the first lesson on assemblies. Don't forget to save your assembly - we'll need it in the next lesson.

You will note that the keyway extends beyond one of the support bushings. Also, the base plate is quite large. In the next lesson we will see how to modify an assembly and its component parts. This will involve creating assembly features (ie. specific to the assembly), as well as making changes to the parts themselves. It is also possible to create new parts while you are in assembly mode (we'll make the key this way, to make sure it fits in the assembly). We'll also find out how to get an exploded view of the assembly, and set up an assembly drawing.

Questions for Review

1. If several identical parts are required in an assembly, do you need a separate part file for each one?
2. What are the six assembly constraints?
3. What is a "packaged" component? How does this restrict what you can do?
4. How do the 3 R's apply to assemblies?
5. What degrees of freedom are constrained by each of the six assembly constraints? Draw a sketch and illustrate the constrained and unconstrained degrees of freedom.
6. Can you use datum planes and/or axes when specifying constraints?
7. What is the difference between applying assembly constraints to individual components versus a subassembly?
8. What is the difference between *Separate Window* and *Assembly*? Where are these options located?
9. How do you select the constraint types?
10. Can you do the assembly operations with a shaded view?
11. If you are in the process of constraining a component and you make a mistake, how can you a) delete, or b) edit a constraint.
12. What does *Move* do, and how is it related to applying assembly constraints?
13. Does it matter what order you create assembly constraints? When you are picking references does it matter if you select component references first?
14. Explain the note at the bottom of page 9-17 in terms of parent/child relations.
15. Find out how many colors you can define on your local system.
16. Which takes precedence: colors assigned at part level or at assembly level?
17. How can you specify the colors of individual components in a subassembly?
18. How do you turn off color display in wireframe mode?

503 - 297 - 5015

Project

Start assembling the vise with this subassembly.

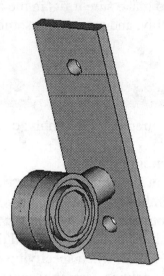

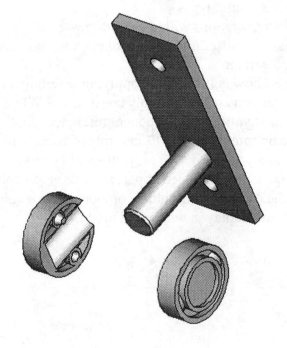

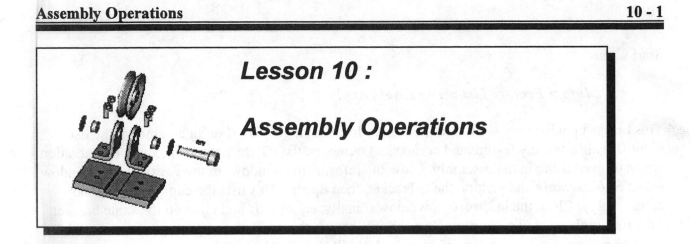

Lesson 10 :

Assembly Operations

Synopsis

Examining the assembly database. Modifying parts in an assembly. Creating parts in assembly mode. Assembly features. Exploded views, assembly drawings, and special display modes.

Overview of this Lesson

In this lesson, we will continue to work with the pulley assembly we created in Lesson #9. We will look at some Pro/E utilities to get information about an assembly (model tree, assembly references, assembly sequence). We will then see how to add features to the assembly, modify the parts used, and create a new part to fit with existing parts in the assembly. We will see how to get an exploded view, and modify it, and how to set up a drawing of the assembly. This seems like a lot, but there's actually not much involved here. Here are the sections of this lesson:

1. Assembly Information
2. Assembly Features
3. Assembly and Part Modifications
4. Part Creation in Assembly Mode
5. Exploding the Assembly
6. Modifying the Component Display
7. Assembly Drawings

To get started, make sure all the part and assembly files you created in Lesson #9 are in your working directory. Then start Pro/E and load the assembly:

> *File > Open > less9.asm*

Shut off all the datums (planes, axes, coordinate systems), colors, and set no hidden lines. Close the model tree.

Assembly Information

In this section we will look at some Pro/E commands to dig out information about the assembly.

Start with

> *Info > Feature List > Top Level | Apply*

This brings up a list very similar to the feature list of a single part. For an assembly, the list identifies all assembly feature and component numbers, the ID, the name, type, and regeneration status of everything in the assembly. Close the information window. In the **Feature List** window, select *Subassembly* and pick on the L-bracket, then *Apply*. This lists the components in the subassembly. Close the information window. Finally, select *Part* and click on the same bracket. This lists individual part features. You can see that we can dig down quite deep into the model structure. *Close* the information window and the **Feature List** window.

To see how the assembly was put together (the regeneration sequence):

> *Info > Regen Info > Beginning*

and proceed through the regeneration sequence with *Continue* until you are back in the ASSEMBLY menu.

If you want to find out more information about how the assembly was put together, in particular the placement constraints:

> *Info > Component*

Pick on the axle then *Done Sel* and follow the prompts and messages in the message window. The **Component Constraints** window will open as shown at the right. This gives you a list of the placement constraints used to position the axle in the assembly. Place the cursor over one of the lines in the table - a pop-up will describe the constraint. If you click on the line, the reference surfaces will highlight in magenta and cyan on the model. Pick on another component, like one of the bolts to see similar information. *Close* the window and *Repaint*.

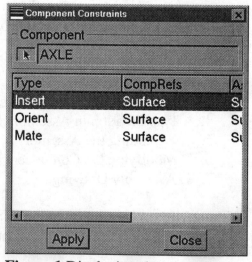

Figure 1 Displaying the component constraints

Another way of looking at the logical structure of the assembly is with the model tree:

View > Model Tree

or use the toolbar button. Click on the small + sign in front of the *support.asm* entries. Note how the individual components are organized in levels. We used two subassemblies - their component parts are on a lower level of the tree. Add the following columns to the model tree: *Feat #*, *Feat Type*, *Status*. Reformat the column widths as in Figure 2.

	Feat #	Feat Type	Status
LESS9.ASM			
BPLATE.PRT	1	Component	Regenerated
SUPPORT.ASM	2	Component	Regenerated
LBRACK.PRT	1	Component	Regenerated
BUSHING.PRT	2	Component	Regenerated
WASHER.PRT	3	Component	Regenerated
SUPPORT.ASM	3	Component	Regenerated
LBRACK.PRT	1	Component	Regenerated
BUSHING.PRT	2	Component	Regenerated
WASHER.PRT	3	Component	Regenerated
AXLE.PRT	4	Component	Regenerated
PULLEY.PRT	5	Component	Regenerated
BOLT.PRT	6	Component	Regenerated
BOLT.PRT	7	Component	Regenerated
BOLT.PRT	8	Component	Regenerated
BOLT.PRT	9	Component	Regenerated

Figure 2 Model tree for *less9.asm*

Select

View > Model Tree Setup > Item Display

and turn on the display of all objects, features, and notes. Now select one of the + signs in front of a part. The model tree shows all the features in the part. Click on any of these features and it will be highlighted on the assembly model. If you right-click on any feature, a small pop-up menu will appear with a number of the utility commands we have seen before (*Modify, Redefine, Reroute, Delete*, and so on). The options are different for subassemblies. For the top level assembly (*less9.asm*), right click and select *Info > Model Info*. Notice that when you close this information window that the data has automatically been written to a file (*less9.inf*). This is useful for model documentation. To exit the model tree window, just turn it off with

View > Model Tree

or use the toolbar button again.

Assembly Features

Creating Assembly Features

An assembly feature is one that will reside *only* in the assembly. You can only create them when you are in assembly mode, and they will *not* be available to individual parts when you are in part mode. Like features in part mode, assembly features will involve parent/child relations (either with other assembly features or with part features) and can be edited, suppressed and resumed. Although we didn't do it here, it may be a good idea to start a new assembly with a set of default datum planes. These would automatically be labeled **ADTM1**, **ADTM2**, and **ADTM3**, for *assembly datums.* If you use an assembly template, these default datums are created automatically and named **ASM_RIGHT**, **ASM_TOP**, and **ASM_FRONT**. The associated views are also created and saved in the view list.

We will create a couple of assembly features in this lesson. The first is composed of a longitudinal cut through the entire assembly in order to show the interior detail.

In the **ASSEMBLY** menu, select

> *Feature > Create > Solid > Cut > Extrude | Solid | Done*
> *One Side | Done*

For the sketching plane, pick the right face of the base plate (assuming you in the default orientation). For the **Top** sketching reference, pick the top face of the base plate. You should now be in Sketcher. Turn the datum planes back on, since we want to do an alignment. Sketch a single vertical line from the top of the pulley to the bottom of the base plate. This should be aligned with a vertical datum plane, with its end points aligned with the top edge of the pulley and the lower surface of the base plate. This is easy to do with the Intent Manager if you select your references as the lower surface of the plate, the outer edge of the pulley, and the vertical datum **TOP** of the pulley, or **FRONT** of the base plate. *Regenerate* your sketch and turn off the datum planes. Your sketch should look like Figure 3.

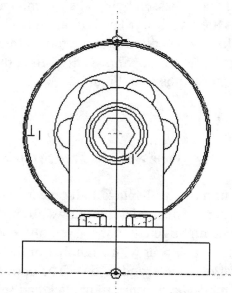

Figure 3 Sketch of first assembly feature (a vertical edge to create a one-sided cut)

Leave Sketcher with *Done* and select the material removal side on the left of this sketched line, and select the depth as *Thru All*. A new menu opens up, called **INTRSCT OPER**. This menu allows you to select which components will be affected ("intersected") by the cut. For now, select the following:

> *Add Model > Auto Sel*
> *Confirm > Done*

to let Pro/E intersect any part it comes across on the cut. The *Preview* button in the elements window does not work quite the same way as it did in part mode - here all it shows is an outline of the cutting surface. Select *OK* in the elements window. The assembly should look like Figure 4 (Why are two bolts left hanging out in space?)

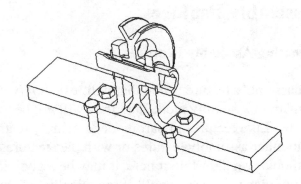

Figure 4 Cut complete

Turn the part colors back on (in the
Environment window), and shade the display.
Note that the keyway in the axle is too long -
extending into the bushings in both directions.
We will fix this a little later.

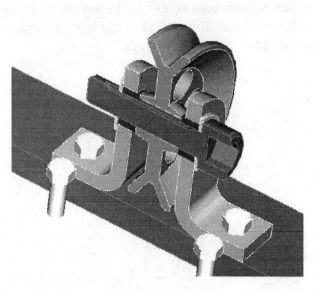

Figure 5 Cut complete - shaded view

Suppressing and Resuming Assembly Features

Assembly features and components can be suppressed and resumed in a similar way as we did
with part features. As before, we will have to watch out for parent/child relations. If we try to
suppress a parent, we will have to take some action to tell Pro/E what to do with the children.

Since we want to do some modifications on the keyway in the axle, let's suppress all components
in the assembly except the axle and the pulley. This is not strictly necessary to do the
modification, but it will remove the visual clutter from the screen. Since line color will be
important here, turn the colors off (*Utilities > Environment > Colors | OK*) and select (in the
ASSEMBLY menu):

> *Component > Suppress*

Click on the left L-bracket. Because of a placement constraint, this component is parent to the
two bolts. You can suppress them both with

> *Suppress All*

Now click on the right L-bracket. This has four children: the two bolts, the axle, and the pulley.
Each will be highlighted in turn, and we must do something about them! We do not want to
suppress either the axle or the pulley, so *Freeze* them. The bolts can be suppressed. Finally,
click on the base plate; freeze the axle (why is it a child of the base plate?) and suppress the cut.
After you select *Done Sel > Done* you should now see the axle and pulley all by themselves.

Notice the keyway extending past the edge of the
pulley hub on both sides. In the next section, we
will modify the dimension of the keyway and add
some other assembly features.

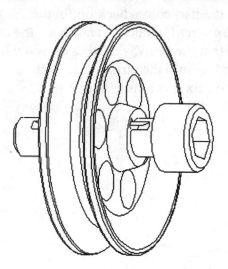

Figure 6 Assembly with suppressed features

Assembly and Part Modifications

Pro/E gives you considerable flexibility in making changes to the assembly. One thing you have
to be careful about is exactly what you are modifying:

- individual part features and dimensions
- subassembly features and dimensions
- assembly features and dimensions

An important thing to note is that for the first type of modification (dealing with individual parts)
your changes will be made **in the part file**. Thus, these will show up if you bring up the part in
Part or **Drawing** modes. If you make changes at the assembly level, even though these may
change part geometry in the assembly, the changes are not reflected in the individual part files.
This will become more clear after we try out some of the commands. Let's start with the first type
of modification...

Changing an Individual Part

We need to shorten the keyway on the axle, and we want to make this a permanent change in the
part (ie. reflected in the part file). From the **ASSEMBLY** menu, select

Modify > Mod Part

and pick on the axle, then *Confirm*. In the **MODIFY PART** menu, select

Modify Dim > Value

and pick on the keyway. The dimensions will show up something like the figure below. If you need to move them to make them clearer select

       Dim Cosmetics > Move Dim

then left click on a dimension to do a drag-and-drop operation to the desired position. If you do this, you will have to re-select *Value*.

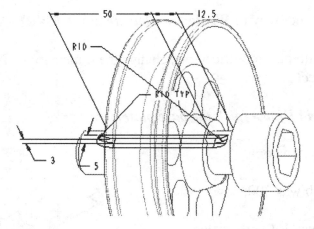

Figure 7 Original dimensions of keyway on axle

Change the following dimensions (click on the old value and enter the new value):

- length of keyway (between the centers of the curved ends) was 50, new value = *18*
- distance from shoulder of the bolt was 12.5, new value = *20*
- radius of rounded end was R10, new value = *R5* (both ends)

Then *Regenerate* the part. Spin the axle/pulley to verify that the keyway does not extend beyond the end of the pulley hub. To get another view of the new keyway, return to the **ASSEMBLY** menu, and select

       Component > Resume
       All > Done

This will resume all the components (including the assembly cut!). If you shade the display, it should look like Figure 8.

Figure 8 Axle keyway with new dimensions

To see what has happened to the *axle* part file, we will bring it in by itself by switching to **Part** mode:

> *Open > axle.prt*

The axle should show up in a new window (read the title bar!). And, voilà, the keyway has changed. If we also had a drawing of this part and brought it up in **Drawing** mode, we would find that it has also been updated. Close the part window by selecting the X at the top right or using *Window > Close*.

Activate the assembly window with *Window > Activate* or use **CTRL-A**.

While we are dealing with part modifications, change the dimensions of the base plate. In the **ASSEMBLY** menu select

> *Modify > Mod Dim > [pick the base plate]*

Change the following dimensions:

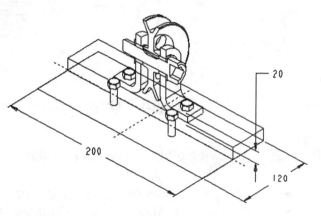

- ▸ overall length was 300, new value = *200*
- ▸ half-length was 150, new value = *100* (if necessary)

The new base plate dimensions are shown in Figure 9.

Figure 9 Base Plate dimensions

Select *Done/Return > Regenerate > Automatic*. Since these changes were made to the part, they will also be reflected in the original part file.

Adding another Assembly Feature

We can also make changes to individual parts at the assembly level. Unlike the ones we did above (changing a part feature dimension), these changes will not be reflected in the part file. We are going to add a U-shaped cut to the base plate in between the L-brackets.

First, suppress the assembly cut. From the **ASSEMBLY** menu select

> *Feature > Suppress > Normal | Select | Sel By Menu | Last Feature*
> *Done Sel > Done*

This brings back the entire base plate. Now create the new cut (you should still be in the **ASSY FEAT** menu):

Create > Solid > Cut > Extrude | Solid | Done
One Side | Done

For the sketch plane, select the long front face of the base plate. For the *Top* sketching reference plane, select the upper surface of the base plate. Make a sketch as shown in Figure 10.

Align the vertical edges of the cut with the inside vertical surfaces of the L-brackets. For the depth, select *Thru All*. The **INTRSCT OPER** menu will open. Instead of letting Pro/E search to see which parts to intersect, do this manually with

> *Manual Sel*
> *[pick on the base plate]*
> *Done Sel > Done > OK*

The assembly should now show the cut in the base plate as shown in Figure 11.

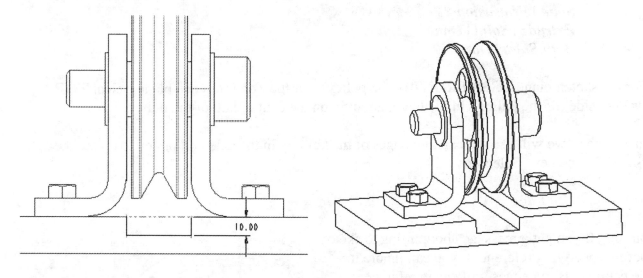

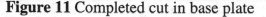

10.00

Figure 10 Sketch of second assembly feature

Figure 11 Completed cut in base plate

In the **ASSY FEAT** menu, select *Done/Return*. Go to the model tree and make sure that

> *View > Model Tree > Item Display*

has checks beside all display objects. You should see that a second cut feature has been added to the assembly at the bottom of the tree. The first one listed is the big cut we made before, and is currently suppressed as indicated by the small black square.

Now retrieve the base plate in **Part** mode. You should find that the dimensions have changed (since we did that at the part level), but the new cross-cut does not appear (since we did that at the assembly level). Close out the base plate part window, and return to the assembly.

What would happen to this cut if we suppressed either L-bracket?

Part Creation in Assembly Mode

When you are working with an assembly, you may want to create a part that must exactly match up with other parts in the assembly. You could, of course, do this by creating individual parts (as we have done up to now) and by very carefully keeping track of all your individual part dimensions and making sure they all agree. You might even use relations to drive part dimensions by referencing dimensions in other part files. Here, we will find out how to create a new part using the assembly geometry as a guide and a constraint.

We are going to create the key for the axle/pulley. To simplify the environment, suppress all the other components and assembly features except the axle and pulley (remember to *Freeze* these children). Turn on the datum planes and hidden lines. To create the new part, select

> *Component > Create > Part | Solid | [key] | OK*
> *Create First Feature | OK*
> *Solid | Protrusion*
> *Extrude | Solid | Done*
> *Both Sides | Done*

For the sketch plane, select **FRONT** of the pulley. For the *Top* reference plane, select **TOP** (yellow side) of the pulley. In Sketcher, zoom in on the central hub of the pulley.

In Sketcher, we will use the existing edges of the keyway in the axle and pulley to create the sketch for the key. Select the

> *Use Edge*

button. If you get a message about trying to sketch before specifying references, you can ignore it. Selecting existing edges will create references automatically. Click on the edges of the keyway in the axle and pulley (some of these are hidden); then *Close* the small window. Be sure to select them all, to create a rectangular, closed section as shown in Figure 12.

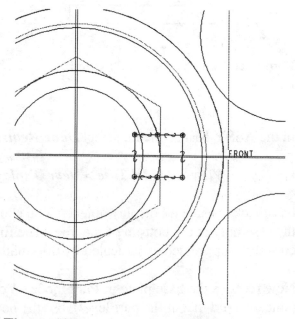

Figure 12 Sketch of rectangular key

Regenerate the sketch. Note that we didn't have to provide any dimensioning information for sketcher - it automatically reads the dimensions from the previous parts. This means that if we change the keyway dimensions in the pulley, the key will automatically change shape. Except note that we have not explicitly connected the width of the keyway in the pulley to the width in the axle. You might think about how you could do this. What would happen if you increased the keyway width in the axle but not the pulley?

For the depth of the key protrusion, select **Blind | Done** and enter a value of *18*. Select **OK** in the elements window.

Check out the model tree - you should see that *key.prt* has been added to the assembly. Let's resume the longitudinal cut to see inside the assembly:

>   ***Component > Resume > All > Done***

and shade the display. You can now see our rectangular key:

Figure 13 New *key.prt* in assembly

Hmmm... why hasn't the key been cut along with all the other parts?

Now is a good time to save everything:

>   ***File > Save***

You will find that the new part file **key.prt** is automatically saved for you. When you select *Save* in assembly mode, every object that has changed since the last save is also saved. Retrieve the key into PART mode; the only dimension shown on the part (with *Modify*) is the length. All the other dimensions are determined by the edges used in the assembly, and therefore can't be modified within part mode. What do you think will happen the next time you start Pro/E if you move the key part file to another directory?

So, here's some advice for creating parts in assembly mode:

IMPORTANT NOTE:
>   If you are going to create parts in assembly mode, try to arrange as many *size and shape* dimensions as possible to be contained within the part. Use other assembly features only for *locational* references (like alignments, or dimensions to locate the new part).

If you load a part containing assembly references, these can sometimes be hard to track down. Let's see what we can dig out for the key. Select

>   *Info > Parent/Child*

and pick on a surface of the key. The References Information Window opens. In the right pane are the parents of the feature. These are the individual features in another part (part names given) in an assembly (name also given).

Exploding the Assembly

A useful way of illustrating assemblies is with exploded views. Creating these is very easy. First, suppress the longitudinal cut:

>   *Feature > Suppress > Query Sel*

and pick on any cut surface.

Getting an exploded view is a snap. You have to be in the **ASSEMBLY** menu to do this by selecting

>   *View > Explode*

All the parts will be translated by some default distance. You should see something like Figure 14.

The assembly has been exploded in directions, and by distances, determined by Pro/E. For a better view, we can change the explosion distances. Select

>   *Modify*
>   *Mod Expld*
>   *Position*

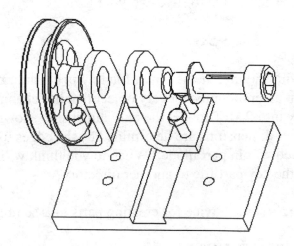

We modify the exploded position of each component by first specifying an explode direction, and then dragging one or more components in the chosen direction. The direction can be defined by an axis, edge, normal to surface, and others. Make sure all the axes are displayed since we will need them to

Figure 14 Default exploded view

define the explode directions. Then, select (in the **Motion Reference** list):

Entity/Edge

and pick on the axis of the axle. The command window will instruct you to "*Select component(s) to move*". Click on the axle and drag it away from the L-bracket. Click again to drop it at the new position. The component is constrained to move in the 3D direction of the axis. Do the same for the bushings and washers. When you are satisfied with these positions, select *Done Sel* and then select (again in the **Motion Reference** list)

Plane/Normal

Now pick on the top surface of the base plate. Move the bolts, pulley, and key upwards away from the base plate. Select *Done Sel* when you are satisfied.

Use a combination of *Entity/Edge* and *Plane/Normal* to produce the exploded view shown below. Of course, throughout all this, the dynamic view controls are active so you can spin and zoom your view to your heart's content! Experiment with the other options for specifying the movement direction and distance. When you are finished, select *Done/Return* and *Done* until you are back in the *ASSEMBLY* menu.

Figure 15 Modified explode distances

Before we continue to the last section, unexplode the assembly:

View > Unexplode

You might also like to save the assembly. All your modified explosion distances will be kept in the assembly file and will be used the next time you explode the assembly. There is no need to create another assembly file (for example using *Save As*).

IMPORTANT NOTE:

Using *Save As* in Assembly mode is very tricky. Be aware that using this command will result in copies of *every* file in the assembly. The default operation appends an underscore character to the new part or subassembly file names. These "new" part files work only in the "new" assembly file. **Do not use *Save As* in Assembly mode unless you really know what you are doing!** If you want to change the name of the assembly file, use *File > Rename*.

Modifying the Component Display

Here is an easy (and impressive) way of displaying a complicated assembly. Select

> *View > Model Setup > Component Display > Create > [display1]*

The model tree will open, and a new menu **EDIT DISPLAY** appears with a number of options. Before we start, expand the *support.asm* components in the model tree. We are going to set the display appearance of each component individually. In the **EDIT DISPLAY** menu, select

> *Shading*

and click on the pulley, axle, and bushing entries in the model tree. The second column in the model tree will indicate the display state of the selected components. Select the following options in the menu and components in the model tree:

> *Hidden Line > lbrack, washer (X2)*
> *Blank > key*
> *No Hidden > bplate*

Now select

> *Update Screen > Done*

and you should get the display shown in Figure 16.

It is not necessary to define a display state for all components. For example, we have left the four bolts undefined. The settings we have made over-ride the main view settings. If not explicitly set in a display definition, component display is determined by the toolbar buttons. Try that out now (wireframe, hidden line, no hidden, and shade).

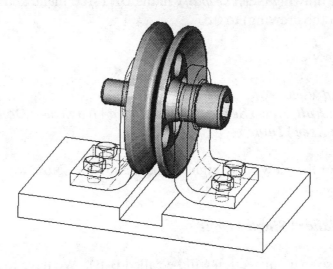

Figure 16 Component display state

To return to the normal display state, select

> *Set Current > Master Rep | OK > Done/Return*

The display state definition we defined is saved with the model, just like the explode state.

Assembly Drawings

Our last task is to create a drawing of the entire assembly. We will not do any dimensioning here, just lay out the views and provide some leader notes. Select

> *File > New > Drawing > [less9asm]*

Deselect the **Use default template** option, and use an empty A-sized drawing sheet. Now select

> *Views > Add View*
> *General | Full View | No Xsec | Unexploded | No Scale | Done*

and pick a view center point on the left side of the sheet. For the **ORIENTATION** select

> *Front > Sel By Menu > [pulley.prt] > Datum > Name > FRONT*
> *Top > Sel By Menu > [bplate.prt] > Datum > Name > TOP*
> *OK*

If they aren't on already, turn on the datum planes (we will need them in a couple of minutes).

Modify the scale of the drawing (select *Modify* in the **DETAIL** menu and pick on the scale legend at the bottom of the drawing) to **0.5**.

Now we'll add a section view:

> *Views > Add View*
> *Projection | Full View | Section | Unexploded | No Scale | Done*
> *Full | Total Xsec | Done*

Make the center point of the view to the right of the main view. Now we have to tell Pro/E what we want to section. Select

> *Create > Planar | Single | Done*

and enter the name *B* (so that our section will be called B-B). We have to tell Pro/E where the section plane will be. If we had an existing assembly datum plane that went through the entire assembly, this would be the one to select. Since we don't (all the datums currently on the screen are part datums and do not extend over the entire assembly), we'll create a make datum:

> *Make Datum > Through | Plane*

and click on any vertical datum plane through the assembly in the view on the left, then *Done*. Now Pro/E wants to know in which view to show the section line and arrows - click on the front view (the view on the left of the drawing). We are finished with the datum planes, so you can turn them off now and repaint the screen.

Let's add one more view - the exploded assembly. You may have to move the two existing views down a bit to fit this one in. Then select

> *Views > Add View*
> *General | Full View | No Xsec | Exploded | Scale | Done*

Place the view near the top of the sheet and, when prompted for the scale, enter *0.25*. Leave the view in default orientation. You can move it around (using *Move View*) until it fits nicely. Notice that this exploded view uses the same explosion distances that you set up in assembly mode.

We're almost finished. You should probably modify the hatching in the section view (see *Modify > Xhatching* and play with the spacing, angle, and hatch pattern), and add some leader notes. Your final drawing might look something like Figure 17.

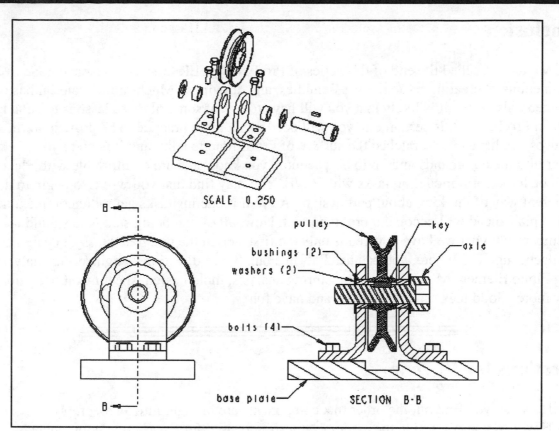

Figure 17 Final assembly drawing

This is a keeper! Obtain hard copy.

A Note about Assembly Templates

Like part templates, assembly templates contain common information used in most assemblies. This includes assembly datums (**ASM_FRONT**, etc), saved views, and so on.

In the last two lessons we have used an empty template to start a new assembly or subassembly. We have then immediately brought in a component, without regard to constraining it. This only works for an empty template! If you use an assembly template, the first component brought in must be constrained. Otherwise, it is considered "packaged" only. Thus, when you are starting a project that involves an assembly, you might like to consider what will be your first component in the assembly, and how to constrain it. This is usually done using the part and assembly datum planes (using *Align*). This is planning "many moves ahead" in the extreme.

Conclusion

Well, we have reached the end of this series of Pro/ENGINEER lessons. We have gone over the fundamentals of creating basic parts, assemblies, and drawings. Much of the material has been presented only once. It is likely that you will have to repeat some of these lessons to get a better grasp on Pro/E, and it is certain that you will need much more practice to be proficient. In some instances, we have only scratched the surface of Pro/E functionality and it is up to you to explore deeper into the commands and options. The more you know and are comfortable with, the easier it will be to perform modeling tasks with Pro/E. You may find that you will also begin to develop a different way of thinking about part design. As your modeling tasks get more complex, the need to plan ahead will become more important. Now, all of that being said, you should also remember that what we have covered is only the first step in the integrated task of design and manufacturing. From here, you can head off in a number of directions: engineering analysis using Finite Element Modeling, manufacturing analysis, mold design, sheet metal operations, and many more. Good luck on your journey and have fun!

Questions for Review

1. How can you find out the order that components are brought into an assembly?
2. How can you determine the assembly constraints used for a particular component?
3. What happens if you left click on a component entry in the model tree? Right click?
4. In the assembly model tree, is it possible to find out what individual features were used to create an individual component?
5. What is an *assembly* feature?
6. Can assembly features refer to individual part features, or only to other assembly features?
7. What kind of features can be created as assembly features?
8. What are the differences between using the default and the empty assembly template?
9. Can you modify individual dimensions of a part while in assembly mode? Is this a permanent modification (that is, is the part geometry changed if you load it alone)?
10. How can you add a feature to a part so that it becomes a permanent feature in the part? What is the alternative?
11. If you change a feature dimension on an assembly drawing, what happens to the part containing that feature a) by itself, and b) in an assembly?
12. How can you get a cut-away view of an assembly?
13. How do you explode an assembly?
14. What does **Auto Sel** do when creating a cut through an assembly?
15. How can you explode some components and not others?
16. Draw a graphical representation of the model tree for the pulley assembly, and trace all the parent/child relations in the assembly.
17. What is contained in an assembly template?
18. If you have appropriate hardware, you may be able to set up the display so that some of the assembly components are transparent. Check this out!
19. If you want a section view in an assembly drawing, does the assembly model require a cut feature along the sectioning plane?

Project

Complete the vise assembly using the parts you made at the end of each lesson. There is one more part to make - the ring shown below. It fits underneath as shown in the second figure. Create this part in assembly mode, using the existing features for dimensional references. A cutaway and exploded view are shown on the next page. The completed vise is on the cover. A VRML model is available on the web at **http://www.sdcpublications.com/tutorial**.

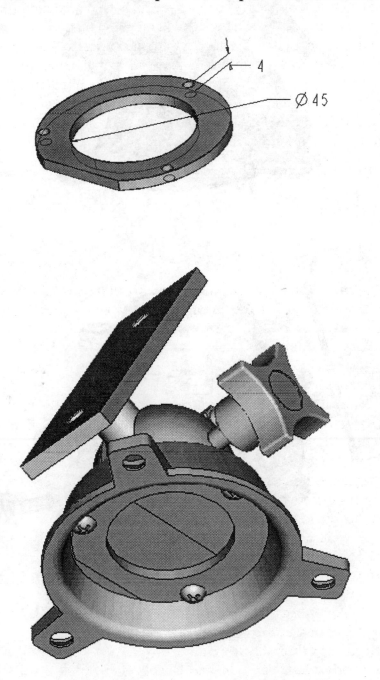

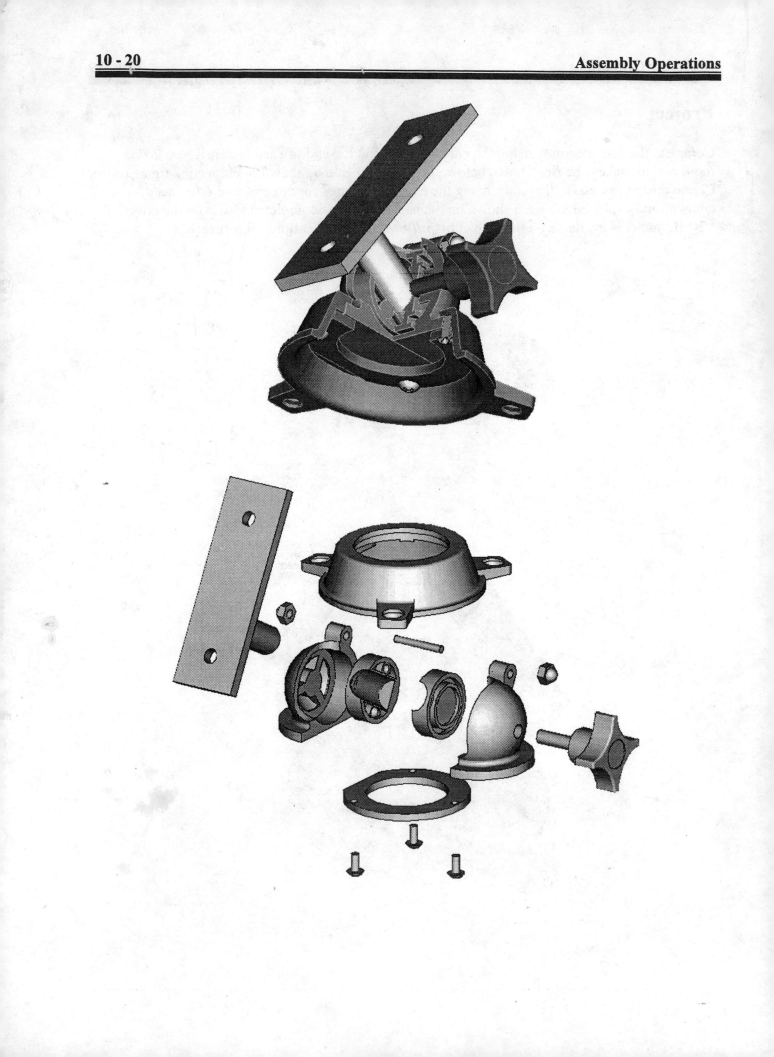